INFOGLUT

"Mark Andrejevic's compelling new book is an impressive survey of the impact of big data on domains extending from bodies and brains to policing, marketing, and sentiment analysis. As it documents the shift from comprehension to correlation, *Infoglut* raises disturbing questions regarding new operations of power and control in a world of algorithms." —Jodi Dean, author of *Democracy and Other Neoliberal Fantasies*

Today, more mediated information is available to more people than at any other time in human history. New and revitalized sense-making strategies multiply in response to the challenges of "cutting through the clutter" of competing narratives and taming the avalanche of information. Data miners, "sentiment analysts," and decision markets offer to help bodies of data "speak for themselves"—making sense of their own patterns so we don't have to. Neuromarketers and body language experts promise to peer behind people's words to see what their brains are really thinking and feeling. New forms of information processing promise to displace the need for expertise and even comprehension—at least for those with access to the data.

Infoglut explores the connections between these wide-ranging sense-making strategies for an era of information overload and "big data," and the new forms of control they enable. Andrejevic critiques the popular embrace of deconstructive debunkery, calling into question the post-truth, post-narrative, and post-comprehension politics it underwrites, and tracing a way beyond them.

Mark Andrejevic is an ARC QE II Research Fellow at the Centre for Critical and Cultural Studies, University of Queensland. He is the author of *iSpy: Surveillance and Power in the Interactive Era* and *Reality TV: The Work of Being Watched*, as well as numerous articles and book chapters on surveillance, digital media, and popular culture.

INFOGLUT

How Too Much Information Is Changing the Way We Think and Know

Mark Andrejevic

Routledge
Taylor & Francis Group

NEW YORK AND LONDON

First published 2013
by Routledge
711 Third Avenue, New York, NY 10017

Simultaneously published in the UK
by Routledge
2 Park Square, Milton Park, Abingdon, Oxon OX14 4RN

Routledge is an imprint of the Taylor & Francis Group, an informa business

Library of Congress Cataloging-in-Publication Data
Andrejevic, Mark, 1964–
Infoglut : how too much information is changing the way we think and know / Mark Andrejevic.
   pages cm
Includes bibliographical references and index.
ISBN 978-0-415-65907-9 (hbk.) — ISBN 978-0-415-65908-6 (pbk.) — ISBN 978-0-203-07531-9 (ebk.) 1. Information society. 2. Internet—Social aspects. I. Title.
HM851.A648 2013
302.23'1—dc23   2012045510

ISBN: 978-0-415-65907-9 (hbk)
ISBN: 978-0-415-65908-6 (pbk)
ISBN: 978-0-203-07531-9 (ebk)

Typeset in Bembo
by Cenveo Publisher Services

Printed and bound in the United States of America by
Edwards brothers Malloy

For Zala, who makes everything clear.

CONTENTS

ACKNOWLEDGMENTS

I am grateful to the University of Queensland for providing me with a UQ Postdoctoral Fellowship that supported this work and for the invaluable research support provided by the Australian Research Council's *Discovery Projects* funding scheme (project number DP1092606).

This book is largely a product of my time at the Centre for Critical and Cultural Studies at the University of Queensland. My profound gratitude to Graeme Turner, who brought me into the centre, and to the wonderfully smart, talented, warm, and supportive colleagues there, including Melissa Bellanta, Mel Gregg, Ben Goldsmith, Anita Harris, Anna Pertierra, Anthea Taylor, Jinna Tay, Hari Harindranath, Abigail Loxham, Morgan Richards, Gay Hawkins, and to the greatly competent, helpful, and supportive administrative staff, including Maureen McGrath and Rebecca Ralph. Fergus Grealy gets special thanks for the time he put into proof-reading the manuscript and grappling with my poor Chicago Style.

The University of Queensland has provided a rich academic community, and I am particularly indebted to the intellectual generosity of Elizabeth Stephens, Nic Carah, Lincoln Dahlberg, Tony Thwaits, Rex Butler, Mark Burden, Maureen Burns, Fiona Nicoll, Tim Keenan, and Liz Ferrier.

I am so grateful to John Durham Peters and Janice Peck for their treasured mentorship and friendship. My time at the University of Iowa provided a foundation for the arguments developed in the following pages (but is not to blame for their shortcomings). In particular, I am grateful for friendship and feedback from Kembrew McLeod, Kristine Munoz, and Hye Jin Lee.

Thanks to all the people who have shared their thoughts with me in conferences and e-mail: a far-flung academic community including, James Hay, Nick Couldry, Jack Bratich, Kelly Gates, Jodi Dean, Christian Fuchs,

Vicky Mayer, Laurie Ouellette, Trebor Scholz, Helga Tawil, Toby Miller, Alison Hearn, Andrew Calabrese, Jason Wilson, Tanya Lewis, and the suspicious mind of Paul Taylor. James Martel's friendship and conversations, which date back more than a quarter century now, continue to sustain me. Slavko Andrejevic provides me with dispatches from the belly of the beast and Helen Andrejevic continues to inspire with her questions, insights, and her abiding concern for the world. Thanks also to those who have helped to make Australia home, including Oliver Vodeb and Vida Voncina, Olivera Simic and Stojan Ignjatovic, Michael Bolger (and Elizabeth again), Chris Turner, Luke Morey, Michelle Dicinoski, Heather Stewart, and Deb Thomas.

My profound thanks to Erica Wetter at Routledge for her interest in the project and for the invaluable help provided by Margo Irvin, Andrea Service, Reanna Young, and the team at Routledge.

In keeping with this book's fascination with the extra-human, I'd also like to acknowledge the lavender shadows of Brisbane's spring jacarandas, the afternoon sunlight on the back deck in Auchenflower, and the waves at Granite Bay.

I am infinitely indebted and grateful to Zala for her patience, her strength, and her perseverance.

1

INTRODUCTION

Infoglut and Clutter-Cutting

Data Overload

After a two-year investigation into the post-9/11 intelligence industry, the *Washington Post* revealed that a sprawling array of public and private agencies was collecting more information than anyone could possibly comprehend. As the newspaper's report put it, "Every day, collection systems at the National Security Agency intercept and store 1.7 billion e-mails, phone calls and other types of communications. The NSA sorts a fraction of those into 70 separate databases."[1] The NSA is merely one amongst hundreds of agencies and contractors vacuuming up data to be sifted, sorted, and stored. The resulting flood of information is, in part, a function of the technological developments that have made it possible to automatically collect, store, and share fantastic amounts of data. However, making sense of this information trove at the all-too-human receiving end can pose a problem: "Analysts who make sense of documents and conversations obtained by foreign and domestic spying share their judgment by publishing 50,000 intelligence reports each year – a volume so large that many are routinely ignored."[2] The so-called "Super Users" who are supposed to have access to the whole range of information generated by the intelligence apparatus reportedly told the *Post* that "there is simply no way they can keep up with the nation's most sensitive work."[3] As one of them put it, "I'm not going to live long enough to be briefed on everything."[4]

The lament is a familiar one in an era of information overload – and not just for intelligence agencies, marketers, and other collectors of databases. The same challenge is faced by any citizen attempting to read all of the news stories (or Tweets, or status updates, or blogs posts) that are published on a given day, or a financial analyst researching all of the available information pertaining to the performance of a particular company. When I was a journalist in the early 1990s, just as computers entered the newsroom, we had available to us several electronic newswires that updated themselves automatically with stories on topics ranging from international news to US politics to sports and entertainment. I remember thinking at the time that it was impossible to keep up with the news as it unfolded on my screen. By the time I had read one wire story, dozens of new ones had been filed from around the world. That was just a tiny taste of the coming information cornucopia. Now an unimaginably unmanageable flow of mediated information is available to anyone with Internet access.

The paradox of an era of information glut emerges against the background of this new information landscape: at the very moment when we have the technology available to inform ourselves as never before, we are simultaneously and compellingly confronted with the impossibility of ever being *fully* informed. Even more disturbingly, we are confronted with this impossibility at the very moment when we are told that being informed is more important than ever before to our livelihood, our security, and our social lives.

This is not to suggest that it might, once upon a time, have been possible to be "fully informed" – in the sense of knowing all the details of the daily events, their various causes, explanations, and interpretations relating to our social, cultural, political, and economic lives. As Jorge Luis Borges's (insomnia-inspired) allegory of the mnemonic phenomenon Funes suggests, every day we are bombarded with more information than we can possibly absorb or recall. The ability to capture and recount all of this information in detail is precisely what made Funes a freak – or a god: "We, at one glance, can perceive three glasses on a table; Funes, all the leaves and tendrils and fruit that make up a grape vine. He knew by heart the forms of the southern clouds at dawn on the 30th of April, 1882, and could compare them in his memory with the mottled streaks on a book in Spanish binding he had only seen once and with the out-lines of the form raised by an oar in the Rio Negro the night before the Quebracho uprising."[5] There are, of course, some drawbacks to total information awareness, Funes-style: it took him a full day to remember a day (and presumably even longer to recall the day spent remembering it). Moreover, Funes was only recording his direct experiences – as yet un-augmented by the Internet and its bottomless reserves of mediated information.

If it has always been impossible to fully absorb the information by which we are surrounded – still more so to be "fully informed" – the palpable information overload associated with the digital, multi-channel era has made us aware as never before of this impossibility. In his book *Data Smog*, David Shenk observed that "It is estimated that one weekday edition of today's *New York Times* contains more information than the average person in seventeenth-century England was likely to come across in a lifetime."[6] He does not say who did the estimating – and it is a formulation whose credibility, such as it is, depends on a particular definition of information: "in mass mediated form." Surely during the

17th century people were absorbing all kinds of information directly from the world around them, as we do today through the course of our daily lives. There is little indication that our sensory apparatus has become more finely tuned or capacious. However, the amount of *mediated* information – that which we self-consciously reflect upon as information presented to us in constructed and contrived formats (TV shows, movies, newspapers, Tweets, status updates, blogs, text messages, and so on) via various devices including televisions, radios, computers, and so on – has surely increased dramatically, thanks in no small part to the proliferation of portable, networked, interactive devices. Even before the advent of these devices, all we had to do was go to the library to feel overwhelmed by more than we could possibly absorb. Now this excess confronts us at every turn: in the devices we use to work, to communicate with one another, to entertain ourselves. Gult is no longer a "pull" phenomenon but a "push" one. We don't go to it, it comes to us. It is the mediated atmosphere in which we are immersed.

When all we had to do to keep up with the news, for example, was to read a daily newspaper and watch the network evening news, it was easier to imagine the possibility that someone like Walter Cronkite could tell us "the way it is" during the half-hour interlude of an evening newscast. By the first decade of the 21st century, the era of the most-trusted man in America was long gone, as evidenced, for example, by a poll revealing that despite (or perhaps because of) the proliferation of hours devoted to television news, not one major news outlet was trusted by the majority of the American people. Poll upon poll have revealed declining levels of public trust in news outlets and a heightened sense of perceived bias on the part of journalists. The researcher responsible for a 2008 poll noted that "an astonishing percentage of Americans see biases and partisanship in their mainstream news sources" presumably because, "The availability of alternative viewpoints and news sources through the Internet ... contributes to the increased skepticism about the objectivity of profit-driven news outlets owned by large conglomerates."[7] It is not just that there is more information available, but that this very surfeit has highlighted the incompleteness of any individual account. An era of information overload coincides, in other words, with the reflexive recognition of the constructed and partial nature of representation.

Cutting through the Clutter

If it is impossible to be fully informed, in the sense of knowing all of the available accounts of the world (and the accounts about the accounts), it is also necessarily impossible for any particular account to be complete and anything other than partial – in both senses of the word. We have all become intelligence analysts sorting through more data than we can absorb with – and this is one of the recurring themes of the book – what are proving to be inadequate resources for adjudicating amongst the diverse array of narratives. We have become, in a sense, like the intelligence analysts overwhelmed by a tsunami of information or the market researcher trying to make sense of the exploding data "troves" they have created and captured.

In this regard, an era of information overload does not merely change our understanding of how much information is available to us; it also corresponds to changes in the way we think about the role of information in our economic, political, and social lives. This book is, in large part, about the nature of these shifts. If it is, indeed, the case that a growing number of people, from intelligence analysts to citizens, are facing the prospect of unprecedented access to mediated forms of information, then it is worth exploring the ways in which people are adjusting to a changing understanding of how information is treated in a data-saturated world.

Unsurprisingly, one of the characteristic responses to the perceived surfeit of information has been the cultivation of techniques for cutting through the information clutter – shortcuts for managing large amounts of information without necessarily having to delve into, engage with, or even understand it. These techniques vary greatly according to one's position with respect to the database: data miners, for example, have access to resources for storing and sorting large quantities of data that are not available to the typical worker or consumer. Nevertheless, the data miner and the Web surfer are united by a common logic – the need to make sense of a welter of information for the purposes of decision-making. The following chapters will explore a range of diverse responses to the challenge of making sense of information in an era of data surfeit – one in which traditional models of representation and comprehension are called into question not just by the sheer volume of data, but by a reflexive awareness of its incompleteness: its partiality.

These approaches to the challenges posed by information overload range across disparate realms of social practice but share a unifying thread: the attempt to find a shortcut that bypasses the need to comprehend proliferating narrative or referential representations, whether these are in the form of descriptive data, first-person accounts, or expert analysis. The range of approaches covered in this book is meant to be indicative, rather than exhaustive, and includes the following: data mining and predictive analytics (which automate information processing and displace explanation with correlation); sentiment analysis (which purports to translate emotional response and individual opinions into machine readable data that can be mined); prediction markets (which replace credentialed expertise with aggregate demand and calls this wisdom); body language analysis (which privileges immediate bodily reactions over the vagaries of narrative content) and neuro-marketing (a form of body language analysis that requires special equipment).

These strategies for cutting through the information clutter vary widely in terms of the resources and techniques they draw on, not least because managing large amounts of data can be an expensive and resource intensive proposition. At the same time, they are united not just by the problem they address – how to make sense of more data than can be fully understood or absorbed (or, and I will argue that this is a related development, how to bypass the contrived character of representation) – but also by the solution they envisage: an attempt to bypass or short-circuit the problem of comprehension and the forms of discursive, narrative representation upon which it relies. This might sound at first like a somewhat opaque formulation, but it is one that will become clearer with the help of the examples and case studies that follow.

Because information is crucial to the functioning of any society – and widespread access to information is an important aspect of a democratic society – the shifting information environment has important consequences for questions of power and politics. Thus, the following chapters will consider the societal implications of a new information landscape in which only the few have access to the infrastructure for storing and making sense of large amounts of data. It will also consider the political implications of the challenges to traditional models of sense-making posed by a reflexive awareness of the partial character of mediated forms of representation.

The Changing Landscape of Information and Power

Once upon a time, in an era of relative media and data scarcity, the political control of information relied upon attempts to define and reinforce dominant narratives that accorded with the interests of those in power. Karl Marx and Friedrich Engels's famous formulation in *The German Ideology* captured this version of ideological control: "The ideas of the ruling class are in every epoch the ruling ideas ... The class which has the means of material production at its disposal, has control at the same time over the means of mental production ... therefore, as they rule as a class and determine the extent and compass of an epoch, it is self-evident that they do this in its whole range, hence among other things rule also as thinkers, as producers of ideas."[8] This understanding of the relationship of ideas to power meant that attacks on dominant interests relied at least in part on challenges to the dominant understandings of the world upon which they depended. Similarly, economic control of information meant securing the most accurate and up-to-date information about prices and the variables likely to affect them. In still another register, police control of information meant targeting wrongdoers: finding the evidence to identify, catch, and prosecute lawbreakers.

In an era of information glut, however, new strategies of control emerge alongside these: in the political realm, information control over information no longer necessarily depends upon sustaining a dominant narrative; in the financial realm, as in that of policing and security, data collection leads to large-scale strategies of correlation, prediction, and pre-emption that would have been impossible in the pre-digital era. This shift, to the extent that it accurately characterizes a changing relationship between ways of knowing and forms of power, heralds a reconfiguration of our understanding of the political implications of challenges to dominant narratives – of the efficacy of "speaking truth to power." It also augers a changed understanding of the role played by data in managing markets and securing the population – themes that will be taken up in subsequent chapters.

Consider an example from the political realm, in which the proliferation of narratives and counter-narratives, of fact-checking and critiques of fact-checking, can all work to multiply the available accounts of reality to the point that it becomes difficult to adjudicate between them based on the constantly moving evidence. The George W. Bush administration relied on a proliferating tangle of multiple and conflicting narratives to manage the revelation that US troops in the initial stages of the Iraq invasion had failed to secure the huge weapons cache at the Al QaQaa facility – a site that the International Atomic Energy Agency (IAEA) had repeatedly warned the administration about, describing it as "the greatest explosives bonanza in history."[9] The revelation of the missing explosives, coming as it did in the midst of the 2004 presidential campaign, might have been devastating to Bush, whose administration had, despite repeated warnings and its alleged goal of discovering "weapons of mass destruction," apparently allowed some 380 tons of high-grade explosives, ideal for the purposes of concealed, portable bombs, to fall into enemy hands, providing ample armaments for an extended and violent resistance.

The way the administration handled the revelation, which it had tried to keep under wraps by preventing the IAEA from inspecting the site, was instructive: rather than providing a "dominant" narrative of what had happened, it did its best to exploit the fog of war to throw up a series of often contradictory explanations. This might be described, following the philosopher Slavoj Zizek's invocation of Freud, as the "borrowed kettle" alibi of power. The term refers to the multiplication of contradictory narratives refuting apparent facts: confronted with the fact that a borrowed kettle was returned with a hole in it, the person accused of breaking it responds with several mutually contradictory excuses: "there was already a hole when I borrowed it; the hole wasn't there when I returned it; I didn't even borrow the kettle."[10] Such forms of narrative multiplication have become a hallmark of the media strategy of what might be described as the postmodern right for handling political debates that they appear to be losing, such as that over climate change: global warming does not exist; even if it does exist, it is not caused by man-made activity; if there is global warming it could have beneficial effects (longer growing seasons, etc.); the world is actually getting cooler, etc.

With respect to the case of the missing explosives, administration officials early on conceded to reporters that in the confusion of the initial invasion (and the frenzied search for weapons of mass destruction – WMDs) the troops had apparently failed to secure the Al Qa'Qaa site. One administration official told the *New York Times*, in its initial story, "It's not an excuse ... But a lot of things went by the boards."[11] Over time, as the damaging import of the revelation became clear, the administration back-tracked, suggesting at various times that the site had been looted before US troops arrived, that Iraqis had smuggled the weapons into Syria, and alternatively that the explosives hadn't disappeared at all, but had been accounted for and disposed of by US troops. Under pressure from reporters, the White House alternatively claimed that the president had not known about the missing cache until a few days before the story broke and that it had embarked on an in-depth investigation once the explosives had been discovered to be missing several months earlier. At one point, the right-wing *Washington Times* floated the unconfirmed story – leaked to them by an unnamed person at the Department of Defense – that Russian special forces had "almost certainly" removed most of the explosives prior to the invasion and sent them to Syria, Lebanon, and "possibly Iran."[12]

As the days passed, the story did not become any clearer – on the contrary, the fog got thicker – with the administration capitalizing on the impossibility of getting the full story (thanks, in part, to its own reluctance to release details) as a means of discrediting critics. As one spokesperson put it, in response to the opposition candidate's charge of negligence: "John Kerry presumes to know something that he could not know: when the material disappeared ... Since he does not know whether it was gone before the war began, he can't prove it was there to be secured."[13] The strategy of sowing confusion extended to deliberately misinterpreting news reports (forcing NBC to issue a clarification explaining how its reporting was to be interpreted) and accusing critics of "insulting" the troops.[14] As time passed, and the administration promulgated various possible explanations, the journalistic consensus became, as a correspondent for *US News and World Report* put it, "there are many more questions than answers regarding this story."[15] As Bush's handlers might have put it: "Mission accomplished!"

Finally, the alleged uncertainty surrounding the story was used to question the *Times*'s motivation in running the story in the first place and to question its release shortly before the election. Although the story had been triggered by a letter reporting the looting of the explosives to the IAEA from an Iraqi official, the administration's challenge seemed to run as follows: since no news story can be complete, this one was not, and therefore should not have been, run. If such a formulation sounds simply like an argument against news in general, it is actually something more: an argument against information-based decision-making in an era of information glut. Not only can we never be fully informed, but, somewhat recursively, we cannot be fully informed about how uninformed we are. Shenk argues that the result of information overload is a kind of paralysis: "The psychological reaction to such an overabundance of information and competing expert opinions is to simply avoid coming to conclusions."[16] This observation is demonstrably false: we continue to draw conclusions all the time, not least because of the ongoing pressure to make decisions based on our reaction to the world around us. The question is not whether we get there, but how we arrive.

Against the background of an indeterminate surfeit of information, the impetus for decision must come from elsewhere. In an article on George W. Bush's famous reliance on gut instinct rather than facts, Brian Massumi outlined the somewhat opaque logic of the data-free decision:

> To admit to discussing, studying, consulting, analyzing is to admit to having been in a state of indecision preceding the making of the decision. It is to admit to passages of doubt and unclarity in a blurry present. It is the blurriness that will continue as a trend into the future … A trustable decision is not made in any dangerously deliberative way. A confident decision strikes like lightning. It *happens* … What's new about it is that the consequences that determine the decision's correctness are directly affective rather than factual.[17]

We might contrast this analysis of Bush's "gut" certainty to an insider's assessment of the indecisiveness reportedly evinced by Bill Clinton – a confirmed policy wonk and data junkie – during White House meetings: "Clinton carried a lot of information in his head … something that didn't always work to his advantage. Reagan, being uninformed, could be utterly clear about his simple goals; Clinton, being exceedingly informed, sometimes got lost in his facts."[18] The following chapters will explore in various ways this formulation of the problem (that more information obscures rather than clarifies the picture) and of some possible solution, including a reliance on intuition and gut instinct rather than informed deliberation, as well as strategies for letting the data, as it were, speak for itself.

Critique in the Era of the Postmodern Right

The Bush administration's response to Al QaQaa represents a generalizable strategy tailored to an era of multiple news outlets and a burgeoning blogosphere that encourage a reflexive understanding of the biased and incomplete character of evidence-based accounts of all kinds, ranging from the journalistic to the scientific. We might describe the "borrowed kettle" response as a ruse of the postmodern right. What it has taken from the postmodern turn is both an obsession with the power of the image and an understanding that not only are all truths constructed, but they are *nothing more* than constructions: the result of imposed closures that can be opened up and unraveled. It turns out that this is a useful strategy not just for debunking dominant narratives, but also for undermining critique. In their book *Merchants of Doubt*, Naomi Oreskes and Erik Conway offer a detailed account of how a small group of right-wing scientists have strategically sought to cast doubt on the scientific consensus on issues ranging from the hazards of smoking to the damage caused by acid rain and the threat of human-induced climate change.[19] The strategy of the scientists involved – who were committed to combating industry regulation – was to "use normal scientific uncertainty to undermine the status of actual scientific knowledge. As in *jiujitsu*, you could use science against itself. 'Doubt is our product,' ran the infamous memo written by one tobacco industry executive in 1969."[20]

The strategy is not limited to scientific knowledge, but can be imported directly into the political realm, in part because it reduces evidence based claims to a matter of politics. As Oreskes and Conway put it, "science, even mainstream science, was [treated as] just politics by other means. Therefore if you disagreed with it politically, you could dismiss it as political."[21] If scientific knowledge is replaced by the more general category of fact- or research-based claims, the pattern is becoming a familiar and oft-bemoaned one in US presidential politics: the alleged uncertainty over whether Barack Obama was really born in the United States; the details of John Kerry's military service; the so-called "death panels" feared by opponents of healthcare reform. In each case, the goal is not so much to propose an authoritative counter-narrative as to use the expanded media space to engulf any dominant narrative in possible alternatives, to highlight the indeterminacy of the evidence by promulgating endless narratives of debunkery and counter-debunkery: not to "cut through the clutter," but, on the contrary, to suck critique into the clutter blender; not to "speak truth to power" but to highlight the contingency, indeterminateness, and, ultimately, the helplessness of so-called truth in the face of power.

Writing in *The Atlantic*, James Fallows has characterized this strategy as the emergence of "post-truth politics" – a term that has started to receive some traction amongst pundits.[22] Post-truthism is fundamentally a "small-c" conservative strategy in the sense that it tends to work in the interest of existing power relations: there's not much point in neutralizing the power of critique if you want to challenge or transform existing power relations. But if you happen to be in power already, the thorough debunking of deliberation and the dismantling of truth claims is more threatening for one's enemies than one's allies. When the truth crumbles around you, the assumption is that you'll still be holding the reins, and what once looked like a threatening form of demystification will have dissipated into a cloud of claims swirling harmlessly like confetti.

Scarcity versus Glut

The way in which we tend to think about the role of information and knowledge in a democratic society took shape during an era of relative information scarcity (at least in the mediated realm): we need newspapers to provide us with information about the world we live in, uncensored history books and encyclopedias to fill in the background, experts to make sense of this information, and a range of information sources to ensure the availability of differing perspectives, arguments, and forms of evidence. Many (but not all) of the historical struggles related to control over information in the history of contemporary democratic societies revolve around issues of scarcity and the restriction of access to information. Attempts to ban books, to license and regulate printing presses, to prevent public access to government records and proceedings, to privatize or censor information, are just some of the ways in which entrenched groups have sought to secure and protect their privileged positions through strategies of enforced scarcity.

This history helps to explain why the Internet has been greeted as an empowering medium: it is received as a scarcity-fighting machine: a means of enhancing public access to information and countering attempts by the state or the private sector to hoard, control, or otherwise monopolize access to information. In many respects, of course, this is an inaccurate portrayal of the functioning of the Internet, which introduces new forms of opacity (regarding, for example, the type of information collected about users by state and private entities) even as it promises transparency. Nonetheless, in myriad ways, both symbolic and concrete, the Internet has had the result of making an unprecedented range of information available to a growing portion of the populace, while also providing it with access to content creation and distribution tools. For this reason the Internet has been called the most powerful and revolutionary communication technology since the invention of the printing press, another technology which eventually facilitated access to a wide range of content previously controlled or monopolized by religious, economic, political, and cultural elites.[23]

With this background in mind, it is worth considering the assumptions that underlie the equation of access to information with empowerment. These include the notion that wider access contributes to forms of knowledge that are convergent (i.e., that more people will come to share more accurate forms of understanding) and efficacious (in the sense that knowledge has some purchase on the operation of power). In political terms, efficacy assumes a degree of accountability: an understanding on the part of the authorities that public knowledge can lead to consequential public action. This is the underlying assumption behind the notion that "sunlight is the best disinfectant" and the role of civil society in a democratic state. Attempts to restrict access to information, in this model, work to prevent both the emergence of shared understandings and the consequences these might hold for entrenched forms of power.

From the perspective of an environment of information scarcity and controlled access to the means of information production and distribution, technologies that make information more readily available and sharable carry with them a potential challenge to entrenched forms of power. As Stephen Coleman puts it, "Interactivity is political: it shifts control towards the receivers of messages and makes all representations of reality vulnerable to public challenge and disbelief."[24] A telling equation is at work in this formulation: that fostering "disbelief" or "challenge" correlates with a shift in control. It is an equation that fails to take into account the way in which strategies of debunkery and information proliferation can work to reinforce, rather than threaten, relations of power and control. Nevertheless, variants of this claim circulate in a range of discourses, from the popular to the academic, and must be understood as forming a keystone of the ideology of the digital era.

The media have been getting in on the act, as evidenced by *Time* magazine's person of the year celebrating "you" – that is, all of us – as "people of the year," thanks to the empowering force of interactive media: "It's about the many wresting power from the few and helping one another for nothing and how that will not only change the world, but also change the way the world changes."[25] Such sentiments follow the path paved by the celebratory claims of media theorists that, "Far from the telescreen dystopias, new media technology hails a rebirth of democratic life."[26] The constellation of themes in these claims take for granted a particular modality of power: one in which information control is exerted in a top-down way that must be protected from feedback – from the ability to question or respond. It is a monolithic, industrial-era model of power, which is why Celia Pearce insists that the revolutionary power of interactivity "is one of intellectual, creative and social empowerment. It is anti-industrial."[27]

Such a formulation recalls the techniques that critics deployed against a top-down model of ideology: attempts to denaturalize and deconstruct, to reveal the forms of power that permeate claims to truth and knowledge. It is in this context that the promise of interactivity emerges not just as a political one, but as potentially subversive and empowering: a tool of demystification perhaps unwittingly crafted by a modern-day Prometheus of the information revolution and duly handed over to the populace at large. Interactivity is political, according to this account, because the hermeneutics of suspicion serve as a tool for empowerment when strategies for control operate in the register of naturalized truth.

What if, however, the modality of control can itself shift in ways that incorporate the very forms of critique that once sought to challenge it by undermining and deconstructing it? Such is the possibility raised by Bruno Latour in his lament on the fate of critique, "Threats might have changed so much that we might still be directing all our arsenal east or west while the enemy has now moved to a very different place."[28] This new "place", Latour suggests, is one in which the forms of challenge, suspicion, and deconstruction mobilized to critique dominant narratives and interests come to align themselves with strategies of control. What if, in other words, that which was once challenged by the deconstructive arsenal now feeds upon it? This is the specter raised by "post-truth" politics and the information practices of the postmodern right that seek to undermine the version of critique as truth telling.

The strategic goal of such approaches is not the reassertion of a naturalized discourse, but the attempt to deconstruct certainty itself, and to "talk back" to the experts. Critique is turned back upon itself. The rejoinder to critique is not the attempt to reassert a counter-narrative about, say, the scientific consensus around global warming, but to cast doubt on any narrative's attempt to claim dominance: all so-called experts are biased, any account partial, all conclusions the result of an arbitrary and premature closure of the debate. Latour describes such developments as a shift in the critical context that warrants new critical tools and approaches: "It does not seem to me that we have been as quick, in academia, to prepare ourselves for new threats, new dangers, new tasks, new targets. Are we not like those mechanical toys that endlessly make the same gesture when everything else has changed around them?"[29]

As deconstructive debunkery becomes automatic and the critiques of totalities and grand narratives become totalizing, mechanical, and taken for granted, these can no longer be unthinkingly equated with progressive politics, or a subversive challenge to power. They may have become, in certain contexts, a ruse of the very forms of power against which they once set themselves. In these contexts, there is no clear-cut political opposition between strategies of naturalization and techniques of reflexive deconstruction: both can serve regressive ends and be deployed as strategies for manipulation, obfuscation, and the reproduction of power relations. The challenge is to trace the relationship between critique and knowledge, to discern how an unreflective critique turns on itself, and to further consider how it might be extricated from this impasse.

The smokescreen approach to political manipulation has a long and storied history, but, as Latour's analysis implies, it has come into its own in an era in which an unthinking "savvy" skepticism aligns itself with the emerging interactive ethos. Yes, the interactive capability of the Internet makes it possible to talk back, to question, to circulate counter-narratives, and consequently to counter dominant narratives. In an era in which the reproduction of social relations relied solely on the unquestioned reproduction of such narratives, we might describe the deployment of interactivity as politically subversive, perhaps even politically empowering.

The Demise of Symbolic Efficiency

It is not difficult to discern that the strategy of disseminating uncertainty relies on shifts in the media environment – on the proliferation of information outlets, the fragmentation of audiences, the way in which interactivity renders "representations of reality vulnerable to public challenge and disbelief."[30] This popularization of a variant of unreflective postmodern debunkery exhibits a certain affinity with the technologies and practices that enable it. Sherry Turkle noted, relatively early on in the Internet era, the link between new media practices and a ready recognition of the constructed character of representation: "technology is bringing a set of ideas associated with postmodernism – in this case, ideas about the instability of meanings and the lack of universal and knowable truths – into everyday life."[31] She suggests that the participatory character of the Internet, and in particular the forms of online socializing that it fostered, were responsible. As users shifted from consuming mediated images to creating them, they gained a self-conscious, practice-based awareness about their constructed character.

This awareness might be described as "post-deferential"[32] insofar as it is associated with an unwillingness to take dominant media representations at face value. Taken to its limit the post-deferential attitude results in the impasse that Slavoj Zizek has described in terms of the decline of symbolic efficiency.[33] As he puts it, symbolic efficiency relies upon "the distance (between 'things' and 'words') which opens up the space for ... symbolic engagement."[34] This paradoxical space of the symbolic acknowledges the possibility that things might be otherwise than how they "directly" seem. The distance opened up between things and words, Zizek suggests, has an important role to play at the level of social and political institutions in which:

> ... the symbolic mask-mandate matters more than the direct reality of the individual who wears this mask and/or assumes this mandate. This function involves the structure of fetishistic disavowal: I know very well that things are the way I see them [that this person is a corrupt weakling], but none the less I treat him with respect, since he wears the insignia of a judge, so that when he speaks it is the Law itself which speaks through him.[35]

The post-deferential attitude short-circuits this logic, brushing aside the symbolic mandate in order to get directly at the "corrupt weakling" behind the black robe. As in the case of virtual reality, it allows for no space between the code and what it defines.

It is not hard to trace connections between the forms of post-deferentialism described by Turkle and Zizek, and the way in which the constructed character of representation comes to the fore in an environment of information glut. The proliferation of content associated with this glut takes several forms, including narrative recycling, the multiplication of alternative narratives, and the reflexive documentation of the story behind the story. None of these tendencies is original or unique to the Internet or the digital era – the difference is more one of quantity than of kind – and yet the form they take in the changed historical context is unique and worth considering. Nor does the assertion of the correlation between post-deferentialism and digital media necessarily imply causality: there are many different ways to use digital networks, and the uses at issue are the result of the current social, economic, and cultural conjuncture.

To the extent that it serves as an enormous content archive, the Internet, ephemeral as it may be in some ways, allows users to step outside the flow of more perishable media such as radio, TV, newspapers, and magazines.

Last week's news is still available online, along with rebuttals, qualifications, alternative perspectives, and so on. It is telling that the dominant metaphors for the Internet tend to be spatial ones ("cyberspace," "websurfing," "hyper-linking," etc.), whereas those for mass media are more temporally oriented (the linear "flow" of TV or radio programming, the fleeting character of yesterday's news, and so on). It is the broad sweep of this information landscape that helps make any particular point isolated from it appear purely partial or perspectival, arbitrarily closed off from an ever-more complex combination of myriad alternative narratives and perspectives. In this regard, the Internet is a medium well suited to an era of media reflexivity – one in which the populace is increasingly savvy about the constructed character of representation.

The "demise of symbolic" efficiency associated with this reflexivity is one of the organizing themes of this book because it highlights the perceived deadlocks of representation associated with contemporary forms of information glut. The term captures a dominant attitude of savvy mistrust and suspicion toward discourse combined with the attempt to bypass representation entirely to get at a more immediate ground for action. Thus, for example, neuro-marketers repeatedly invoke the unreliability of interviews and self-report: if people's words are unreliable, their brains might provide more direct access to the truth of their desires, their preferences, their fears and anxieties, hopes and dreams – all the things marketers want to tap into. In this regard, neuromarketing updates the Groucho Marx question so often invoked by Zizek: "What do you trust: my words or the ability of your eyes to 'see' my brain in action?"[36] Perhaps the defining symptom of the demise of symbolic efficiency is the attempt to bypass mediation and its vagaries by gaining direct access to a pre-discursive "truth" not yet caught up in the tangles of representation. This is the case of body language analysis and neuromarketing (discussed in Chapters 5 and 6, respectively). Another characteristic symptom is the attempt to use information in ways that obviate the need for comprehension – to relegate the process to an impersonal system that does the "knowing" for us – such as a machine-learning algorithm that makes sense of the data for us, or a decision market in which the inscrutable workings of the market allegedly assess the available information more efficiently and effectively than the experts (data mining and decision markets are taken up in Chapters 2 and 6).

We might describe the automation of sense-making as a variant of the "interpassivity" described by Zizek in which belief is offloaded onto the figure of the "other" who believes for us.[37] The challenge to comprehension, sense-making, and referentiality posed by information glut leads to the offloading of knowledge-generating processes onto the figure of the sorting machine or the allocating market. We no longer have to take responsibility for making sense of the data – the apparatus does this for us. In both cases – that of the algorithm and that of the market – the autonomous sense-making procedure is incomprehensible in the sense that it cannot be reduced to a model or predicted in advance. What differentiates data mining from the historical use of databases is that the former is meant to generate previously unknown patterns (patterns that cannot be perceived prior to running the algorithms or actualizing the market). To the extent that they are used for forecasting, both data mining and decision markets are strategies of simulation – not in the sense of modeling or imitating an existing reality, but rather in that of generating a process as unpredictable as reality – in order to be able to predict and manage it.

The (Re)Turn to Affect

The significance of emotion, affect, and sentiment, are, furthermore, foregrounded by the demise of symbolic efficiency insofar as they come to represent cognitive shortcuts through the deadlock of representation (the reflexive recognition that all representations are partial, and that the goal of being fully informed is an impossible/infinite one). As will be discussed in more detail in Chapter 5, in the recent literature on decision-making, emotional responses are portrayed as shorthand summaries of learned preferences that allow information to be winnowed down subconsciously. These visceral shortcuts are portrayed as much more efficient than rational forms of cognition and comprehension. Emotional responses become the subject of renewed interest in the context of information overload both as a means of managing information and consequently as an avenue of influence.

The renewed recognition of the role of affect and emotion as decision-making drivers – means of cutting through the clutter – is reinforced by recently developed monitoring strategies for tracking and measuring sentiment and opinion. The advent of social media creates a data trove (or glut) of affective response: millions of messages about people's reactions to news events, products, popular culture, and the events of everyday life. At a moment of renewed interest in the role of emotion in decision-making, more data than ever before can be captured about people's emotional reactions and opinions. Thus, the popularity of social media has inaugurated a prolifically productive category of demographic information in the register of the affective rather than the descriptive: the challenge becomes how best to measure and describe it in machine-interpretable form.

The Fate of Critique

The case studies of different ways of managing data glut – and of the ways of "knowing" associated with these strategies – presented in the following chapters are meant to get at two related concerns: the power relations associated with emerging regimes of "knowledge" in the era of "big data" and the fate of critique in the era of the demise of symbolic efficiency. The two are closely related because the notion of critique hearkens back to a particular way of knowing: the Enlightenment use of reason as a challenge to tradition. Kant famously formulated the motto of Enlightenment as "dare to know": "*Sapre aude!* Have courage to use your own reason!" (*Sapere aude!*).[38] What happens when we offload our "knowing" onto the database (or algorithm) because the new forms of knowledge available are "too big" for us to comprehend? Likewise, what happens when reason turns back on itself, tracing its own limitations and indeterminacies in ways that reproduce the allegedly surpassed binary of reason and emotion, privileging the latter in strategies for sense-making and clutter cutting? In Chapter 7 I argue that when a particular version of the split between reason and emotion is reinscribed so that affective "truths" come to stand in for debunked discursive ones, the result is the collapse of critique into conspiracy theory – a fundamentally conservative (in the sense of reinforcing existing power relations) result of the demise of symbolic efficiency. This is not to recapitulate the worn-out celebration of reason at the expense of emotion; rather, it is to call into question the reconfiguration of the relationship between these two categories. Although emotion is endowed with a certain kind of cognitive power, this is portrayed, suggestively, as inaccessible to conscious forms of cognition – as a kind of learned reflex.

The conclusion argues that this external relationship between thought and emotion is conserved in recent formulations of affect – as well as in the measures of aggregated "sentiment" developed by data miners. The conclusion proposes an alternative way of thinking this relationship by drawing on Walter Benjamin's notion of the "mimetic" faculty – and its uptake by Theodor Adorno. The framing of such an alternative is meant to address the question of what it might mean to imagine a form of cognition that traverses the feeling/knowing distinction and thereby to address some of the challenges posed by information overload, including the default of critique to conspiracy.

It is important not to overstate the case: we do not (yet) inhabit a world in which symbolic efficacy is finally and effectively lost. Indeed, it would be hard to imagine such a world. The notion designates a tendency more than an endpoint, and the tendency is far from being a universal one – it coexists and clashes with others, marking perhaps a deeper manifestation of the so-called "culture wars." The journalist Ronald Suskind provides one of the defining popular representations of this clash in his interview with a top aide to former President George W. Bush for an article about the latter that parallels Massumi's description of Bush's tendency to make important policy decisions based on gut instinct and "feel," rather than on careful consideration of the available research. This tendency is reflected in the administration's calculated promotion of Bush's visceral appeal over his expertise, in his self-described ability to directly access the "souls" of others (Putin), and in his famed reluctance to "overthink." As Laura Bush put it, "He has good instincts, and he goes with them. He doesn't need to evaluate and reevaluate a decision. He doesn't try to *overthink*. He likes action."[39] This is the aspect of Bush's vital talent that reporters such as Suskind too often overlook, according to the Bush aide (later reported to be Karl Rove):[40]

> The aide said that guys like me were "in what we call the reality-based community," which he defined as people who "believe that solutions emerge from your judicious study of discernible reality." I nodded and murmured something about enlightenment principles and empiricism. He cut me off. "That's not the way the world really works anymore," he continued. "We're an empire now, and when we act, we create our own reality. And while you're studying that reality – judiciously, as you will – we'll act again, creating other new realities, which you can study too, and that's how things will sort out."[41]

The aide uncannily (and presumably unknowingly) echoed Jean Baudrillard, who makes similar use of the notion of Empire (but as a form of critique rather than celebration) in his description of the logic of simulation.[42] Baudrillard opens his discussion of simulation with a reference to Jorge Luis Borges's fable about an Empire whose ambitious cartographers make such a detailed map that it covers the entire territory. As the Empire goes into decline, the map similarly falls into ruins, with only its shreds remaining dispersed across the territory. Baudrillard updates and inverts the fable for an era in which simulation displaces reality, claiming that "today it is the territory whose shreds slowly rot across the extent of the map." He goes on to anticipate the post-reality-based Empire described by Rove: "even inverted, Borges's fable is unusable. Only the allegory of the Empire, perhaps, remains. Because it is with this same imperialism that present-day simulators attempt to make the real, all of the real, coincide with their models of simulation."[43]

At stake, then, in the diagnosis of the decline of symbolic efficiency is a reconfiguration of the relationship between forms of knowledge and power. Two aspects of this relationship are of particular concern: first, the increasing asymmetry between those who are able to capture, store, access, and process the tremendous amounts of data produced by the proliferation of digital, interactive sensors of all kinds; and, second, ways of understanding and using information that are uniquely available to those with access to the database. The dystopian version of information glut anticipates a world in which control over the tremendous amount of information generated by interactive devices is concentrated in the hands of the few who use it to sort, manage, and manipulate. Those without access to the database are left with the "poor person's" strategies for cutting through the clutter: gut instinct, affective response, and "thin-slicing" (making a snap decision based on a tiny fraction of the evidence). The asymmetric strategies for using data highlight an all-too-often overlooked truth of the digital era: infrastructure matters. Behind the airy rhetoric of "the cloud," the factories of the big data era are sprouting up across the landscape: huge server farms that consume as much energy as a small city. Here is where data is put to work – generating correlations and patterns, shaping decisions and sorting people into categories for marketers, employers, intelligence agencies, healthcare providers, financial institutions, the police, and so on. Herein resides an important dimension of the knowledge asymmetry of the big data era – the divide between those who generate the data and those who put it to use by turning it back upon the population. This divide is, at least in part, an infra-structural one shaped by ownership and control of the material resources for data storage and mining. But it is also an epistemological one – a difference in the forms of practical knowledge available to those with access to the database, in the way they think about and use information.

The type of "knowledge" generated by these databases and controlled by those with access to them might possibly be challenged, qualified, and shaped by more human forms of knowing and policies that derive from considered discussions about how best to put this new power to work for the whole of society. However, it is precisely the purchase of discursive deliberation and the nature of comprehension that is called into question by the demise of symbolic efficiency. William Connolly, for example, has described the challenge posed by "the insufficiency of what might be called intellectualist and deliberationist models of thinking."[44] The proliferation of information upon which new strategies for information processing and knowledge production rely thereby contribute to knowledge practices that inoculate themselves against the forms of critique that might hold them in check. Furthermore, the novelty of emerging data-mining techniques poses a challenge deriving from the lack of widespread knowledge about their potential power. It is one thing to understand that a broad array of information about our behavior and communications is being collected and archived, and quite another to anticipate how this information will be used. As one privacy consultant put it, "What I don't see people thinking about are the privacy issues that will result from applying the data analytics tools of tomorrow to the data being collected today."[45] The claims of data mining suggest that such issues are, to some degree, unknowable. We cannot anticipate the type of patterns that will emerge until we run the algorithms: in this regard, we are at the mercy of our databases.

Things are not, however, as dystopian as they seem. I will argue that the critique of symbolic efficiency and the related development of knowledge practices that attempt to bypass the deadlocks of representation have not been sufficiently self-reflexive. My goal in exploring in some detail several attempts to bypass forms of discursive or narrative representation is to extract from these the resources for considering the ways in which they conserve the symbolic logics they claim to surpass. In doing so, I embark upon a critique of an overly quick, popularized embrace of deconstructive debunkery and the post-truth politics it underwrites. The journey starts in the digital depths of the data mine.

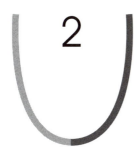

2

INTELLIGENCE GLUT

Policing, Security, and Predictive Analytics

In our society we have no major crimes ... but we do have a detention camp full of would-be criminals.

John Anderton in "The Minority Report" (Dick, 1994)

What Is Total Information Awareness Good For?

Once upon a time when a mass shooting took place in the United States, the familiar media response was often one of bewilderment on the part of those who knew the perpetrator: "Who would have guessed that such an impulse lay dormant, waiting to emerge, in the heart and mind of a neighbor or co-worker." And the familiar refrain went something along the lines of, "He just seemed like an ordinary guy ... I never would have believed he could have done *this*." The implicit and somewhat disturbing message was that, "you never can tell": maniacal tendencies may be lurking under the surface anywhere, perhaps everywhere, waiting to be triggered. In the post-9/11 era, this potential threat seemed to align itself with the unpredictable character of terrorism, which could potentially strike anywhere at any time, along any threat vector.

In keeping with this connection to the unpredictability of the terrorist threat, and, more specifically, with the proposed solution provided by new monitoring and surveillance technologies that have received much publicity in the interim, the bewilderment in the face of mass murder is now supplemented with an additional question: would it have been possible to predict that the shooter might one day cause mayhem and tragedy despite the trappings of ordinariness? This is a significant shift in the tone of the response: from shock and surprise to data-driven forms of prediction and pre-emption. As a *Wall Street Journal* columnist put it shortly after the mass shooting at a midnight movie screening in Colorado that left 12 dead and 58 injured: "Aside from privacy considerations, is there anything in principle to stop government computers, assuming they have access to the data, from algorithmically detecting the patterns of a mass shooting in the planning stages?"[1] After all, we are increasingly regaled with evidence of the power of new forms of data mining and so-called "predictive analytics" in the big data era: retailers can figure out when a young woman is pregnant even before she has told her family, and marketers claim to be able to anticipate our desires before we know them ourselves. If they can anticipate what brand of cereal we are likely to buy and what interest rate will induce us to get a new credit card, shouldn't they be able to predict when someone is planning to do something a lot more dramatic and dangerous?

The question recalls the post-9/11 data-driven plans of Admiral John Poindexter for a Total Information Awareness program that would sift through a giant database of databases in search of threat indicators. Indeed, the *Wall Street Journal* opens its op-ed piece about the Colorado shooting with the question, "Would Total Information Awareness have stopped James Eagan Holmes [the suspect in the Colorado shooting]?"[2] Put that way, the question sounds almost rhetorical: "total information awareness" implies a high degree of predictive power: if you could keep an electronic eye on everyone's actions all the time, surely you could unearth the symptoms of eventual wrongdoing. Set aside for a moment that the version of security on offer requires willing submission to "total" surveillance and simply consider the fantasy of pre-emption opened up by the technology: "a future landscape of surveillance without limits – everything visible in advance, everything transparent, sterilized, and risk-free, nothing secret, absolute foreknowledge of events."[3] If this sounds futuristic and vaguely absurd, consider the claims that are currently being made on behalf of so-called predictive policing, which uses past crime patterns and related data to guide the deployment of police patrols: "It is now possible to predict the future when it comes to crime, such as identifying crime trends, anticipating hotspots in the community, refining resource deployment decisions, and ensuring the greatest protection for citizens in the most efficient manner."[4] It is perhaps a telling sign of the power of the promise of new information and communication technologies, based on their ability to collect, store, and process huge amounts of data, that one of our first reactions to the unexpected has become: "could the database have predicted it?" – and the automatic corollary: "could the database have prevented it?"

Lurking in these two questions is an assumption about the character of knowledge in the digital era: the notion that the only limit on our predictive power is the ability to effectively organize all the available information. If this were indeed the case, then the development of technological information storage and processing technology might compensate for the shortcomings of the human brain by ushering in new forms of aggregate "knowledge" and predictive power. Such forms of "knowing" would, in a sense, exceed the limits of human comprehension. It would no longer be a question of comprehending the data or using it to understand, in referential fashion, the world to which it refers, but rather of putting the data to use. The promise of automated data processing is to unearth the patterns that are far too complex for any human analyst to detect and to run the simulations that generate emergent patterns that would otherwise defy our predictive power. The form of "knowledge" on offer is limited to those with access to the database and the processing power, and it replicates the logic of "knowing without knowing" insofar as it can serve as the basis for decisions while exceeding the processing power of any individual human brain.

In keeping with the logic of digital convergence, this form of knowledge is portrayed by its proponents as universal insofar as it is generalizable across the political, economic, and social domains. It can be used to predict consumer behavior as well as the spread of disease, or the likelihood that someone will need to be hospitalized within the coming year. Keeping this convergent background in mind, this chapter will focus on the somewhat narrower example of policing and security in order to explore the knowledge practices associated with data mining and predictive analytics in the era of "big data." In particular, the focus will be upon the version of distributed, predictive "knowledge" that emerges from the database. As McCue puts it in her discussion of the use of predictive analytics for security purposes, "With data mining we can perform exhaustive searches of very large databases using automated methods, searching well beyond the capacity of human analysts or even a team of analysts."[5]

In the wake of the development of database technology, there is an emerging tendency to devalue individual comprehension in comparison with the alleged predictive power derived from "super-crunching" tremendous amounts of data. This development has significant implications for the promise that because new information and communication technologies are less or non-hierarchical, they are therefore forces for democratization and user empowerment. If the (allegedly) more powerful and productive forms of knowledge associated with "big data" are limited to those with access to the database and processing power, digital-era knowledge practices could prove to be even more exclusive and asymmetrical than those they promise to displace. Widespread access to digital media would go hand-in-hand with what might be described as the emergence of a "big data" divide – one that could not be ameliorated by any relatively simple technological fix (such as more widespread broadband access) or by enhanced forms of education and training. In this respect, the knowledge practices associated with big data represent a profoundly *un-*democratic shift insofar as they are reliant upon access to huge and costly databases as well as to the processing power and technological know-how to make use of the data.

Simulation as Deterrence

The French cultural theorist Jean Baudrillard famously defined simulation as a form of deterrence, taking as his model the Cold War logic of "mutually assured destruction" (MAD). The deterrent effect of simulation has been a recurring theme in popular science fiction that received perhaps its most iconic pop-culture treatment in the movie *War Games*, which portrays a computer game that goes awry, accessing the United States missile defense system and transforming a game of simulated nuclear war into the real thing. Disaster is averted when the program considers all possible outcomes of the "game" of global thermonuclear war and discovers that, as in tic-tac-toe, if both sides play rationally, attempting to win, there can be no winner. The computer, which is programmed to learn, describes its assessment of "global thermonuclear war" in the movie's finale: "A strange game! The only winning move is not to play." Or, more accurately, the only right way to play is by not playing: the game is already being played, as it were, prior to any missile attack. The logic of mutual assured destruction relies on the ability to avoid a possible future by modeling it. Simulation stands in for a kind of knowledge about the future that exerts control in the present: "What stirs in the shadow of this posture under the pretext of a maximal 'objective' menace, and thanks to that nuclear sword of Damocles, is the perfection of the best system of control which has never existed."[6]

Simulation as deterrence, then, operates in a paradoxically counterfactual realm: that of the proven negative. On the one hand is the promise of information as control that stipulates a kind of mechanistic causality, on the other is the claim to intervene in the mechanism of causality itself. This is why, taken to their limits, strategies of simulation invoke both total control and its eclipse: a kind of smothering stasis in which all possibilities are fully saturated – everything has been modeled in advance, including the modeling process itself. As Baudrillard puts it in his discussion of the virtualization of reality via simulation, "What is the idea of the Virtual? It seems that it would be the radical effectuation, the unconditional realization of the world, the transformation of all our acts, of all historical events, of all material substance and energy into pure information. The ideal would be the resolution of the world by the actualization of all facts and data."[7] The apparent obstacle to such a resolution is the limit of human perceptions, analytic ability, and time. The ability to overcome such limits is relegated to the realm of the superhuman. As Laplace, the pioneer of mathematical probability, put it, "Given for one instant an intelligence which could comprehend all the forces by which nature is animated and the respective situation of the beings who compose it – an intelligence sufficiently vast to submit these data to analysis … for it, nothing would be uncertain and the future, as the past, would be present to its eyes."[8] The name for that intelligence, viewed through one historical lens, would be God. In the digital era, it is the computer and the database.

In the era of predictive analytics, popular fiction continues to experiment with the paradoxes of simulation. Consider, for example, the television show *Person of Interest*, in which a renegade computer programmer taps into the government's data-mining apparatus (which he created) in order to predict when and where life-threatening crimes will occur. The show's premise is that automated surveillance has become both ubiquitous and multifaceted – all spaces and practices are monitored via technologies ranging from smart cameras equipped with facial recognition technology to telephones with embedded voice-stress analyzers. The seemingly distributed network of commercial, public, and personal sensors and communication devices (closed-circuit surveillance cameras, Webcams, smart phones, and so on) has been covertly colonized by a centralized monitoring apparatus. This apparatus – which becomes increasingly "subjectivized" over the course of the series – can watch, listen, and communicate with the main cast members through the full range of networked devices. It is as if all of our various smart devices have teamed up to create an emergent machine intelligence. The show's opening sequence represents the monitoring process at work by portraying the view from the perspective of the all-seeing surveillance apparatus. We see quick intercut shots of people viewed in grainy surveillance video overlaid with terms meant to suggest the various forms of monitoring at work: "voice capture stress percentage"; "GPS (global positioning system): active, tracking location"; "searching: all known databases"; etc. In this world, the environment itself has been redoubled as both setting and spectator. No one in particular is watching, but everyone is watched all the time. The result is what Bogard describes as "the impersonal domination of the hypersurveillance assemblage."[9]

On the show, this assemblage comes to serve as a technologized version of the mutant, prescient "pre-cogs" in Steven Spielberg's 2002 movie *Minority Report*, based on the Philip K. Dick story that envisions a world in which crime is prevented before it takes place. Dick's story stages the paradox of simulated deterrence in a discussion between two officials engaged in fighting "pre-crime": "You've probably grasped the basic legalistic drawback to pre-crime methodology. We're taking in individuals who have broken no law … So the commission of the crime itself is absolute metaphysics. We claim they're culpable. They, on the other hand, eternally claim they're innocent. And, in a sense, they are innocent."[10]

The difference between the modeling of possible futures proposed by *Minority Report* and the strategies of simulated deterrence currently under development in the United States and elsewhere is that between determinism and probability. The fictional portrayals envision a contradictory world in which individual actions can be predicted with certainty and effectively thwarted. They weave oracular fantasies about perfect foresight. Predictive analytics, by contrast, posits a world in which probabilities can be measured and resources allocated accordingly. Because forecasts are probabilistic, they never attain the type of certitude that would, for example, justify arresting someone for a crime he or she has not yet committed. Rather, they distribute probabilities across populations and scenarios. The mobilization of such forms of data mining are anticipated in Michel Foucault's description of the rise of apparatuses of security, governed by questions such as "How can we predict statistically the number of thefts at a given moment, in a given society, in a given town, in the town or in the country, in a given social stratum, and so on? Second, are there times regions, and penal systems that will increase or reduce this average rate? Will crises, famines, or wars, severe or mild punishment, modify something in these proportions? … What is the cost of suppressing these thefts … What therefore is the comparative cost of theft and of its repression … ?"[11]

What emerges is a kind of actuarial model of crime: one that lends itself to aggregate considerations regarding how best to allocate resources under conditions of scarcity – a set of concerns that fits neatly with the conjunction of generalized threat and the constriction of public-sector funding. The algorithm promises not simply to capitalize on new information technology and the data it generates, but simultaneously to address reductions in public resources. The challenges posed by reduced manpower can be countered (allegedly) by more information. As in other realms, enhanced information processing promises to make the business of policing and security more efficient and effective. However, it does so according to new surveillance imperatives, including the guidance of targeted surveillance by comprehensive monitoring, the privileging of prediction over explanation (or causality), and new forms of informational asymmetry. The data-driven promise of prediction, in other words, relies upon significant shifts in cultures and practices of information collection.

From Marketing to Policing

Predictive analytics and data mining exemplify convergent strategies of digital information processing. Since the methods for processing large data sets are topic-agnostic, they can be used in any context that calls for the extraction of useful patterns from large collections of data, ranging from climatology to criminology. From the perspective of the statistician, the step from target marketing to terrorism-tracking is all but non-existent. As McCue puts it, "The same tools and techniques that are used to determine credit risk, discover fraud, and identify which consumers are likely to switch cell-phone providers also can be exploited in the fight against terrorism and the protection of homeland security."[12] The convergent character of database monitoring makes so-called function creep – the repurposing of data collected for one purpose for new and perhaps unanticipated ones – all but irresistible. In this regard, the data itself might be described as a highly convergent resource insofar as information about everything from people's locations in time and space to their Web browsing habits can be used for purposes ranging across the spectrum from marketing and healthcare to political campaigning and policing. The very premise of "total information awareness" is that data collected for one purpose (transactional information about book purchases or movie rentals, geo-locational information about travel destinations, food preferences, and on and on) might reveal unexpected correlations that are useful for other unrelated purposes (such as target marketing or targeted surveillance). A crude example of this kind of repurposing – but one that reveals aspects of a data-driven security mindset – is the FBI's attempt to identify covert Iranian operatives by data-mining grocery purchases in the Bay Area: "the FBI sifted through customer data collected by San Francisco-area grocery stores in 2005 and 2006, hoping that sales records of Middle Eastern food would lead to Iranian terrorists."[13] The program was reportedly discontinued, but surely persists in some form in the ever-expanding database-driven intelligence industry.

For an indication of how predictive analytics operates in the context of retail marketing, consider the example of its use by retail giant Target to determine which of its customers might recently have become pregnant. Market research suggests that the birth of a child is a life-changing event that disrupts consumer habits and allows for interventions that might reshape them.[14] So Target searched through its giant consumer database to determine what patterns of purchasing correlate with the eventual appearance of female shoppers on its list of customers with babies (reportedly, these new shopping behaviors included distinct purchase patterns including large amounts of unscented lotion, dietary supplements, scent-free soap, and other goods).[15] Then Target's researchers determined what patterns of advertising were the most effective, conducting controlled experiments by creating different combinations of advertising appeals.[16] The potentially intrusive character of this type of research was indicated by an anecdote reported to the *New York Times* about a man who complained to Target after his teenage daughter started receiving advertisements for baby products: it turned out that the store knew before he did that his daughter was pregnant.[17]

The example of Target's marketing to pregnant women remains just a tiny foretaste of a world to come – one in which marketers rely on the detection of details of psychological and physiological changes that render consumers more susceptible to particular types of stimuli, and use data mining to deliver these stimuli in the most effective contexts, times, and places. One of the more suggestive details revealed in the coverage of Target's database marketing efforts was the lengths the company took to disguise the detailed knowledge it had of consumers by embedding baby-related advertising appeals amongst other content in their customized mailers.[18] The goal was to target expectant mothers without letting them know they were being singled out: in effect, to turn the details of consumers' own behavior back upon them in order to change their behavior, but to do so in ways that were opaque. As Bogard observes, "For every technology of surveillance, a parallel technology of simulation; for every effort to observe, a method of foiling or disguising observation."[19]

If the imperative of data mining is to continue to gather more data about everything, its promise is to put this data to work, not necessarily to make sense of it. Indeed, the goal of both data mining and predictive analytics is to generate useful patterns that are far beyond the ability of the human mind to detect or even explain. As McCue puts it, "With data mining we can perform exhaustive searches of very large databases using automated methods, searching well beyond the capacity of human analysts or even a team of analysts."[20] In short, the promise of data mining is to generate patterns of actionable information that outstrip the reach of the unaided human brain. In his book *Too Big to Know*, David Weinberger describes this "new knowledge" as requiring "not just giant computers but a network to connect them, to feed them, and to make their work accessible. It exists at the network level, not in the heads of individual human beings."[21] He is, in this regard, describing another version of what Malcolm Gladwell calls "thinking without thinking": knowing without understanding.[22] The question of what it might mean to know something without comprehending it is, perhaps, one of the defining questions of the big data era, although it is certainly not without precedent. Traditional forms of "knowledge" arguably function in this way: we may know, for example, that folk remedies work without knowing why. Typically such forms of knowledge can be described in terms of their instrumental power. We know what we need to know: that is, that they can get something done with a certain degree of probability.

Thus, data miners are careful to point out that their findings are not explanatory in the familiar meaning of allowing users to understand it. If, simply put, data mining refers to the automated discovery of "unknown patterns and trends" in data, and predictive analytics establishes the durability of these patterns over time, in neither case is there a promise to explain these patterns to users.[23] It is not simply that the patterns in huge data sets cannot jump out, as it were, to the unaided human eye; rather, it is that even when the patterns are discovered, there is no guarantee that an underlying explanation comes along with it. Perhaps it is true that a large percentage of people who buy a particular brand of razor vote Republican – the data do not say *why*. The upshot is that data-generated patterns cannot necessarily be reverse-engineered or, by the same token, predicted. Sometimes the data just has to be run in order for the pattern to emerge. Data mining, then, is to be distinguished from data queries that make use of pre-existing structured categories to sort and correlate information. In a sense, what data mining does over time is to generate the categories themselves: "data mining distinguishes itself from queries by its exploratory nature of discovering patterns rather than developing a hypothesis and searching for entities that match the hypothesis."[24] In other words, the claim is that, ideally, you do not start with educated guesses; you start with the data and let the data speak for themselves.

Given its exploratory character, it is perhaps not surprising that accounts of data mining tend to start out by referencing its business and marketing uses. Accounts of the history of computational techniques for data mining generally refer back to work on machine learning and "knowledge discovery in databases" in the 1980s – the roots of the algorithms used to discern previously unknown trends and patterns in data. However, O'Harrow argues that the precursor of contemporary forms of data mining is the large-scale market research of the mid-20th century: "By the early sixties, some 250 businesses began specializing in brokering almost any details they could acquire. Fueling this nascent industry were magazine publishers, hoteliers, car dealerships, and other businesspeople, who soon understood they could make extra cash just by selling the names, addresses and preferences of their regular customers."[25] Two aspects of this genealogy of data mining help to render it compelling: the first is the generation of data as a transactional byproduct. Organizations that collected information for one set of purposes (keeping track of hotel guests or mailing magazine subscriptions) found that they had generated large collections of data that might have other productive uses. The second is what might be described as the populational scope of the data collection. Whereas policing surveillance at the time relied on targeted monitoring, information "winnowing," and surveillance – thanks in large part to material and technological limitations – businesses were collecting information about entire populations of consumers. Tapping phone lines, tailing cars, and doing detailed record searches in large pre-digital databases required a clearly defined and relatively small set of targets. Retailers and distributors, by contrast, collected transactional data and market research about entire segments of the population as part of the bureaucratic process of doing business. Governmental agencies also collected large amounts of data, but had a less clearly defined incentive to mine it.

For marketers, the fact that information was often gathered as a transactional byproduct of business activities meant that its resale was pure gravy: revenue derived from data whose costs had already been defrayed. Of course, the government also collects transactional and research data with economic value (marriage and birth registries, voter registration and driver registration information, police and court records, the census, and so on), much of which has been folded into marketing databases as it has been digitized. Prior to digitization, it was possible, in a rudimentary fashion, to "query" this data: to provide national averages, for example – but not to mine it. There just wasn't any practical or effective way of sorting it as a whole in order to extract unknown patterns.

However, the advent of digitization made the data searchable and sortable using automated systems. Not only the sorting of the data could be automated, but in many cases the collection could be as well. Consequently, the amount of information generated as a byproduct of interactions and transactions grew exponentially at the same time as it became possible to automatically sift, sort, and aggregate population-level data. The advent of data storage and processing on a gigantic scale led to the development of data mining as we have come to know it over the course of the past few decades. By 2010, IBM estimated that 90 percent of the world's stored data had been generated in the preceding decade – and that information continued to be generated at an unprecedented scale: the equivalent of 4,000 Libraries of Congress each day and accelerating.[26] In the end, it took the arrival of powerful computers and cheap storage to make detailed population-level monitoring practical on a national and international scale for the purpose of law enforcement and national security.

"Foreknowledge is Supremacy"

Law enforcement remains a promising market for data mining in an era of digital convergence – one in which the boundaries between formerly distinct information cultures have become more porous than ever before. What worked for marketers could work for cops and spies. By the first decade of the new millennium, it was possible for a police consultant to proclaim – in an article entitled "Next Step for Police: Predicting Crime": "Preventive policing, that's where the future is."[27] Several major metropolitan police forces in cities including New York, Chicago, Los Angeles, Minneapolis, and Memphis have implemented various versions of database-driven predictive policing, as have so-called Fusion Centers that share data across jurisdictions and agencies. IBM, which has positioned itself as a market leader in predictive analytics by spending upwards of $14 billion acquiring startups that work in the area, promotes its SPSS predictive analytics packages to business and law enforcement alike.[28] In a white paper devoted to the benefits of predictive analytics for Fusion Centers, which promote data-sharing between police and security agencies, it claims to be able to "Allow local and state entities to better forecast and identify emerging crime and public health trends in support of important operational and policy decisions," as well as to "Maximize the ability to detect, prevent, investigate and respond to criminal and terrorist activity by finding previously unknown patterns and linkages."[29]

The leap from marketing and policing might, at first glance, seem longer than it is. If policing is about deterrence – pre-empting an undesirable outcome before it takes place – isn't marketing just the opposite: the attempt to produce a desired outcome (usually a purchase)? If one deters, doesn't the other, by contrast, "precipitate" or induce? It might be possible to argue that these are just two sides of the same coin (selecting one outcome means deterring its alternative); but there is a deeper connection between the two realms, and another way of conceiving of the role played by deterrence in marketing. Consider the oft-repeated mantra of database marketers: "Advanced analytics helps retailers know what their customers want to buy before the customers do."[30] In the world of database-driven targeting, the goal is, in a sense, to pre-empt consumer desire: "Your Internet experience will continue to get more personalised.

With your information following you as you move around the Internet, your online world will get more and more targeted to your lifestyle and preferences. Searches will know what you want before you do."[31] Or, as another paean to data mining put it, "Imagine if a retailer could promote a product as personal as perfume and match it to your preferences before you've ever smelled it."[32]

These formulations bring us a bit closer to the notion of deterrence: a kind of pre-emption of the core experience of desire itself – what gets averted is the moment of lack with which this experience coincides. Taken to its limit, the goal is to relegate desire to the pre-empted status of crime in "The Minority Report": "pure metaphysics." If you're jailed before you committed the crime, are you really guilty? If the database knows what you want before you do, did you really want it? The lack is filled before it is subjectively perceived. Would the crime really have happened? Was the desire really there? Is that purchase/search term really what the subject wanted prior to the precipitation of the moment of consumption or search? The mutants and the statisticians say yes, and who is to prove them wrong?

In his description of what he describes as the simulation of surveillance, Bogard argues that predictive analytics is not simply about predicting outcomes, but about devising ways of altering them. In policing terms, the goal of predicting the likelihood of criminal behavior is to deter it. In marketing or campaigning terms it is to anticipate desire before it happens – to precipitate an accelerating range of latent desires that were allegedly "already there." Transposed into business jargon, as one digital marketing executive put it, "In the early days of digital marketing, analytics emerged to tell us what happened and, as analytics got better, why it happened. Then solutions emerged to make it easier to act on data and optimize results."[33] The more data that can be processed faster, the better for turning "big data into a big opportunity."[34] The promise of predictive analytics is to incorporate the future as a set of anticipated data points into the decision-making process: "Historically all Web analytics have reflected data from the past which has been to a certain extent like driving a car using only the rear view mirror … for the first time we can be marketers using data in a manner that allows us to drive while facing the road ahead."[35]

It is a vision of a future in which the structure outlined by predictions is subject to modification along certain pivot points. If, for example, a credit card company can predict a scenario that might lead to losses, it can intervene in advance to attempt to minimize these, as in one example described by the *New York Times*: "credit-card companies keep an eye on whether you are making purchases of that kind [indicating marital problems], because divorce is expensive and they are paranoid that you might stop paying your credit-card bill. For example, if you use your card to pay for a marriage counselor, they might decrease your credit line."[36] Similarly, in the book *Super Crunchers*, Ian Ayres describes how the credit card company CapOne uses data mining to predict the smallest possible reduction in interest rates that can be used to retain customers.

When someone calls in with a complaint about a card's high interest rates, a computer uses detailed information about the consumer combined with information about how similar customers have behaved in the past to rapidly generate a range of rates likely to pre-empt the consumer's cancellation request: "Because of Super Crunching, CapOne knows that a lot of people will be satisfied with this reduction (even when they say they've been offered a lower rate from another card)."[37]

The fact that marketing analogies are so frequently used to introduce the topic of predictive analytics reflects both the pioneering role played by the commercial sector and what might be described as its ordinariness: the way in which the use of data mining has incorporated itself into our understanding of how the world works in the digital era. Customized recommendations on Amazon.com and targeted advertising on the Internet, not to mention targeted mailings and customized coupons in the supermarket, have become the commonplaces of everyday life in contemporary, information-rich societies. What once might have seemed slightly creepy – Google scanning our email, for example, to figure out how best to market to us – has become a normal and largely overlooked part of daily life for millions of email users.

This level of normalcy helps to pave the way for forms of population-level police surveillance that might previously have seemed intrusive or otherwise inappropriate. As a report for the National Institute of Justice put it, "Walmart, for example, learned through analysis that when a major weather event is in the forecast, demand for three items rises: duct tape, bottled water and strawberry Pop-Tarts … Police can use a similar data analysis to help make their work more efficient … some in the field believe it has the potential to transform law enforcement by enabling police to anticipate and prevent crime instead of simply responding to it."[38] If we are submitting to detailed monitoring to help enhance Pop-Tart sales, surely we can do it for public safety and national security. Viewed from a slightly different perspective, it is hard to avoid the notion that we are living in an era of rampant surveillance creep. Whereas once upon a time it might have seemed strange to allow police to scan and store license plate numbers of everyone who drives by a particular location, this now takes place as a matter of course. Predictive policing, in this regard, is just piggybacking on the "new normal" of digital, interactive monitoring.

Reinforcing this normality are the claims made on behalf of predictive policing. In Boston, officials reported that serious crime in the Cambridge area in 2011 dropped to its lowest level in 50 years after police adopted a data-driven predictive policing program (tellingly, the claim does not distinguish between correlation and causation). The murder rate actually increased – but police said this was a result of domestic disputes that they could not (yet?) predict.[39] In Santa Cruz, police reported a significant drop in burglaries after adopting a predictive policing program developed by mathematicians, an anthropologist, and a criminologist based on models for predicting earthquake aftershocks.[40]

In Memphis, officials reported a 15 percent drop in serious crime over four years after adopting a database-driven predictive policing program.[41] Police are experimenting with a growing range of variables to predict crime, ranging from weather patterns to building code violations. In Arlington, Texas, police reported that every unit increase in physical decay of the neighborhood (measured by code violations) resulted in six more residential burglaries in the city.[42] For the moment, however, the most common indicator seems to be past patterns of behavior. In Santa Cruz, for example, two women were taken into custody for peering into cars in a parking garage that the computer indicated would be at risk for burglaries that day: "One woman was found to have outstanding warrants; the other was carrying illegal drugs."[43]

If, for the moment, the methodologies seem relatively crude (but potentially effective – at least on occasion), it is worth keeping in mind that current systems rely on only a tiny current of the swelling information flood. However, recent regulatory shifts propose to make much more data available. As of this writing, legislators in the UK have proposed giving intelligence agencies access to the phone records, browsing details, emails, and text messages of all Britons without a warrant.[44] In the US, updated "guidelines" for the National Counter Terrorism Center allow the organization to collect data about any American without a warrant and keep it for up to five years. It also permits the center to data mine this information for the purposes of investigating terrorism.[45] Total Information Awareness as a named program may have disappeared, but as an unnamed initiative it continues to develop apace.

From Policing to Security

Another form of convergence in the digital era is the blurring of lines between criminality and "terrorism," and thus between national security and policing. As McCue puts it, "Terrorism and efforts to support it also encompass other crimes including fraud, smuggling, money laundering, identity theft, and murder, which have been investigated successfully with the use of data mining and predictive analytics."[46] The indeterminate definition of terrorism allows a wide range of activities to be folded into its embrace. Just as anyone is a potential suspect in the diffuse "war on terror," so too is any crime potentially encompassed by an overarching terrorist plot. The formation called "War 4.0" becomes increasingly reliant on the data capturing power of the Web and the techniques for data mining and forecasting. McCue describes this convergence in ominous terms: "The distinction between war and peace will be blurred to the vanishing point. It will be nonlinear, possibly to the point of having no definable battlefields or fronts. The distinction between 'civilian' and 'military' may disappear."[47] When the battlespace is no longer delimited and the boundary between military and civilian blurs, monitoring and surveillance, like the threat they are meant to address, become generalized and ubiquitous. In part, data mining is necessary for a kind of cognitive mapping – for helping to orient oneself in this newly de-differentiated landscape: "Using predictive analytics, we can accurately model complex interactions, associations or relationships and then use these models to identify and characterize unknown relationships or make reliable predictions of future events." The model of deterrence is, once again, at work in these formulations. As McCue puts it, "if knowledge is power, then foreknowledge can be seen as battlespace dominance or supremacy."[48]

The tendency of such formulations to recall the fantastical premise of "The Minority Report" obscures the probabilistic character of predictive analytics. Consequently, the form of warfare envisioned by predictive analytics is not necessarily that of total pre-emption, but one in which tactical advantage goes to those with access to the database. In a recent study published in the online Proceedings of the National Academy of Sciences, researchers working with a trove of data about the Afghanistan war (retrieved from dispatches leaked by Wikileaks) demonstrated their ability to predict the location and intensity of future conflicts.[49] One analyst for *IT World* responded to these findings with the proclamation that "Predictive analytics has moved into dangerous terrain. It's now able to forecast battles in a war zone."[50] As in the case of pre-emptive policing, the significance of such a finding lies in (among other things) the ability to allocate manpower as efficiently as possible: "For years now predictive analytics has been used to anticipate where in a city a police department should deploy officers in order to prevent violent and property crime ... This is the first time I've encountered analysts using unstructured data to predict the location and level of violence in a war zone."[51] The broader lesson of the research was, accordingly, that "the benefits should also be apparent to leaders of almost any kind of organization. Given the right kind of unstructured information and the right analytics model, valuable insight can be gleaned."[52] The tendency of promotional rhetoric is to portray predictive analytics as a crystal ball whose view of the future becomes clearer with every new piece of data about the present – as if at the very point when we can capture the entirety of the present in a database, the future will simultaneously be pinned down. More cautious accounts suggest that it would be more appropriate to describe the predictive power of data mining as a form of forecasting. "Forecasting is different from prediction ... You can forecast an earthquake but not predict it."[53]

The convergence of data-driven policing and securitization was highlighted by the 2012 release by Wikileaks of emails it obtained from the private intelligence agency Stratfor referring to another company called TrapWire that markets database research to "law enforcement, financial services corporations, the armed forces, and intelligence agencies."[54] A relatively small player in the intelligence field, TrapWire nonetheless received attention for its strategy of piggybacking on available surveillance cameras and license-plate scanners to detect suspicious activity and, in particular, behavior that seemed to indicate preparatory surveillance directed toward potential terrorist targets: cameras watching cameras, in other words.

The exploitation of the existing infrastructure of sensors and databases is a hallmark of data mining and predictive analytics for both marketing and policing purposes. Such practices have surpassed Bogard's description of the complementary relationship between surveillance and simulation. When information and communication technologies are digitized, networked, and interactive, their "primary" functions are redoubled by their capacity to be used for monitoring purposes. One and the same device serves as the monitoring device and its alibi. The supermarket scanner prices your groceries and monitors your consumption patterns at the same time; Facebook allows you to keep track of your friends while it keeps track of you; a bit of code that allows a Website to "remember" a particular user can simultaneously be used to monitor the activities of that user; mobile phones that ping the nearest cell towers simultaneously register the location of their users. The need for concealment is displaced by multitasking and the offer of convenience. We might describe this as a self-fueling cycle of monitoring-based rationalization: transactions and interactions are rendered more efficient by automated forms of information processing, which, in turn, generates data that can be used to further rationalize the process.

This functional redoubling is not unique to digital technology – an analogue landline phone can also generate data; but the proliferation of networked devices, many of which are associated with unique users, makes the monitoring ubiquitous and increasingly precise. What might be described as convenience creep – the ways in which digital devices make our communication and information search and retrieval practices ever more efficient and frequent – underwrites the proliferation of data available for marketers and intelligence agencies. At this point, it seems only realistic to assume that *anything* one does on a digital, networked device generates a record that some entity has captured and stored for any of a variety of purposes (indeed, some jurisdictions *require* that this information be stored in case law enforcement or intelligence agencies request it).

As interactive, networked devices proliferate and as the applications they run become increasingly specialized and customized, the data they collect will become correspondingly broad ranging and detailed. Just as the rise of social networking has generated a new category of data to be "mined" – that of expressed "sentiment" or "opinions" on a mass scale – the development of new "app" capabilities that rely on "mood" data or biometric data will continue to expand the range of data that is captured. Devices that can "read" facial expressions in order to respond to users' mood are already under development, as are technologies for facial recognition, voice pattern recognition, iris scanning, surface body temperature monitoring, and other forms of biometric tracking. In the not too distant future, when you talk to or watch your smart phone, it will be watching and listening back, collecting information about your stress level, your eye movements, and your body temperature in addition to your viewing history, your search patterns, and all the other types of information currently collected by phone applications.

The future, then, is one that is converging toward what Bill Gates once described as a fully documented life – one in which our actions, our movements, our words, our bodily responses, even our moods will be captured and recorded, generating a trove of data that will be orders of magnitude beyond the size of current databases.[55] To handle the burgeoning supply of data, the National Security Agency (NSA) is building a huge data center in Utah and the Pentagon is reportedly attempting to build out its capacity in order to process information on the order of yottabytes (10 to the 24th power – a scale so large that "no one has yet coined a term for the next higher order of magnitude").[56] Despite the rapid growth of the private database sector, it is unlikely that any commercial entity can come close to the scale of information collection, storage, and processing envisioned by the NSA project. However, as the Central Intelligence Agency's (CIA's) Chief Technology Officer Gus Hunt has observed, the state has relied on the creativity of the marketplace for strategies to make sense out of all of its data: "We have these astounding commercial capabilities that have emerged in the market space that allow us to do things with information we've never been able to do before."[57] And the ability to do these things coincides, perhaps not un-coincidentally, with the mobilization of a newly unpredictable and diffuse threat – one that intelligent analysts say is difficult to detect, but relatively easy to thwart once it's detected. According to Hunt, it is the threat environment of ubiquitous risk that underwrites the paradigm shift from search to data mining: "It's about the fact that we have enemies who are very intelligent and sophisticated and we never know what they plan to do next, hence a need to do things like pattern analysis and pattern detection ahead of time."[58]

Surveillance in the Era of Big Data

If it is hard to even conceive of the magnitude of the data being collected, imagine trying to *make sense* of its contents. This process will, of necessity, become the province of automated forms of data mining, sorting, and analysis – which reframes sense-making according to a very narrow definition: that of finding patterns, trends, and correlations. In this regard the digital era opens up a new form of digital divide: that between those with access to the databases and those without. For those with access, the way in which data is understood and used will be fundamentally transformed. There will be no attempt to read and comprehend all of the available data – the task would be all but impossible. Correlations can be unearthed and acted upon, but only by those with access to the database and the processing power. Two different information cultures will come to exist side by side: on the one hand, the familiar, "old-fashioned" one in which people attempt to make sense of the world based on the information they can access: news reports, blog posts, the words of others and the evidence of their own experience. On the other hand, computers equipped with algorithms that can "teach" themselves will advance the instrumental pragmatics of the database: the ability to use tremendous amounts of data without understanding it.

If it turns out that data mining and predictive analytics are the powerful information strategies that their populizers portray them as, those with access to the proprietary and classified databases will gain a relative advantage over those without. The following sections of this chapter explore some of the salient features and potential consequences of this new way of understanding and using data. The too-big-to-know strategies of data mining and predictive analytics reveal the outlines of what might be described as the post-comprehension era of information processing. The sheer volume of the data that we generate and use gets in the way of our being able to comprehend it. This is the paradox of "total documentation" – although we cannot construct the vantage point from which to comprehend the increasingly complete picture of everything that takes place, we can develop technological extensions that allow us to put it to use in ways hitherto unavailable.

The Target is the Population

The defining shift associated with big data is rapidly making itself felt in both the commercial and government sectors: the move from targeted to population-level data capture. If targeted surveillance or monitoring was, in a sense, exceptional (only conducted on particular individuals who had been singled out for special treatment), "populational" surveillance, by contrast, only works if it is normalized and ubiquitous: if everyone is captured in the monitoring embrace. This shift explains why police and intelligence agencies around the world are seeking warrantless access to data about the entire populace and not simply about suspected criminals or terrorists. Often such initiatives are portrayed as treating everyone as if they are a suspect. Although there is an element of truth to this accusation, insofar as no one is ruled out in advance as a potential target, it is not the main explanation for the imperative to widen the breadth and depth of monitoring activity. In population-level intelligence-gathering, authorities count on the fact that the vast majority of those whose details are collected are innocent because it is against this background of unsuspicious or normal activity that the anomalies of deviant and particularly threatening behavior are meant to emerge.

To imagine that everyone who is monitored is a suspect (at least in the realm of policing) is, in a sense, "old school" thinking that hearkens back to the day when suspects were first identified and then tracked. In such a context, the very fact of tracking was evidence of suspicion. Data mining flips the sequence around: tracking comes first and targeting later. Big data surveillance uses the monitoring process itself to generate the targets. For even a few confirmed targets of suspicion to emerge, data about the rest of the population must be put to work. The transitional moment from targeting to predictive analytics arrives with the advent of "big data" sorting: when security agencies such as the NSA track all the signals they can capture, sifting through communications for suspicious keywords. Signals intelligence systems that have been in place for decades rely on the "collect and query" model, amassing large amounts of information that can be sifted for keywords or other indicators. The model is one of collect and winnow: cast the net as wide as possible and then throw out everything but a few suspicious leads.

Data mining relies on the same scope of data capture (anything and everything that can be collected) but moves beyond human or automated attempts to query the data based on existing categories (suspicious key words, locations, and so on). As the CIA's Chief Technology Officer Gus Hunt put it, predictive analytics means "moving away from search as a paradigm to pre-correlating data in advance to tell us what's going on."[59] This approach to targeting unites marketing and security-based forms of monitoring, and the fact that it has been embraced by both sectors means that emerging surveillance strategies will continue to push for data access at the level of entire populations as opposed to, say, that of suspicious (or, from a marketing perspective, desirable) groups or individuals. It is not simply the fact that new technologies make it possible to collect and store huge amounts of data that is driving ongoing attempts by state and commercial entities to collect population-level data, but also the change in the pragmatics of monitoring. The reversal of the relationship between targeting and comprehensive surveillance means that we are likely to see ongoing pressure from the security and policing realm for greater warrantless access to a wide range of data.

Data Collection without Limits

Because predictive analytics is, as it were, model agnostic, it does not rule out in advance the relevance of any kind of information. All data is potentially relevant no matter how seemingly trivial, irrelevant, personal, or invasive it may seem. Moreover, because it relies on population-level monitoring, data mining does not exclude any category, group, or individual. All information about everyone is potentially germane – if not now, perhaps sometime in the future. In keeping with this logic, the CIA's chief technology officer says that the traditional detection model based on collecting information and then winnowing it down "fails spectacularly" in the era of "big data": "If I just use what I want to now and throw away the rest, I will end up throwing information away that critically matters tomorrow."[60] Data mining is, in this regard, speculative as well as comprehensive: data is captured not solely for current use, but also to take into account the possibility of any and all future scenarios and technologies.

Just as information about the entire population makes it possible for anomalous patterns to emerge, information about the full range of human activity generates an increasing range of dimensions to detect such anomalies. That is, there is no dimension of human activity, no matter how private or personal, that is ruled out *a priori*. The proliferation of interactive applications and services expands the available range of data collection. When a company like Google, for example, offers a new category of online services, it is also creating a new category of data collection. When it stores your documents, it also learns about the ways in which you use them; when it provides email, it also learns about the details of the content of your messages and your communication patterns; when it provides you with online videos, it learns about your viewing habits and preferences, and so on. Similarly, when apps rely upon biometric or affective feedback, they also collect biometric and affective data that creates new populational norms against the background of which suspicious or anomalous behavior can start to emerge. All aspects of life that can be captured within interactive environments enter into the database with their potential relevance to be determined by their contribution to robust patterns of correlation. If it turns out, for some inexplicable reason, that an apparently meaningless detail, such as one's preferred combination of toiletries, is highly correlated with a trait or behavior of interest to marketers or law enforcement, then this information enters into the scope of sorting and prediction algorithms. The appetite of the database, whether for purposes of marketing, policing, national security, healthcare, or any other application, is, for the foreseeable future, insatiable, limited only by practical limitations on storage capability and processing power. Since, as the CIA's Gus Hunt puts it, when it comes to "connecting the dots", "we cannot know the value of a future dot today," and "We cannot connect a dot we don't have," all data points must be collected and stored with an eye to a future in which their currently obscure relationship might become clear.[61]

From a policy perspective, familiar norms of individual privacy threaten the data mining model to its core. For data miners, they reek of the "quaint" and "outdated" – once useful social norms that co-existed well with regimes of targeted monitoring, but that collide head-on with the big data paradigm. In a context in which data about innocent people can be used to develop criteria for identifying guilty ones, existing privacy protections become subject to challenge and revision. What once seemed scandalous – the warrantless wiretapping of Americans by the George W. Bush administration – has subsequently been retroactively approved by ongoing renewals of the Foreign Intelligence Surveillance (FISA) Amendments Act, which provided immunity to those communication companies that cooperated with government spies.[62] The measure, which allows what amounts to unlimited monitoring of Americans' overseas communications, has been defended on the grounds that "sweeping NSA surveillance of our digital 'papers' is constitutionally unproblematic precisely because it does not 'target' the Americans whose papers are searched."[63] Because the monitoring is universal, no particular targets are identified in advance – no one is targeted until the algorithm does its work. This is precisely the rationale of big data surveillance: "we are not collecting information about you because you are a suspect, but because you can help us to identify who the real suspects are." Exempting individuals from monitoring would be tantamount to discarding data points that become useful in the future. Furthermore, if any discarded data point has the potential to become critically important, the future is, in a sense, always now: the collection of the next bit of data might itself reveal a previously undetected pattern.

The Fiction of Anonymity

The days in which it was possible to joke with the famous *New Yorker* cartoon that "nobody knows you're a dog" on the Internet are fast being relegated to the pre-history of the big data era.[64] There are still ways of acquiring an anonymous online identity and encrypting one's communications, but for those who do not take such measures, anonymity is fast becoming little more than a useful fiction. Marketers like to tell us in various "terms of use" agreements that much of the data collected about individual users is anonymized before being resold or otherwise put to use. This is useful as a strategy for alleviating privacy concerns, but it is fictitious insofar as it suggests that the practical impact of data use does not affect us. Marketers do not have to know our name in order to target us based on detailed knowledge about us.

Consider the example of the Heritage Health Prize, a crowd-sourcing competition that offers a grand prize of $3 million to whoever can most accurately predict whether and how long people will be hospitalized within the coming year based on their medical histories. Hosted by Kaggle, a company that specializes in crowd-sourcing the development of predictive algorithms (their motto is "We make data science a sport"), the contest supplies contestants with anonymized data from real patients.[65] The team that is best able to use the data to correctly predict which patients were hospitalized in the year following the period from which the data is drawn (and meeting criteria for sufficient success) wins the prize. The winning algorithm is meant to pre-empt costly medical treatment by identifying candidates for early intervention – but it has other potential applications as well, especially for private healthcare providers interested in screening health insurance applicants to avoid costly payouts. It is possible, then, that someone might find themselves subject to medical intervention – or, perhaps, denied coverage based on anonymous data about other people. As Bogard puts it, "Oftentimes to be effective, these technologies do not have to be intrusive at all (even though in many cases they justify or enable intrusion, and on a massive scale)."[66] Even when data is anonymized, in other words, it can be used to shape the opportunities available to and the interventions visited upon others.

Other forms of anonymity are purely symbolic. Thus, for example, third-party advertisers can target Website visitors based on a range of anonymous data about past searches, location, purchases history, and so on. This type of targeting is anonymous in the narrow sense that the advertiser does not know the name of the person being served a targeted ad – the goal is to reach a particular customer and not a named individual. But this does not mean that the identity of the target is unknown – in many cases, the collected data can be traced back to a uniquely identified device such as a smart phone. For anyone with access to the data who wants to identify a particular user, it is often a simple matter to reverse engineer the data. After America Online released anonymized data about what search terms its users were entering into Web browsers, the *New York Times* was easily able to pick one batch of search terms out and identify the user within a matter of hours.[67] Similarly, Netflix was sued by a subscriber and investigated by the Federal Trade Commission (FTC) after releasing anonymized movie rental data as part of a contest designed to crowd-source the creation of a better recommendation algorithm for its users. It turned out that the data could be reverse engineered to identify individual users and the movies they had rated and rented.[68]

Reverse engineering is often not necessary, given the development of "digital fingerprinting" techniques that profile users' online behavior in order to create profiles that allow them to be tracked across different devices: "these companies can tell it's you whether you're surfing the web on a computer, iPad or phone."[69] When this type of technology is in place, users will be anonymous in name only: devices and service providers will know the details of their past behavior, their movements, and their communications, if not necessarily their names. The step from creating a digital profile to identifying a name is all but non-existent in many cases: once unique users are identified it is a relatively simple matter to find a piece of data that links to their names and other identifying information. "The more online data trackers know about you, the anonymous web surfer, the easier it becomes for them to tie it to you, the person … From there, data brokers can easily take online information offline, where they can obtain information such as a residential address from public documents."[70]

The trajectory of tracking technology and data mining is on a collision course with anonymity in any meaningful sense of the word. There is something anachronistic about the notion that as long as we are not identified by name, we are somehow undetected and protected from the monitoring gaze. For surveillance purposes, a name is simply one way of getting at the constellation of information associated with it; but if you can access that information directly, the name is superfluous in many instances and can be added whenever necessary. Those engaged in the monitoring practices are often not as interested in individual names as they are in probabilistic categories of behavior. If someone's profile matches up with the characteristics that are correlated with vulnerability to a particular type of message or the tendency to behave in a certain way, this person can be subjected to various types of sorting-based targeting, exclusion, or suspicion without being named (or being named only after the fact). Some forms of monitoring require that a particular individual be tracked in ways that can easily lead to identification, but others need only rely on "scraping" anonymous data off the Internet.

Just as database monitoring focuses on the population and not on targeted individuals, the results it yields are probabilistic and not individualistic. Mining big data does not provide any definite answers about what particular individuals will do or how they will react. Rather, it provides probabilities about what someone in a particular category is likely to do. As one data miner put it, "I can't tell you what one shopper is going to do, but I can tell you with 90 percent accuracy what one shopper is going to do if he or she looks exactly like one million other shoppers."[71] Such strategies allow for aggregate rather than individualized prediction. Decision-making based on these strategies assigns probabilities to particular individuals: someone who may not ever miss a credit card payment might be denied credit because 90 percent of those who share similar characteristics are considered to be high-risk consumers. Any attempt to build a protective bulwark against big data surveillance on the foundation of privacy must confront the increasingly fictitious status of anonymity. We will be told that, at least in some instances, the databases do not know our names; but this does not mean that they do not know who we are.

Post-Referentiality and the Triumph of Correlation over Causation

A further corollary of the shift to "populational" surveillance is the privileging of correlation over causation, predictability over referentiality. The goal of populational surveillance, despite its ubiquity, is not to generate an accurate "map of the territory," but to unearth useful, reliable correlations. Perhaps the best description of this shift is provided by Chris Anderson's diagnosis of the fate of theory in the so-called "petabyte" era: "Out with every theory of human behavior, from linguistics to sociology. Forget taxonomy, ontology, and psychology. Who knows why people do what they do? The point is they do it, and we can track and measure it with unprecedented fidelity. With enough data, the numbers speak for themselves."[72] We might push this formula even further: forget about trying to describe a world (and the various impasses this poses) and focus on predicting it.

Data, in this context, becomes detached from what might be described as "referentiality" – describing not the world beyond it so much as the data's own patterns of inter-relationships. Here's how Chris Anderson describes what I am calling post-referentiality, using the model of Google for guidance: "Google's founding philosophy is that we don't know why this page is better than that one: If the statistics of incoming links say it is, that's good enough. No semantic or causal analysis is required. That's why … it can match ads to content without any knowledge or assumptions about the ads or its content."

In the realm of market research this approach was anticipated by Paco Underhill, famous for developing the so-called "science of shopping" based on his large database of films that document what people do when they enter the physical space of a shop.[73] Underhill looks for predictable patterns, measuring, for example, how long it takes people to slow down and start browsing once they enter a store; or which direction they typically take when they enter a store, which Underhill dubbed the law of the "Invariant Right" after the habit of shoppers in the United States. Like data miners (which is what Underhill is, in a pre-digital sense), he searches for previously unknown robust patterns with predictive power and uses them to formulate generalizations about shopping (hence, "the science of shopping"). But, as one profile points out, Underhill makes no attempt to explain or interpret the "laws" he discovers: "Uncovering the fundamentals of 'why' is clearly not a pursuit that engages him much. He is not a theoretician but an empiricist, and for him the important thing is that in amassing his huge library of in-store time-lapse photography he has gained enough hard evidence to know how often and under what circumstances the Invariant Right is expressed and how to take advantage of it"[74] Underhill was a man ahead of his time: the goal is not to understand the world but to correlate its elements.

This shift from comprehension to correlation is at the heart of many of the arguments in this book because it amounts to a way of thinking about and using data that is uniquely available to those who have access to the database and the processing power to put it to use. The way of thinking it augers dispenses with the forms of information-based comprehension that, once upon a time, underwrote the allegedly democratizing potential of the Internet, understood as a medium that could promote greater public understanding of the surrounding world and thus facilitate more enlightened forms of democratic self-governance. The data-mining model of correlation and prediction promises to deliver a form of symbolic power that allows those with access to the database to bypass the vexed task of comprehension – at a time when the impasses of representation weaken its claims. Data mining, then, comes to serve as a kind of "post-comprehension" strategy of information use that addresses the challenges posed by information overload. Access to this particular strategy, however, is limited to the few, leaving the many left with the challenge of devising less costly and technically demanding strategies for dealing with an environment of data glut.

3

EMOTIONAL GLUT

Opinion Mining and Sentiment Analysis

Data-Mining Sociality

Viewed through the lens of market research, platforms such as Facebook and Twitter are much more than sites of networked sociality: they are the world's biggest focus group, generating more data than any market researcher could ever hope to read and analyze. When a movie comes out, when a political candidate makes a gaffe, when a new product is introduced, data scrapers comb the Web for opinions, reactions, criticism, and praise. They are not the only ones; intelligence agencies such as the National Security Agency (NSA) comb the social Web for clues of possible security threats, health organizations search for epidemiological patterns, and the list continues to grow. Many of the types of conversations that generate this data have been taking place since time immemorial, though some take place in recently developed formats – the 140-character bursts of Tweets, the personal and potentially mass medium of blogs, the status updates to networks of online friends, and so on. What is really novel, however, is the fact that because these forms of communication take place within what I have elsewhere described as a "digital enclosure" – the interactive embrace of networked devices that record everything that takes place upon them – they can be captured, stored, sorted, and processed.[1] It's as if the casual conversations of daily life that once disappeared into the ether have now been captured and fixed on searchable, sortable, aggregate-able recording tape. The utterances might seem as casual and fleeting to us as comments we make to friends at the pub or around the water cooler, but once they are captured by the digital enclosure their temporal and spatial reach expands far beyond what we likely imagine. These casual remarks can be sought after as evidence for a court proceeding; they can contribute to police investigations or to background checks by potential employers or prospective dates.

If we approach these conversations from the perspective of sociality, we can see an efflorescence of a new kind of semi-public sphere in which people feel comfortable publicly sharing matters of all kinds, often with minimal public import. Suggestively, one of the hallmarks of the proliferating forms of semi-public disclosure is that, in important respects, they are *less* interactive than more private forms of communication. This is, in part, a contextual limitation: the imperative of social media is one of the hyper-production of opinions, observations, and responses, but as the flow of communication increases, it becomes increasingly difficult to keep a coherent conversation going – to keep up with the pace and scope of the multi-party conversation. Platforms such as Twitter and Facebook have a stake in facilitating the development of large networks of connections for the purposes of boosting their membership and, also, ultimately for gathering information about users. What is important, from their perspective, is not so much the content of the conversation or the expression, but the fact that it can be registered, archived, and mined. At the same time, it is not hard to get the impression that there is a lot more talking going on than listening – the ongoing imperative to publicize oneself and the appeal of the "democratization" of publicity-as-celebrity yield a new landscape of glut. It is becoming more difficult to trace the distinction between the pre-Internet era in which only the few were heard because of the relative scarcity of communication and the coming one in which so few are heard because everyone is talking. Perhaps one of the key differences is the silicon incarnation of the "big Other" that listens for us: the medium registers our comments – they are "out there" in the database.

For those who have access to the database, of course, the result is a fresh trove: the perpetual production of data that can be repurposed to meet the needs and interests of a vast array of enterprises both private and public. In India, for example, IBM has developed "a new social sentiment capability" to help municipal governments "understand public opinions on key city issues and services such as public transportation, education, etc."[2] The United Nations has announced a Global Pulse initiative that, "will conduct so-called sentiment analysis of messages in social networks and text messages – using natural-language deciphering software – to help predict job losses, spending reductions or disease outbreaks in a given region."[3] It is hard not to detect a note of excitement in the widespread embrace of this new category of data mining – there is proselytization in the air: now that the world of human sentiment has opened up to the sensors, this potentially valuable feedback offers new vistas of possibilities. The realm of sentiment and emotion was the crucial dimension of human response that had not yet opened itself up to automated forms of mass quantification, collection, and mining. The opening came just in time, it turns out, to address the turn to affect in an era when emotional response allegedly holds the key to cutting through the clutter of available information (as will be discussed in more detail in Chapter 6). As the abstract for a presentation at a 2012 Predictive Analytics World conference put it, "For the first time in human history a collective measurement of sentiment can be taken from Twitter and the social Internet."[4] Best of all, thanks to the structure of the Internet, "The data is often free and available for everyone to see. The challenges for prediction is collecting, normalizing, and analyzing the unstructured data" – in this case, for the purpose of guiding investment decisions.[5] Thanks in large part to the imagined economic payoff of delving into the sentiment mine, the *Harvard Business Review* has proclaimed "data scientist" to be "the sexiest job of the 21st Century": "Think of big data as an epic wave gathering now, starting to crest. If you want to catch it, you need people who can surf."[6]

It is telling that the advent of "big data" is figured as a force of nature: a wave, a flood, a gusher – a found resource that miners are tapping and harnessing. This formulation backgrounds the hyper-productivity of people (at least in the case of sentiment analysis) who spend an increasing amount of their time commenting, linking, posting, blogging, and Tweeting – for the most part without a thought as to how their communication is captured and redoubled as a fresh data source. It is as if the energy of suppressed response left over from a non-interactive, top-down media world has been unleashed and tapped. People have always been active, communicative, and creative in their reaction to the events around them – now these responses can be channeled, captured, and put to work, thanks to the interactive capability of new platforms for expression, communication, and interaction. There is something hyper-efficient about this capture and repurposing of the fruit of human creativity and activity: the information-era equivalent of noting that every day humans expend all kind of energy that might be captured and harnessed. The energy is being expended in any case – just like the data is being generated – why not capture it and put it to use? Facebook, Google, *et alia* form a symbolic version of *The Matrix*, living not off the physical or biochemical energy of their pod people, but from their communicative productivity. As in the case of the matrix, this relationship is not without consequences for those whose data is captured.

The newfound interest in sentiment data is not simply a function of the developing technological infrastructure. It fits well with related trends in the information-era economy: first, the increasing importance attached to emotional response as a means of navigating a landscape of information glut; and, second, the role of information about preferences, opinions, and emotional response in the management, marketing, and provision of a wide range of goods and services associated with a mass customized economy. Because activities such as online social networking, Tweeting, blogging, and so on have the capacity to generate value, we might include them in the broader categories of "affective" and "immaterial" labor: not the manufacture of material products, but rather the production of networks of sociability, taste, and communication. Maurizio Lazzarato describes immaterial labor as the "activity that produces the 'cultural content' of the commodity," noting that it "involves a series of activities that are not normally recognized as 'work' – in other words, the kinds of activities involved in defining and fixing cultural and artistic standards, fashions, tastes, consumer norms, and, more strategically, public opinion."[7] Such labor corresponds to what Michael Hardt (also following Lazzarato) describes as an "affective" form of immaterial labor: "the production and manipulation of affects," which "requires (virtual or actual) human contact and proximity."[8] They have in mind a range of industries devoted to entertainment, management, education, therapy, self-help, and so on – industries that produce not material products such as cars and lamps, but the promise these products started to trade on of providing a sense of security, well-being, entertainment, and so on. The argument for including the production of the raw data of sentiment analysis in this category is the ancillary role it plays in the provision of these services. The manufacture of material products is tied in to the collection and use of this kind of data, as was driven home to me during a presentation by a corporate anthropologist featuring a close-up image of a computer chip her company had designed. Her extensive ethnographic research had actually shaped the construction of the chip in significant ways that influenced its capabilities and specifications, she said.[9] She had spent hundreds of hours interviewing people, photographing them, studying them in their natural habitat – and the final project of all of this labor was a mass-produced industrial object installed in millions of devices around the world.

The promise of sentiment analysis is something of a similar order: the ability to capture human response and activities in ways that influence everything from policing and healthcare practices to the creation of goods and services. In contrast to ethnographic research, however, data mining quantifies the analysis in order to run it in real time on a huge scale, sidestepping the interpretive and narrative character of anthropology. It doesn't tell stories but reveals patterns with allegedly predictive power – and can do so in a wide range of human endeavors. As the director of Harvard's Institute for Quantitative Social Science put it: "It's a revolution … We're really just getting under way. But the march of quantification, made possible by enormous new sources of data, will sweep through academia, business and government. There is no area that is going to be untouched."[10]

Perhaps unsurprisingly, it is the marketing world in the interactive era which is at the forefront of attempts to capitalize on the capture of sentiment, emotion, and what might be described as the Internet's background feeling tone. As a *New York Times* article devoted to the marketing trend put it, "An emerging field known as sentiment analysis is taking shape around one of the computer world's unexplored frontiers: translating the vagaries of human emotion into hard data."[11] But this description is not quite right: the goal of marketers is not to gauge personal, "human" emotion, but rather to probe an affective landscape without having to pore over the individual contributions of millions of Internet users. Sentiment analysis relies on technological advances that make it possible to sift through all these forms of expression without actually reading them. The goal is a kind of thin-slicing or pulse-reading of the Internet as a whole. Pioneering companies in the field develop applications that troll through Twitter feeds, blogs, social networking sites, online forums, bulletin boards, and chat rooms, probing the emotional pulse of the Internet. The industry places a premium on speed and volume: processing as many posts and messages as possible in real time in order to deliver "relevant and actionable answers fast."[12]

As in the case of other examples explored in this book, the model is not a descriptive, referential one (that would aim to accurately describe how individuals are feeling), but a predictive, correlational one. Applied to sentiment analysis, the goal of data mining is both pre-emptive and productive: to minimize negative sentiment and maximize emotional investment and engagement – not merely to record sentiment as a given but to modulate it as a variable. The process relies on giving "populations over to being a probe or sensor"[13] to provide the raw material for tracking the emotional indicators that correlate with desired outcomes – and for developing ways of inducing them. This latter intervention comes not at the level of evidentiary appeal, but at that of intervention in an aggregate feeling tone: the attempt to channel or shape the ambient sentiment around particular issues, products, and so on. What Patricia Clough describes as the "modulation" of affect comes to serve as a strategy for management and control.[14]

It is perhaps not surprising, then, that the "investment arm" of the US Central Intelligence Agency (CIA), an organization called In-Q-Tel, has already provided backing for a sentiment analysis company called Visible Technologies, as "part of a larger movement within the spy services to get better at using 'open source intelligence.'"[15] In this context, "open-source" refers to the public availability of online data such as Tweets and of blog posts and other messages that can be "scraped" from relevant sites and platforms – data that is already "out there" and readily available – as opposed to data that has to be directly generated by researchers through surveys, focus groups, and so on.

The modulation of affect is a convergent strategy – a management mode that lends itself to the realms of politics, policing, and marketing alike. Whether or not it turns out to be a successful strategy, it gestures in the direction of a different way of thinking about information – not as the raw material of rational-critical understanding and not as contributing to an ongoing process of deliberation based on an evidentiary, representational view of the world (one in which facts tells us about something beyond themselves). Rather, it fits with the post-referential world of what Brian Massumi has described as the "affective fact":

The breakdown of logico-discursive reasoning and the accompanying decline of the empirical fact does not of course mean that there is no longer any logic – or any facts. There is a tautological logic that tends to prevail, and a new order of facts associated with it emerges. We have witnessed the birth of the *affective fact* as a key political operator.[16]

Massumi's examples, drawn from George W. Bush's presidency, recall Suskind's account of right-wing, postmodern performativity: "we'll act again, creating other new realities," leaving the slow thinkers, the ones lingering in the realm of symbolic efficiency, one step behind.[17]

The logic of the affective fact persists into the Obama era in the form, for example, of the so-called "birthers," who claim to have uncovered a conspiracy to hide the fact that the president was not born in the United States and is ineligible to be president. So-called "birthers" have Websites filled with readily falsifiable evidence to "prove" their claims, but it is a self-stoking proof immune to challenge (the type of "proof" associated with conspiracy theory, which will be taken up in Chapter 7). Each piece of counter-evidence is treated as further proof of the magnitude of the conspiracy to conceal the truth of Obama's birth. There is no evidence-based way of dismantling the beliefs of the birthers: refutations merely end up reinforcing them, a dynamic that illustrates the demise of symbolic efficiency in action. As Massumi puts it, the "pretension to certainty" is "actually far more trustably achieved by affective facts than empirical ones due to the tautological logic they share with pure decision or command."[18]

In the era of the affective fact, power relies not on the attempt to control and monopolize the realm of empirical facts, but upon channeling this tautological logic: monitoring and modulating the ambient feeling tone that endows non-facts with their "truthiness." As Clough puts it, "affective modulation and individuation displace subject formation and ideological interpellation as central to the relation of governance and economy."[19] The proliferation of strategies for cutting through the clutter by gaining access to the realm of the circulation of emotions and affective intensities come to serve the modulation of affect. The rise of sentiment analysis, in other words, accords with the exigencies of monitoring and managing a populace enjoined to rely on their emotions, their gut instinct, and their thoughtless thoughts, to anchor themselves in a flood of information.

Consider, for example, the change in the register of news from the factual to the affective represented by Fox News. In early 2010, when Fox News was attempting to mobilize anti–Obama sentiment in the United States by providing a public platform for conservative political figures and commentators who, among other things, sought to cast doubt on whether President Barack Obama had really been born in the US, a survey conducted by Public Policy Polling revealed that Fox was the "most trusted" of the country's news operations.[20]

It would have been more accurate to call Fox, with its close ties to the Republican Party and its coterie of right-wing political analysts, the least "mistrusted" news operation, given the finding that less than half of the respondents (49 percent) said they trusted Fox. The survey revealed that Fox was the only major TV news organization that more respondents trusted than distrusted. In response to the findings, which perhaps also help to explain Fox's commercial success, the polling organization's president observed that "A generation ago you would have expected Americans to place their trust in the most neutral and unbiased conveyors of news … But the media landscape has really changed and now they're turning more toward the outlets that tell them what they want to hear."[21] Fox is tapping into the reactions – the intense sense of anxiety, fear, indignation, superiority, or anger that they feel or want to feel. Its viewers are seeing themselves, perhaps, more as discriminating consumers choosing the brand of impassioned (and outraged) "news" than as citizens enduring the outdated ritual of listening to a dispassionate accounting of the facts, as determined in some distant newsroom.

One ready explanation for such a shift is the multiplication of media outlets and the fragmentation and "nichification" of audiences. Legal scholar Cass Sunstein, among others, has voiced his concern that audience fragmentation and mass customization threaten a shared public understanding of current events that relies on common reference points provided by the mass media.[22] As consumers choose to cut through the commercial media clutter by selecting information and media outlets that reflect their political persuasions and preferences and cater to both a particular understanding of the world and an impassioned reaction to the day's events, audiences run the danger of insulating themselves from information and perspectives that might challenge their own. The result, Sunstein argues, is the prospect of greater divergence of opinion in the place of an information-driven consensus: "the consequence will be further balkanization, as group members move one another toward more extreme points in line with their initial tendencies. At the same time, different deliberating groups, each consisting of like-minded people, will be driven increasingly far apart, simply because most of their discussions are with one another."[23]

The success of Fox news – the supposed trustworthiness of an aggressively partisan news outlet – is, in part, a result of its willingness to embrace what Sunstein terms "balkanization" by ensuring that audience members consistently receive information, analysis, and rhetoric that reinforces their worldview. Such a strategy does more than carve out a niche audience for the news; it markets news as branded entertainment that relies on emotional engagement. Sunstein describes the resulting logic of divergence and polarization as a technologically driven one: in a world in which audiences can customize their information consumption, they will, through the force of selective exposure and selective retention, become increasingly fragmented and polarized in their worldviews.

This ready explanation has become popular in accounts of the obvious forms of polarization and political and cultural disconnects that have come to characterize political discussion in the United States. In a plea to resuscitate a version of science-based symbolic efficiency, New Jersey Congressman Rush Holt published an article in the scientific journal *Nature* in 2012 bemoaning the unwillingness of his fellow legislators to "think like scientists" and defer to the facts: "What is lacking is this most basic idea that scientists have that it's not how strongly you believe something, it's what the evidence says ... they know that when other scientists substantiate opposing ideas, then they have to yield, they have to be open to evidence."[24] Referring to one of his Congressional colleagues who has dismissed the scientific evidence behind global change for its alleged anti-business bias and described the attempt to intervene in climate change as an act of hubris that amounts to a challenge of God's will, Holt highlighted the incompatibility of their discourses: "I just don't know where to go in an argument with Senator Inhofe."[25] What has been lost in political deliberation, he continued, is a sense that "it's not ideological certitude that counts, it's the evidence that resolves the argument ... When one realizes that our knowledge is provisional and can be checked against evidence, then it makes it possible to achieve more optimal decisions."[26]

Holt is here describing something quite different from Sunstein's account of fragmentation and polarization, and in this regard, Sunstein's explanation falls short: it does not account for an important condition for the logic of fragmentation – that is, for the role played by the background understanding on the part of viewers that facts, information, and news, have become a matter of choice, faith, or contingent commitment. That is to say, the proliferation of media outlets, on its own, does not directly account for the alleged generational shift identified by Public Policy Polling's study of news outlets' credibility. The willingness to choose one's news depends not just on the multiplication of available choices, but also on a reconceptualization of news as a customizable commodity subject to the vagaries of taste that govern other forms of consumption.

The technological shift that facilitates the multiplication of news outlets and narratives goes hand-in-hand with an ideological shift – with the familiar, knowing debunkery of the seemingly quaint and outdated assumptions of someone like Rush Holt and his plea for science. This shift also accompanies a reflexive understanding of the contrived and selective character of all and any news. It is this shift that Jenkins's notion of "affective economics," outlined in *Convergence Culture*, might help to illuminate – with the help of some tweaking, interpretation, and critical elaboration. There is perhaps more at work in the notions of "affective economics" and "emotional capital" than Jenkins accounts for.[27] A shifting logic of media engagement is accompanied by revamped strategies for managing and manipulating audiences. Although Jenkins's account starts to address these shifts, it does not get at the asymmetries that characterize interactive marketing in the database era. In order to develop further an account of the emerging interactive media economy and aspects of what this book has described as the displacement of representation by correlation, the following sections explore Jenkins's notion of affective economics as a means of thinking about the commercial logic of customization in which marketers seek to manage consumers by tapping into a dominant feeling-tone or "sentiment." The emerging practices of sentiment analysis, opinion mining, predictive analytics, and "super-crunching" rely on a model of affect quite different from that envisioned by Jenkins in his account of affective economics.

Affective Economics and "Emotional Capital"

The notion of affective economics is not a thickly developed one in *Convergence Culture*, which presents it largely as a re-appropriation of marketing rhetoric. The book's glossary defines affective economics as "A new discourse in marketing and brand research that emphasizes the emotional commitments consumers make in brands as a central motivation for their purchasing decisions."[28] Since strategies of mobilizing emotional commitment have been around for a long time, the newness of this discourse seems to hinge more on its urgency in a multiplatform, multi-outlet era than its originality.

The chapter in *Convergence Culture* devoted to the popular TV show *American Idol* similarly invokes marketing discourses, referring to a "new configuration of marketing theory ... which seeks to understand the emotional underpinnings of consumer decision-making as a driving force behind viewing and purchasing decisions."[29] For Jenkins, the shift is more than merely discursive or theoretical: it refers to a real if perhaps not yet fully realized transformation in the way the media economy works. If it is a discursive or theoretical development, it nevertheless has concrete effects, "allowing advertisers to tap the power of collective intelligence [of viewers]" and, at the same time, "allowing consumers to form their own kind of collective bargaining structure that they can use to challenge corporate decisions."[30] What Jenkins seems to have in mind here is not so much the newness of advertisers' attempts to mobilize emotional engagement (again, a topic that long predates the advent of so-called convergence culture and the emergence of "sentiment analysis"), but the enhanced ability of consumers to participate in the process.

As an example of the workings of the affective economy, Jenkins describes the way in which shows such as *American Idol* rely on audience participation and the creation of brand "communities" supported by interactive media in the form of chat rooms, social networks, blogs, bulletin boards, and so on. The ambivalence of affective economics for Jenkins – the fact that it has "both positive and negative implications" – hinges on the multivalent character of the "emotional capital" (another marketing buzzword) that serves as its currency. In some of the formulations he invokes, control over this form of capital apparently lies in the hands of producers, as suggested by the account of

Coca-Cola president Steven J. Heyer's vision for the fusion of entertainment and advertising: "We will use a diverse array of entertainment assets to break into people's hearts and minds ... the ideas which have always sat at the heart of the stories you've told and the content you've sold ... whether movies or music or television ... are no longer just intellectual property, they're emotional capital."[31] If producers control this capital, then they should be heartened by the observation of Saatchi & Saatchi CEO Kevin Roberts that "emotion is an unlimited resource."[32]

However, Jenkins argues, producer control is far from complete. Audiences who invest their emotional capital in a particular show or brand can also withdraw it, or even use it as a resource to build brand communities to influence media producers. Viewed from this perspective, it is not the producers who control this capital, but the viewers. Emotional capital is, in other words, a slippery concept. If for Heyer it can be owned like intellectual property, for Jenkins it is a consumer investment that can be withdrawn at will and reinvested elsewhere: "If a program is going to become, in Heyer's terms, the 'emotional capital' of its consumers, then we can expect consumers to make different investments in the program than the producers do."[33]

The point is not to belabor a term that was never meant to serve as anything more than a boardroom buzzword, but to suggest that the confusion surrounding it may be more than the result of the shallowness of marketing hype. The ambiguity in the notion of emotional capital (is it the audience's investment in the show, the emotion-invoking storyline owned by producers, or the relation between these?) echoes the ambivalence in Jenkins's account of affective economics. If audiences control the capital, they can use it to bargain with producers, if producers control it, they can use it to exploit audience engagement. Although Jenkins's notion of affective economics refers simply to the role played by emotion in an interactive context, the version of emotion he invokes has the diffuse character of affect invoked in Smith's Deleuze-inflected account. According to Smith, affects:

> ... are not your own, so to speak. They are, if I can put it this way, part of the capitalist infrastructure; they are not simply your own individual mental or psychic reality ... Nothing makes this more obvious than the effects of marketing, which are directed entirely at the manipulation of the drives and affects: at the drug store, I almost automatically reach for one brand of toothpaste rather than another, since I have a fervent interest in having my teeth cavity-free and whiter than white, and my breath fresher than fresh – but this is because my desire is already invested in the social formation that creates that interest.[34]

This formulation begs the notion of desire by pushing it back a level, but it usefully invokes the economic logic of affect in ways that, while foreign to

Jenkins's account, may help to illuminate the emerging commercial uses of interactivity. In an affective economy, a circulating, undifferentiated kind of emotion (neither solely "in" the stories nor "of" the audience) comes to serve as an exploitable resource, a part of the "infrastructure." This is not to say that the reliance of marketers on attempts to mobilize affect in the sense described by Smith is new (indeed, Smith has ready access to the history of marketing as a means of illustrating his account); rather, it is to claim that the economic and technological environment has shifted in ways that rely upon and enable a new array of techniques for its monitoring and management. Clough, for example, associates the recent history of capitalism with emergent forms of control that aim "at a never-ending modulation of moods, capacities, affects, potentialities assembled in genetic codes, identification numbers, ratings profiles and preference listings."[35] She describes such forms of control as:

> ... determinant of and a response to the tendency to smooth out the separations between the nation and civil society, the state and the economy, the public and the private domains, due in part to the disorganization of nation-based capitalism effected since the 1970s by globalization, the increased complexity added with flexible accumulation of capital, and flexible employment of labor power but also due to the ongoing social responses to these changes locally and globally.[36]

These are the shifts that set the stage for the forms of flexible and customized marketing facilitated by the commercial deployment of interactive digital technologies in the era of convergence. If this analysis remains at a relatively high level of generality and abstraction compared to Jenkins's specific media examples of affective economics, recent developments in interactive marketing neatly illustrate the ways in which, as Massumi puts it, "affect is a real condition, an intrinsic variable of the late capitalist system, as infrastructural as a factory."[37]

Sentiment Analysis, Vibology, and Buzz Volume

Jenkins references but does not engage with an ongoing conversation around the notion of affect by invoking the term. Still, in making the term central to his account of the changing logics of commercial media in the digital era, he is tipping his hat to its currency in cultural and media studies circles. As Massumi notes:

> There seems to be a growing feeling within media, literary, and art theory that affect is central to an understanding of our information- and image-based late capitalist culture, in which so-called master narratives are perceived to have foundered ... belief has waned for many, but not affect. If anything, our condition is characterized by a surfeit of it.[38]

In the wake of the demise of the narratives that prop up symbolic efficiency, a preoccupation with affect comes to the fore.

If, as Shouse puts it, affect might be described as a, "a non-conscious experience of intensity" (not in the sense of *sub*-conscious, but in the sense of non-reflexive and non-articulated) – "a moment of unformed and unstructured potential" – the goal of affective economics, as espoused by the practitioners of so-called "sentiment analysis," is to channel and structure that intensity.[39] If affect is "prepersonal," the role of affective economics is to personalize it, to fix it in the form of an emotion. As Massumi puts it, "An emotion is a subjective content, the sociolinguistic fixing of the quality of an experience which is from that point onward defined as personal."[40]

The refrain of the marketing industry (at least for public consumption) is that advertising does not instill desires or emotions, but merely taps into already existing, perhaps latent, ones. If someone is moved by a targeted campaign to make a purchase that wouldn't have been made in the absence of the ad, the marketers have merely helped a consumer to realize his or her (latent) desire. This is the apparent indeterminacy of consumer desire in marketing accounts: on the one hand, reliant upon the ministrations of marketers, on the other, an un-coerced invocation of subjective autonomy. Even as advertisers work to gather more information about consumers in order to manage their responses, they refer to their own increasingly slavish devotion to the whims of their targets. Perhaps the question of whether a desire pre-exists a particular stimulus in latent or unrecognized form is the wrong one. The real question is how does a specific desire get articulated to circulating forms of "pre-personal" intensity – what Clough calls an "affective background" – or, more simply, how does affective economics piggyback on affect?[41]

In what Massumi describes as an era of affective "surfeit," one characterized by the apparent decline of those master-narratives that underpin representational models of reality (such as "objective journalism," "scientific research," and so on), market research turns to strategies for surveying the background intensity of the affective economy. Clough discerns in these strategies shifting potentials for social control: "the probabilistic measuring of sociological methodology shifts from merely representing populations, even making populations, to modulating or manipulating the population's affective capacities."[42] Forms of ideological manipulation give way to the modulation of affect: "affect and its modulation displace socialization and disciplining as central to sociality, a displacement which has been essential to installing a conservative neo-liberalism," and facilitating new strategies for the mobilization of affective economics.[43]

Strategies for affective modulation rely on instantaneous and ongoing mechanized monitoring of aggregate flow rather than on discrete analysis of individual responses. One sentiment analysis company described an application that, "automatically evaluates conversations based on sentiment ... to deliver feedback about your products and brands. By automating the process, we can significantly reduce the time needed to analyze conversation."[44] This is typical of the framing of sentiment analysis: the promise that the ability to provide a "real-time" analysis of huge amounts of data outweighs the lack of granularity or individual specification. Automation means that no actual people read the content of individual posts; rather, proxies for sentiment are used to gain a general overview of the aggregate. Typically this means coding particular words or word combinations and situating them within a distance to mentions of the brand, event, political candidate or issue being studied. Once trends are determined, data miners can drill down deeper to isolate individual responses as anecdotal "evidence."

Thus, sentiment analysis relies on what might be described as non-content-based analysis – something similar to the way in which, according to Jodi Dean, "word-clouds" (which measure the frequency with which certain words appear in particular texts) operate: "In word-clouds, frequency and proximity displace meaning ... Words matter, not stories and not narratives ... Word-clouds shift away from a space of linguistically constituted meaning, away from a language constituted out of sentences that are uttered in contexts according to rules that can be discerned and contested."[45] In such approaches statistical proxies for affective intensities displace reference, meaning, and comprehension. The word-cloud is a great equalizer in the sense that it can be applied to anything from the most profoundly moving texts and speeches in human history to technical manuals and promotional flyers: they all look pretty much the same after running through the frequency tabulator. What gets lost in the process, according to Dean, is, "The ability to distinguish between contestatory hege-monic speech. Irony. Tonality. Normativity ... Critique. The terms prominent in a discourse can be discerned but not what they mean."[46] Word-clouds automate the process of reading without reading – signification without com-prehension. They find a way to sidestep meaning while simultaneously creating "actionable intelligence" – that is, correlations that either warrant a response or demonstrate the effectiveness of a particular strategy or campaign.

Sentiment analysts claim to push beyond frequency distributions by attaching a valence to certain words that appear in proximity to key terms being studied. Of course, the goal is to automate the process – to bypass comprehension and thereby the need to read through all the available data. Suggestively, startups frequently invoke the language of "listening" (to the opinions and feelings expressed online) with its overtones of attentiveness, dialogism, and response. But it is a particular kind of listening in which no one individual message is being heard. What takes place instead is an ongoing search for patterns. Thus, the rhetoric of listening readily slips into that of visibility, with its connotations of monitoring and oversight. For example, the tagline for a sentiment analysis site called The Listening Station, which "Listen[s] to Conversations about Brands" is "Providing Visibility into Social Media."[47] This tagline appears over a row of graphs that purport to provide an overview of sentiment patterns as revealed by online search algorithms that sift through the "over one billion conversations stored."[48] A company called Jodange, which bills itself as "The World's First Opinion Utility," features an application which it calls Opinion Lens[TM] for visualizing its data, and another company, Scout Labs, offers "buzz tracking" to allow customers to "*See at glance* which searches are up or down. The Scout Labs dashboard offers real-time metrics for buzz volume, customer sentiment, and competitive share of voice across the web."[49] The company places its clients in the digital cockpit so they can fly by instruments over the emotional landscape. Keeping up with the tech trends, a customer relations management company called 24/7 Customer has introduced a sentiment analysis program called TweetView[TM] that "measures the combined influence of tweets on a company."[50] The goal is not so much to listen to the myriad voices of the members of what Jenkins refers to as a "brand community" as it is to monitor and oversee them, to aggregate and mine them in order to trace signals in the noise and to extract information to improve its marketing campaigns.[51]

Sentiment analysis represents the commercial embrace and reconfiguration of the feedback that Jenkins associates with convergence culture: the ability for consumers to make their voices heard via interactive technologies. It creates *ad hoc*, astro-turfed brand communities, built not by consumers with shared interests but by search algorithms that assemble conversations or posts about particular brands and topics. If Jenkins credits brand communities with empowering groups," to assert their own demands on the company," marketers envision the possibility of creating instant *ad hoc* focus groups writ large. There is a similarity in these accounts: in both cases interactive feedback is envisioned as a way of enlisting consumer participation.[52] But there are significant differences in tone and genealogy: Jenkins traces the version of participation he is interested in back to the progressive politics of the counterculture, underground/alternative media and the participatory ethos of fan culture; marketers hearken back to the scientific management of production and consumption. If fan communities fostered active engagement with media content, marketers have long been gathering information about consumers in order to develop strategies for fostering what Jenkins describes as "a stronger emotional engagement with their brands."[53]

The history of commercial strategies for harvesting consumer feedback and harnessing consumer engagement (ranging across the development of consumer monitoring techniques, the use of mail-in contests, the sponsorship of fan clubs and focus groups, and so on) is largely absent from Jenkins's account of affective economics, which, despite its fascination with the de-differentiation of the realms of production and consumption, remains a consumer-side fan-inflected account. The absence is significant insofar as it marks what might be described as a difference in tone and perhaps in the political potential of consumer-generated participation, on the one hand, and the interactive monitoring envisioned by sentiment analysts, on the other. If convergence marks the mainstreaming of participatory fan culture, it has the potential to cut both ways: the increasing influence of participatory consumers on the production process, and the facilitation of monitoring-based regimes of control. If, as Jenkins observes, "We need to confront the social, cultural, and political protocols that surround the technology and define how it will get used,"[54] then we must consider the ways in which participation contributes to what Clough describes as "the ongoing setting to capitalist exchange of attention-work of all kinds."[55]

Sentiment analysis piggybacks on the formation of relatively engaged, self-aware communities, dispersing and dissolving them into the wider discussions on the Internet. The goal of data-mining sentiment is not to capture the articulated feedback of self-consciously constructed brand and issue communities, but to gain an overview of myriad (decontextualized) ongoing conversations – a perspective within which emotions are abstracted from individuals. One start-up sentiment mining application, for example, claims to "understand *how the web feels*" via a "vibology meter."[56] This version of prosopopoeia – attributing an imagined and unified voice to a dispersed and invisible aggregate that cannot speak for itself – enacts the fetishistic disavowal of contemporary capitalism, according to Slavoj Zizek: the simultaneous dismissal of the ability to comprehend or represent a totality and its reassertion as an autonomous, anonymous imaginary entity. For example, when "the people speak" through aggregate voting results that allegedly provide a candidate with a "strong mandate," this combined sentiment may not reflect that of any particular individual or group (since widespread weak support combined with significant strong opposition might result in the apparent mandate). As Zizek puts it, "no one is personally responsible for it, all just feel the need to accommodate themselves to it. And the same goes for capitalism as such."[57] The logic of aggregation is distinct from that of collectivity – the former seeks to create an imagined consensus out of an overview that makes up for what it lacks in depth, comprehension, and meaning with breadth, speed, and predictive power. The intent, according to one CEO of a sentiment analysis company, is to capture enough data to discern an overall tendency, or an aggregate sentiment: "If we're right 75% to 80% of the time, we don't care about any single story."[58] In the end, being "right" does not refer to representational accuracy but to correlational confirmation. If, for example, increased sales are correlated with shifts in a particular measure of sentiment, there is no need to interrogate the underlying reasons, but simply to influence this measure.

Whereas Jenkins, building on the model of fandom, envisions brand communities knit together by their shared engagement in a TV program, consciously campaigning for their interests, sentiment analysts seek to eavesdrop on the entire wired populace. The result is not an approach based on collective bargaining with interest groups but one that relies on covert and pre-emptive opinion tracking on an unprecedented scale: speed-reading a "body" of data as if it might inadvertently reveal its hidden truths when it doesn't realize it's being watched. The language of "community" and "engagement" echoes Jenkins's fan-inspired version of participatory viewership in an interactive era, but repurposes these as strategies for managing interactive audiences. As one testimonial for a sentiment analysis company puts it:

> There's one reason why we use Scout Labs: it helps us turn conversations into action. Buzz monitoring is one thing, but the ability to collaborate with our clients in real-time to reach far across the social web to engage our customer communities is the ultimate capability. Our clients are genuinely excited by the ability to stimulate word of mouth among their influencers and track our programs' effects over time.[59]

This testimonial points to the way in which sentiment analysis pushes beyond the goal of representing or modeling the populace. The goal is not to describe but to affect and effect – to stimulate word of mouth, to promote engagement and, in some cases, to thwart it. One sentiment analysis company, for example, promises, "Real-time tracking of 'Detractors' to minimize the impact and velocity of negative word-of-mouth."[60] The press release does not indicate how such detractors are dealt with. Presumably the company has ways of drowning them out or pre-empting critique. A complementary application seeks out influential members of brand communities (those whom Jenkins, using marketing lingo, refers to as "inspirational consumers") in order to amplify positive reviews. The application: "harnesses a brand's customers – and their followers – to quickly and effectively spread the word on the brand and its products."[61] It "encourages consumers – at the time they're most likely to share their opinions – to publish their product reviews on Facebook, Twitter and blogs."[62] Strategies of detailed tracking are designed not just to monitor audience feedback, but to modulate its volume and circulation by intervening pre-emptively, adjusting in real time so as to alter the information landscape.

The goal of predictive analytics is both pre-emptive and productive: to manage risks before they emerge or become serious while at the same time maximizing sales. Such approaches, in other words, seek to integrate possible futures into present behavior. As Massumi puts it, "Preemption does not prevent, it effects. It induces the event, *in effect*. Rather than acting in the present to avoid an occurrence in the future, preemption brings the future into the present."[63] Applied to sentiment analysis, the goal is to minimize negative sentiment and maximize emotional investment and engagement: not merely to record sentiment as a given but to modulate it as a variable. Modulation means constant adjustment to bring the anticipated consequences of a modeled future into the present in ways that account for the former, and thus alter the later.

To treat a population as a probe is not so much to measure and record it as to subject it to ongoing experimentation. This is the form that predictive analytics takes in the age of what Ian Ayres calls super-crunching: not the attempt to get at an underlying demographic or emotional "truth," but to search for correlations.[64] Marketers and advertisers use interactive environments to subject consumers to an ongoing series of randomized, controlled experiments. Bearing out Clough's observations about the role of sociology in the modulation of affect, Ayres notes that experimental methods continue to migrate from the scholarly world to the commercial one: "Academics have been running randomized experiments inside and outside medicine for years. But the big change is that businesses are relying on them to reshape corporate policy. They can see what works and immediately change their corporate strategy."[65] The goal of such experiments is to generate what the various startups and marketers call actionable intelligence: if one seemingly minor variable is changed, how might this affect consumer response? Access to the database is crucial for generating this kind of information. As Ayres puts it, "The sample size is key" – the bigger the better, which is what makes the Internet such a rich site for this kind of research.[66] Recall Chris Anderson's description of a "petabyte era" in which, with enough data, the numbers "speak for themselves."[67]

This is a way of thinking about data that fits neatly with what Massumi calls the waning of belief (and Clough describes as the shift away from logics of representation and ideological interpellation): there is no need to rely on models of reality to interpret the data.[68] Data-crunching in the incunabulum of the petabyte era envisions the interactive modulation of affect: a world in which feedback is not just collected, but constantly generated thanks to ongoing experimental variation. The goal is to craft an interactive mediascape that triples as entertainment, advertising, and *probe*. The promise of super-crunching vast amounts of data, according to Ayres, is to "predict what you will want and what you will do."[69] Such is the data-driven fantasy of control in the affective economy: the more emotions are expressed and circulated, the more behavior is tracked and aggregated, the greater the ability of marketers to attempt to channel and fix affect in ways that translate into increased consumption. Commercial control over the infrastructure of the data that it generates lies at the heart of this version of affective economics.

Betting against Ourselves

Marketers may have something quite different in mind from Jenkins when they speak of engagement and community. Not a grass-roots formation with a range of ties to other community members, but dispersed individuals who can be engaged and enlisted for the purpose of brand management, constituting myriad data points whose online activities and interactions generate "actionable" findings available exclusively to those who mine the databases. If the Internet is supposed to be the great equalizer, the rise of super-crunching in the data mine reintroduces asymmetry in the form of the database. If, for Jenkins, affective economics refers to the recognition of fan activity as a model for the interactive media economy, for marketers it partakes of the logic of control outlined by Massumi and Clough.[70]

For Jenkins, the notion of affect appears to refer to shared individual emotional engagement and investment. However, the development of sentiment analysis, opinion mining, vibology, and predictive analytics treats what Jenkins calls affect as something perhaps less clearly defined: an ambient sentiment that can be productively modulated and manipulated in ways that impact upon the desires, emotions, and preferences of individual viewers and consumers. In this version of an affective economy, "there is an ongoing subsumption of the social reproduction of biological and social life into capitalist production and exchange, such that affect must be thought of as 'an impersonal *flow* before it is a subjective content.'"[71] This version of affect is both meta-individual and pre-personal. As Clough puts it, neatly anticipating the logic of sentiment analysis:

> ... this is a dynamic background, a probablisitic, statistical background which provides an infra-empirical or infra-temporal sociality, the subject of which is, I want to propose, the population, technologically or meth-odologically open to the modulation of its affective capacities. Sociality as affective background displaces sociality grasped in terms of structure and individual.[72]

Against this background, a version of the "politics of participation" built around "consumption communities" looks like a throwback to a surpassed context: one in which participation, insofar as it thwarted centralized, institutional forms of authority, carried with it overtones of subversion and the prospect of the democratic empowerment that Jenkins invokes.[73] He marks the passing of this context when he criticizes the politics of culture jamming for clinging to the "rhetoric of opposition and co-optation" in a transformed world where "the new digital environment expands the scope and reach of consumer activities."[74] But the celebration of participation *per se* as empowerment is simply the obverse of this disavowed politics (which wants to imagine that we do not *need* to oppose once we can participate). It presupposes what it ostensibly surpasses – what Clough describes as a politics of ideological representation, "where resistance to these identities and the transgression of the institutional norms that support them, was possible, even enabled by the instability of the strategies of disciplining."[75]

A context in which control relies increasingly upon expanded opportunities for participation requires a rethinking of the oppositions that place participation *per se* on the side of democratic empowerment. If a regime of ideological control gives us Walter Cronkite's sober assessment of "the way it is," one of affective modulation gives us the impassioned commentators of Fox News. Fox is perhaps the paradigmatic example of a "news" brand attuned to the surfeit of affect: what it provides that the other networks do not (though MSNBC is trying) is a level of intensity that makes up for what Massumi describes as the waning of belief. In the era of the reflexive critique of grand narratives (and the forms of representation they underwrite), Fox relies on the mobilization of intensities that congeal in various contexts into fear, anger, indignation, patriotism, pride, and so on. Perhaps the most frenetic performer in this symphony of intensities was the emotionally labile Glenn Beck – an affective strange attractor who channels, in turn, anxiety, anger, grief, indignation, wounded curiosity, pride, and humor, careening from one to the other, but manifesting above all an unstable hyper-intensity.

These intensities circulate in a plane distinct from that of the various under-lying "factual" claims (true or otherwise) to which they are ostensibly attached. They have the uncanny persistence of Massumi's "affective facts": they persist and even thrive on the debunking of the empirical claims to which they are attached (that Barack Obama is not really a US citizen, that his proposed healthcare system includes "death panels," that there is a direct connection between Iraq and the 9/11 attacks, and so on). This persistence is perhaps one of the drawbacks of taking the pleasures of popular culture as a model for a resuscitated politics. The populist logic of Fox is to treat the debunking of the empirical fact as if it were an (elitist) attack on the affective attachment to it (amounting to an assault on one's taste). The resulting ersatz democratization exempts itself from the logics of media monitoring and deliberation that play an important role in Jenkins's account of the convergent relationship between new media and old. This is not to deny that the ongoing process of fact-checking, critique and debunkery plays an important role in the interplay between, say, the blogosphere and the cable news networks. Rather, it is to suggest that what emerges is not so much a convergence upon a shared version of the facts, but the multiplication of divergent narratives tied to affective facts.[76] The issue here is not so much the process of nichification but rather a vernacular postmodern savviness about the constructed character of mediated representation and the arbitrary closure of truth narratives that serves as its condition of possibility.

The notion of affective economics, then, raises (at least) two major concerns that are worth incorporating into an understanding of "the social, cultural, and political protocols that surround the technology" of convergence culture.[77] The first has to do with the role played by participation in the modulation of affect as a modality of control. In concrete terms, it is not clear that the emergence of participatory forms of interactivity has coincided with widespread forms of economic or political empowerment. On the contrary, the early decades of convergence culture have coincided with the dramatic concentration of economic power in the US, increasing income disparity, and profound challenges to public accountability by the executive branch, security agencies, and commercial entities. The least mistrusted news organization in the country has in many instances worked to mobilize support for these changes. Against this background, Jenkins's admonition against complacency rings increasingly urgently: "Too often, we have fallen into the trap of seeing democracy as an 'inevitable' outcome of technological change rather than as something which we need to fight to achieve with every tool at our disposal."[78]

The second concern has to do with the affective economic model of convergence culture. Although the Internet and various online services have relied on a variety of different forms of economic support, there is little mainstream debate over the direction in which it seems to be headed, and the invocation of the potential of commercial popular culture reinforces this tendency. A commercial Internet will rely upon the effectiveness of online advertising, and this, in turn, depends upon strategies of data mining and predictive analytics as effective tools for managing the populace. As traditional forms of commercial support are threatened by the Internet, data-driven customization, forecasting, and targeting become the default model for financing the commercial media infrastructures of the digital era. Media convergence means that models developed for interactive devices are being adopted by producers across the media spectrum. The wager is that data-driven, targeted forms of advertising will one day prove effective enough to make up for the decline of traditional forms of commercial revenue. It is an odd wager in this regard: we are betting on our own susceptibility to new forms of control and manipulation as a means for supporting the burgeoning digital media economy. If the promise of the power of data-crunching and predictive analytics turns out to be nothing more than misplaced marketing hype, the commercial future of media convergence is in jeopardy. On the other hand, if it comes true, we find ourselves active participants in our own interactive submission and manipulation. The wager on the commercial future of affective economics and sentiment analysis, in this regard, feels like a bet against ourselves.

FUTURE GLUT

Marketocracy

Who Needs Experts?

In the thick of the 2008 presidential campaign, Hillary Clinton offered a populist rejoinder to the criticism that her proposed reduction of the federal gas tax was not supported by economic experts: "I'm not going to put my lot in with economists," she told George Stephanopolous of ABC's *This Week*, "We've got to get out of this mindset where somehow elite opinion is always on the side of doing things that really disadvantage the vast majority of Americans."[1] Attacking the experts was an out-of-character tactic for a candidate who had made her political reputation on the basis of her intellect, her wonkishness, and political expertise. In mocking the wisdom of the experts and their support for taxes that "hurt" the American people, Clinton was borrowing a page from George W. Bush's 2000 campaign strategy of portraying politicians and bureaucrats as overweening elitists: "My opponent and the folks up in Washington want to empower bureaucrats and make the health decisions for America. They want more power in Washington. They want the planners and deciders, the folks that are telling you how to think, in power."[2] Long before Clinton, Bush made it clear that he certainly was not going to throw his lot in with the experts, the deciders, or planners: "We don't trust bureaucrats in Washington, D.C. We don't believe in planners and deciders making decisions on behalf of America."[3]

This approach to expertise of all kinds was a familiar staple of Bush-era Republicanism as practiced by various vociferous climate science naysayers, Iraq war supporters, and creationists. Someone who purported to know better than "you" – the everyday citizen – was portrayed as someone who thought they were better than you (and anyone else who thought like you or simply did not agree with them). This variant of ersatz democratization claims the scalp of expertise in the name of the demise of symbolic efficiency. To paraphrase the faux-news anchor Stephen Colbert, in the universe of the postmodern right, the "facts" were portrayed as having a well-known tilt toward elitism, probably because they were repeatedly being used to challenge people's deeply held beliefs and desires.[4] In a representative example of this practiced skepticism toward expertise, cable-news commentator Bill O'Reilly asked comedian Jon Stewart during a 2010 discussion of political issues, "But you believe in global warming – man made?"[5] The framing of the question took it squarely out of the domain of expertise and science, and into the realm of individual opinion, ideological predisposition, and faith. To make man-made global warming a matter of faith is, of course, to put it on the same playing field with Santa Claus – a personal matter of faith or belief in which the intervention of fact-oriented experts looks like an unwelcome and interfering intrusion. In this realm – the realm of what we know simply because we passionately believe it, even in the face of the well-established opposing opinions of "the experts"; Rush Limbaugh can be just as much a climate-change expert as anyone else. Those who would seek to challenge our faith with their science have simply chosen a different faith. Anyone who attempts to educate or argue us out of our chosen belief system can be dismissed as a condescending elitist whose efforts are simply evidence of disrespect for our faith and values.

This is the familiar savvy appeal of populist rhetoric: "the experts are elitists who do not respect how you think, and that means they do not respect who you are." In the book *Data Smog*, Shenk claims that "The proliferation of expert opinion has ushered in a virtual anarchy of expertise," but this does not seem quite right – something must have first shifted to make this proliferation possible.[6] You don't simply get more experts because there are more opinions and proliferating alternative narratives – the point of expertise is to adjudicate between these. It is only when the basis of adjudication – of expertise itself – is called into question that the proliferation described by Shenk takes place. In this regard, he is not describing the proliferation of expertise so much as the dissolution of the criteria for identifying experts. This dissolution, as I argue at various points in the book, has political implications. The pundit and political analyst Josh Micah Marshall associates the populist mainstreaming of a savvy postmodernism with the tactics of the political right in the Bush era, which seemed predicated on "the belief that … [i]deology isn't just the prism through which we see the world, or a pervasive tilt in the way a person understands a given set of facts. Ideology is really all there is."[7]

The Market Knows Best

If the Internet has helped to create the conditions for the revamped populism of the postmodern Right, it has also contributed a substitute for the void created by generalized debunkery in the form of the non-expert expertise of the marketplace. As Hillary Clinton was asserting her mistrust of the economic experts, her chances were being tracked day-by-day, statement-by-statement in the prediction markets – part of a range of futures markets devoted to speculation on events ranging from elections to the spread of the latest flu virus and the paths of hurricanes. Electronic prediction markets devoted to politics have been around for a while now – the best known of them, the Iowa Electronic Markets, has tracked presidential elections since 1988, but these markets have come into their own thanks in part to the rise of the Internet, which enables ease of access to online trading and the ability to circumvent US gambling restrictions by basing operations overseas (the Iowa Electronic Markets has been given an exemption from gambling restrictions for educational purposes). Suggestively, the *New York Times* has attributed the rise of prediction markets to a declining faith in expertise in the past decade, triggered in no small part by the decision of Bush's "best and brightest" to advocate invading Iraq: "The rise of prediction markets started in the middle of the last decade, brought about by a combination of politics, psychology and technology. The politics came mostly from the aftermath of the Iraq war, when the collective, pro-invasion opinion of Washington experts came to look tragically wrongheaded … The only good alternative to a few flawed opinions, some researchers argued, was a vast number of flawed opinions. The biases often canceled one another out. The legitimate information rose to the surface."[8] But only, apparently, under the pressure of cash.

During the 2008 presidential campaign, recourse to the analysis of the pundits and polls increasingly came to be supplemented by the wisdom of so-called prediction markets. As one news account put it in a frequently echoed background paragraph: "The Iowa Electronic Markets, the oldest prediction market and the only major prediction exchange based in the United States, has an impressive track record: Compared with 964 polls conducted over five presidential elections since 1988, the exchange has been closer to the real outcome 74 percent of the time."[9] A political reporter for *The New York Times* noted the role that prediction markets were having on the 2008 presidential campaign: "In recent months, when I have asked former advisers to Bush or Bill Clinton what they think will happen in 2008, they have often talked about Intrade [an online prediction market] … Journalists – me included – have praised Intrade as a miniature version of the stock market, where the collective wisdom of the masses reveals a larger truth."[10]

Prediction markets such as Intrade provide one response to the perceived information glut associated with the Internet-facilitated information society: let the market sort it out. They promise to aggregate large numbers of dispersed signals into an easily digestible, readily quoted number. Moreover – and this is apparently a large part of the appeal – they can generate truths without comprehension. The market serves as the master algorithm, effortlessly making sense of large numbers of signals in real time. Like a data algorithm, the prediction markets need to be allowed to run their course in order to generate an outcome – one that cannot be modeled in advance. As Intrade CEO John Delaney puts it, "We are in a world of information overload and prediction markets can summarize, aggregate, distill a huge amount of thought, opinion and expert view into single probabilities."[11] Futures markets thereby address the proliferation of narratives and evidence of all kinds online. They offer a strategy for automatically making sense of huge amounts of information without having to adjudicate between rival interpretations in deliberative fashion. They allow for aggregation without collectivization and for exchange without deliberation because they create a statistical "consensus" out of competition.

In this regard, prediction markets are an ideal decision-making mechanism for an era in which enhanced access to communication resources results not in convergence upon shared understandings, but in the proliferation of irreconcilable narratives without any agreed-upon principle for adjudication. They generalize the promise of the invisible hand as a decision-making mechanism for a "divergence culture" in which the logic of economic rationality is generalized to the realms of the political and the social. From the perspective of the decision market, we are all viewed as discrete, individual, profit-maximizing actors.[12] Such markets equate the search for meaning with profit maximization, replicating the assumptions of neoclassical economics: all meanings (like tastes) are treated as individual (something over which the individual is sovereign), competition trumps collaboration, and the notion of collectivity is dismissed as dependent decision-making – a lack of freedom and autonomy (that invokes the specter of the "culture of dependency" so often used to discredit the Welfare State). As James Surowiecki, the author of *The Wisdom of Crowds*, puts it: "the people in the crowd need to be independent, so that they pay attention mostly to their own information ... when people start paying too much attention to what others in the group think, that usually spells disaster."[13] So much for the power of deliberation and the goal of collective action.

"Futarchy" and "Predictocracy"

One economist frequently quoted in the coverage of prediction markets has proposed a political system dubbed "futurachy," in which policy decisions are left to the wisdom of speculative markets: "Elected representatives would continue to define and manage national welfare, but their policy decisions would be made by market speculators. 'In futarchy, democracy would continue to say what we want, but betting markets would now say how to get it.'"[14] Government by the market for the market represents the culmination of the principle of voting with one's wallet: "Those who know they are not relevant experts shut up … And those who do not know this eventually lose their money and then shut up."[15]

Another recent book called *Predictocracy* argues that prediction markets ought eventually to displace alternative means of making predictions in a variety of contexts for both the private and the public sectors.[16] The book purports to demonstrate "how bets can serve as a foundational alternative to votes in the construction of institutions … prediction markets offer the possibility of a new way of thinking about structuring decision making, and this approach can be used for problems large and small."[17] "Predictocracy" and "futarchy" envision a world in which speech is replaced by money, experts by winners, deliberation by market competition, and commitment by wealth (though some advocates argue for *subsidized* prediction markets – a practice that can introduce its own distortions). Amidst the debris of expert knowledge, the distortions of representation, and the deadlocks of deliberation, the market emerges as the last institution standing – an allegedly post-ideological arbiter for a post-ideological era.

It is the (highly questionable) status of the market as the non-ideological ideology, the anti-grand narrative, that allows it to fill in the void left by the critique of expertise symbolic systems upon which it relies. The savvy and ostensibly subversive critique of expertise is characteristic of what I have been describing in this book as a vernacular postmodernism, composed of a mistrust of the arbitrariness of closure and of master narratives, along with the revelation of the alignment of truth (in scare quotes) with powerful interests. Grand narratives, however, are sticky, tricky things, and even the story of their demise takes on a certain inescapable grandeur. The goal of this chapter is to consider how the populist critique has embraced the rise of so-called prediction markets and their ability to harness what Surowiecki calls "the wisdom of crowds."[18] The promise of such markets is their ability to at one and the same time dispense with expertise and arrive at the right answer, while catering to the equation between democracy and the idealized "free" market. As Surowiecki puts it, "Markets are made up of diverse people with different levels of information and intelligence, and yet when you put all those people together and they start buying and selling, they come up with generally intelligent decisions."[19]

The market compensates for its role in undermining master narratives by offering itself up as a post-narratival replacement for grand narratives. In an era of thinking without thought, knowledge without knowing, communication without referents, and information without comprehension, the market serves as a post-deliberative and post-political decision-maker. This double role of the market – as the "un-narrative" narrative – underwrites the promise of its efficacy as a decision-making mechanism able to fill the vacuum created by savvy critique of the claims to disinterested rationality, expertise and scientific knowledge. The following sections consider both the conditions of possibility for the embrace of prediction markets and some consequences of their proposed use as a means of addressing the challenges of information glut.

Decision Markets and Vernacular Postmodernism

One of the significant conjunctures of the late 2000s was that of the proliferation of prediction markets in areas ranging from internal business planning to politics, epidemiology, and meteorology with the highly publicized, large-scale failure of financial markets triggered by the collapse of the sub-prime mortgage market. The persistence of the narrative of the wisdom of markets in the face of their palpable folly was striking. On the one hand was the repeated assertion that markets are reliable forms of information aggregation and prediction since, as Surowiecki puts it, "investors do not need to be rational and markets do not need to be perfect for markets to still be excellent at problem solving," and, on the other, a dramatic illustration of the abysmal failure of markets to predict and assess risk.[20] The point is not just that, as Michael Lewis observed in his book about the few investors who saw the collapse coming, "The big Wall Street firms, seemingly so shrewd and self-interested, had somehow become the dumb money."[21] It is that the free market system, left to its own increasingly deregulated devices, had imploded. Even the "smart" money – those investors who profited tremendously by betting against the US economy, could not have won without large-scale government intervention. That is to say, they would have won in theory, but would not have received much of a payout if a large part of the finance sector they were betting against collapsed. Just one part of the assistance package – the promise to guarantee $306 billion of Citigroup's assets – represented "nearly 2 percent of the U.S. gross domestic product, and roughly the combined budgets of the departments of Agriculture, Education, Energy, Homeland Security, Housing and Urban Development and Transportation."[22] In other words, the costly collapse represented not simply the fraudulence, ignorance, or stupidity of particular investors, but the failure of the combined wisdom harnessed by the system: the idiocy of markets. In the heyday of the triumph of global capitalism, after a long period of deregulation capped off by the heady atmosphere of free-market worship cultivated by the eight-year Bush administration, the finance system took all the rope it was given and would have simply hung itself if not for the intervention of the highly visible hand of the state.

One symptom of an ostensibly post-political formation in the era of the savvy critique of grand narratives is its uncanny ability to survive the de-legitimation of its ideological underpinnings. We might describe this persistence as another pathology of the demise of symbolic efficiency, the success of ideology without referent. In the wake of the sub-prime mortgage crisis and the near collapse of the financial system, the stories about the effectiveness of the market in aggregating complex information and efficiently allocating resources ought to have been significantly discredited; yet, not only is the political will to transform speculative financial markets lacking, but the narrative of the wisdom of markets persists as a substitute for debunked expertise. Ideology critique is futile against affective facts such as the wisdom of "free" markets or the efficacy of trickle-down economics, which have proven their ability to withstand repeated onslaughts by the "reality-based-community."

Market fundamentalists are apt to argue that the collapse of the sub-prime mortgage market was the result of the opacity and novelty of the financial instruments involved – but this argument would defeat their claims. The whole point of prediction markets is that they are supposed to provide a powerful and efficient way to unearth intelligence about future events, especially those which are opaque even to the so-called experts. The concealed flaws and the fundamental unsoundness of the bundled sub-prime mortgage securities was precisely the type of hidden truth that speculative markets are supposed to be so good at unearthing.

Above all, we are told, futures markets are more accurate than opinion polls because they mobilize self-interest: "People predict a lot more with their heads than their hearts" when they wager on prediction markets, according to an Intrade official, "because their money is really on the line."[23] Unlike cable news shows and opinion polls, such markets are supposed to weed out unsuccessful participants (assuming that they have limited funds): "The consistently wrong are chased from the market; those who have a pattern of guessing right stick around for more."[24] A certain denigration of discourse is at work here – a theme that runs through several of the chapters in this book. Compared to bets – real monetary commitments – mere words are empty and unreliable, subject to the vagaries of various social pressures and distortions: mouths with no money behind them. As Abramowicz puts it, the willingness to bet (to put one's money where one's mouth is in a country where spending is treated as a form of speech) attests to sincerity. Therefore, he goes so far as to claim that "a refusal to bet ... suggests insincerity."[25] In such a context, risk aversion becomes a serious problem because it can be conflated with lying or deception, and citizenship training for participation in a "Predictocracy" requires that such tendencies be curtailed. This version of neoliberal market fundamentalism relies on a particular type of participants – the speculative citizen – who replaces speech with money and lets the market sort out the results.

The Spread of Prediction Markets

In accordance with the omnivorous character of exchange value, prediction markets can be constructed around any measurable, detectible outcome and have so far been applied to the search for a shipwreck, the anticipated damage caused by hurricanes, and the future success and profitability of new product lines. Notoriously, shortly after the 9/11 attacks, media reports described a Pentagon anti-terrorism initiative to create a futures market in terrorism that would rely on speculators to aggregate intelligence about the likelihood of particular types of terrorist attacks. Although the plan was scrapped after Congressional concerns about encouraging speculation on future harm to the US and its citizens, it retained the support of those who viewed markets as an efficient information processing mechanism. As one aggrieved commentator put it, "Outraged senators who whine about our inability to anticipate threats while denying us new ways of gathering intelligence can hardly claim to be concerned about protecting the homeland."[26] As a form of preventative homeopathy, an embrace of speculative risk in futures markets proposes to detect (and pre-empt) other forms of risk: threats to national security, the spread of disease, and unsuccessful product launches, to name a few.

From the perspective of prediction markets, the full range of social and political life can enter the embrace of speculation. The only barrier – and this is a giveaway – is government restrictions on speculation: "Imagine the president had a crystal ball to predict more accurately the impact of broader prescription coverage on the Medicare budget, the effect of more frequent audits on tax compliance – or even the consequences of a political settlement in Iraq on oil prices. Now, stop imagining: Such crystal balls are within our grasp. But they can't be used without running a gauntlet of federal and state regulation."[27] If only deregulation of the financial markets had turned them into equally accurate fortune tellers!

There is something disconcertingly faith based about the renewed interest in prediction markets in the wake of the spectacular speculative failure that ushered in the so-called Global Financial Crisis. The mistrust of regulation and the agents who would promulgate it goes hand-in-hand with a confirmed faith in that elusive (because fictive) ideal of the free market. Savvy cynicism and credulity go hand-in-hand. I have been describing this combination throughout the course of the book as symptomatic of a vernacular or populist postmodernism. The critique of expertise parallels the demise of symbolic efficiency. The savvy debunkery of expertise "sees through" the insignia and credentials of the expert, reducing these to the various interests and contingencies attached to a particular individual. At stake is not simply individual authority – the fate of the expert – but rather the symbolic system that confers expertise and underwrites the function of representation. The demise of symbolic efficiency, then, refers to the erosion of the guarantees of the narratives – religious, scientific, or otherwise – that support a particular symbolic order. To refer to this demise is not to suggest that such narratives have disappeared or ceased functioning entirely, but that their claims to general assent (whether realized or not) have succumbed to the reflexive critique of representation.

As previous chapters have argued, one of the symptoms of the deadlock of the demise of symbolic efficiency is the multiplication of attempts to bypass the level of discursive representation altogether – the resurgent popularity of body language analysis and other detection techniques, as well as the development of so-called neuromarketing technologies that promise to bypass the potentially misleading level of conscious discourse. I have included in this formation the fascination with television police procedurals (which focus on forensic investigation techniques rather than on narrative) and the "democratization" of access to various surveillance technologies (nanny cams, global positioning system (GPS) tracking devices). Prediction markets fit into the same category insofar as they promise to generate a meaningful aggregate picture of the world without relying on a background of shared presuppositions, information, or worldview – or even the need for deliberation. For Surowiecki, the market-based wisdom of crowds depends on the lack of collaborative decision-making. Markets do best, he argues, when individual participants pursue their own viewpoints and interest in order to avoid "the perils of dependent decision making."[28]

The Speculative Citizen

Accounts of prediction markets portray the active speculator as, of necessity, more motivated and, hence, responsible and participatory than the passive polling subject, implicitly a welfare state product (prone to dependency and, presumably, the pathology of "dependent decision making"). Because money is on the line (a condition which would be considered to skew polling results), "You are incentivized to be careful and methodical," according to Intrade CEO John Delaney.[29] Economics professor Robin Hanson, responsible for devising the notion of the speculation-based form of governance he terms "futarchy," contends that real money wagers serve as a measure of commitment and a means of promoting the cultivation of clear-thinking analysis and self-motivated forms of market research: "Markets give incentives to think carefully."[30] Moreover, they provide the incentive for speculative citizens to educate themselves about the issues. For good greed to work its magic, it needs to be legal, and the celebration of prediction markets goes hand-in-hand with the deregulatory impulse. Several news accounts have insistently noted that economists from the American Enterprise Institute and the Brookings institute have "urged deregulation of predictive markets as different from gambling on poker and other games," although the difference is not always clearly spelled out.[31]

The goal of opening up such markets, they argue, is not an economic one – since they recommend that these be administered by non-profit organizations – but a policy-oriented one. Deregulation would make it possible to bet on a whole range of policy initiatives: whether, for example, a particular proposal might raise or lower standardized test scores or lower infant mortality rates. Such markets replicate the logic of pre-emption insofar as they are used to model outcomes so as to avoid them. Imagine, for example, a prediction market devoted to evaluating a new educational or tax policy: the point of running such a market would be to help decide whether to implement the policy in the first place. If the market bets in favor and the policy is adopted, then the predictive power of that particular set of speculations can be assessed at some later point (did the market accurately predict the initiative's success?). However, if the market turns against the policy, the failed status of the policy is like that of the future criminal's guilt in "The Minority Report": hypothetical. As one news account put it, "Suppose that a foundation is thinking of paying \$5 for every child vaccinated against a certain disease. Information markets can be used to estimate the number of children who will suffer from the disease both with and without the bounty. That gives a market-based estimate of the benefit to be had from paying the bounty."[32] All of which raises the somewhat disturbing prospect of speculators placing bets on and profiting from predictions about the number of people who will fall ill or die – whether as a result of storms, epidemics, healthcare reforms, or terrorist attacks. Speculative citizens, in other words, must adopt a certain calculative logic for the purposes of the common good, although they do not need to make this shift from the individual to the collective themselves: the prediction market does it for them.

The logic of prediction markets follows that of other neoliberal reforms where a speculative citizenry is inculcated in the "norms and values of the market including those of 'responsibility, initiative, competitiveness, risk-taking, and industrious effort.'"[33] As in the case of, say, the proposed privatization of social security in the United States, the advent of prediction market-based policy initiatives requires members of the citizenry to take on the responsibility of training themselves to more effectively manage their own marketplace wagers. The difference, of course, is that while private Social Security accounts remain individualized benefits, prediction market speculation shapes broader forms of social and economic policy. As an article on prediction markets in the *Journal of Economic Perspectives* puts it, "the power of prediction markets derives from the fact that they provide incentives for *truthful revelation*, they provide incentives for research and *information discovery*, and the market provides an algorithm for *aggregating opinions*."[34] By truthful revelation, the artcile means evaluations revealed by dint of wagers. Whereas as poll respondents may not say what they are actually thinking, speculative citizens have every incentive to bet according to their actual assessments, according to the advocates of prediction markets. The way to create an informed citizenry is to make it pay.

The goal of prediction markets is a time-annihilating one: to collapse the future into the present via the process of speculation. This creates some recursive temporal loops in policy futures markets that not only predict specific outcomes, but in so doing help to shape these outcomes. Thus, for example, a model for policy markets proposed by the economist Robin Hanson would rely on conditional probability contracts which are paid off only if a given pre-condition also occurs. A conditional probability contract for an election, for example, might invite wagers on the likelihood of a Republican victory if a particular candidate is nominated (i.e., the probability that Republicans will win the White House if John McCain is the nominee). A contract for a policy proposal would offer wagers on the likelihood of a particular outcome if a policy is adopted (the likelihood, say, that national reading scores will rise more than 5 percent if a new reading program is adopted). If the initial condition does not obtain (McCain is not nominated or the reading program is not adopted), the contract is called off and the parties keep their money. To the extent that decision market results are used to choose whether to adopt a particular proposal (or nominate a particular candidate), the wager on a future outcome (unlike, say, a wager on the roll of the dice) determines, in part, the outcome being wagered on.

In this regard, prediction markets function as simulation machines to model various possible futures in the present. For them to function properly, the realization of a social good must necessarily come at the expense of a subsection of the speculative citizenry – that which bet against its realization. There must be some losers in order to generate the best forecast. By the same token, every failure to achieve desired social goods will end up benefiting some sector of the speculative citizenry, just as a few canny traders benefited tremendously from well-placed bets on the collapse of the finance system shortly before the sub-prime mortgage market blew up. As if to confirm the anti-collectivist tendency of the prediction markets, their well-functioning relies on the tension between individual profits and social benefits. Without a few dramatic failures to keep the long-shot betters going, the markets will not function: someone has to take the other side – the losing side – of the bet.

Prediction markets might be described as the neoliberal analogue of a public sphere for an era characterized by the demise of symbolic efficiency. Unlike the classic Habermasian version of a public sphere, they are tailored to a logic of de-differentiation that subsumes the social and political to the economic. Consequently, they rely on the market to translate social goods into personal gain, while eschewing the impasse of representation, since they thrive on the competition between alternative worldviews, narratives, and evidentiary claims. They lend themselves to a climate characterized by a generalized reflexive savviness in which economic incentives structure strategies for risk assessment and management.

In keeping with the mistrust of representation of which they are symptomatic, prediction markets promise to dispense with (public) deliberation by offloading it onto the market. There is a technocratic, post-political distaste for the "friction" of politics, deliberation, and the human at work in such accounts. The goal is to format decision-making discourse for the marketplace by operationalizing it. Hanson's account of futarchy carves out some remaining space for democratic deliberation by maintaining a distinction between the political and the technical: deliberation sets values and goals (the political process), while the market supplies the favored means for achieving them. However, the distinction starts to erode under closer scrutiny. In order to create prediction markets, outcomes need to be defined in ways that render them amenable to speculation. When it comes to national well-being, for example, "Hanson suggests that a good measure of this, by which the bets could later be settled, might be gross domestic product ... So only those policies predicted to maximise GDP [gross domestic product] would be implemented."[35] The economic definition of well-being is determined by the means to achieve it. The use of economic techniques for adjudicating between policy alternatives results in the goal, perhaps unsurprisingly, of maximizing economic performance. Hanson goes on to propose the creation of indexes for policies designed to address questions of "happiness, inequality, health, leisure, and environmental measures."[36] To make them amenable to the betting process, all of these would have to be allocated measurable proxies, providing the speculative public with a range of economic metrics to assess, monitor, and maximize.

Back to the Futarchy

It is hard not to discern a deeply conservative and instrumental pragmatism in the celebration of futures markets as a means of addressing the impasse of representation associated with the demise of symbolic efficiency. The shift from deliberation and opinion polling to betting not only places policy decisions in the hands of those with the means to devote their time and resources to speculation, it also represents a shift in emphasis from a concern with what *should* happen to what *will* happen.[37] This slippage passes largely unnoticed in the celebratory accounts of prediction markets, which compare bettors to poll respondents – the former (duly incentivized) bet with their heads, the latter are asked to reveal their hearts. The difference between the two reflects changes in the marketing world, which has become increasingly reliant, in the interactive era, upon the monitoring of revealed patterns rather than research on stated preferences. What emerges are a series of substitutes for discursive expressions: bets, blood flow in the brain, involuntary micro-expressions, and aggregations of quantified sentiment correlated with desired outcomes.

Opinion markets fit well with the emerging ethos of interactivity insofar as they foster active "participation" rather than passive response. Similarly, they cater to the promise of overcoming the industrial-era alienation associated with the top-down management of management expertise. Hence, the repeated dismissal of expertise and the invocation of the democratic character of the marketplace: "Markets offer a way to tap into the collective wisdom of a population. Markets don't care who is the loudest, who is the most aggressive, who is the most powerful, or who is the most persuasive; markets only care about accuracy ... In this way, the good information filters to the top, yielding forecasts that reflect about as good a vision of the future as can be found by any other means."[38]

In an era in which the norm of objectivity has fallen into disrepute and that of truth has retreated behind scare quotes, the market takes on the role of objective arbiter. The resurgent interest in prediction markets (which had a lengthy history in US presidential elections up until the passage of mid-20th-century gambling restrictions) evinces the double-sided character of vernacular postmodernism: the default of savvy debunkery to a direct faith in market objectivity and efficacy. To paraphrase Zizek, the market allows us to offload faith onto an external mechanism: we do not have to believe because the market, in a sense, believes for us.[39] But this is a bit more complex than it might first appear: the catch is that, at least in our deeds, we have to act as if we believe in the market. In a reflexively savvy era – the triumph of what Zizek terms cynical ideology – is marked by the split between our self-consciously disillusioned attitude and the palpable illusions simultaneously sustained by our actions (this formulation is surely another way of approaching the combination of canny skepticism with the default to a naïve empiricism). As Zizek put it, there "is a distortion which is already at work in the social reality itself, at the level of what the individuals are doing, and not only what they think or know they are doing."[40] By way of example, he updates the Marxist formulation of commodity fetishism: "When individuals use money, they know very well that there is nothing magical about it – that money, in its materiality, is simply an expression of social relations … So, on an everyday level, the individuals know very well that there are relations between people behind the relations between things. The problem is that in their social activity itself, in what they are doing, they are acting as if money, in its material reality, is the immediate embodiment of wealth as such. They are fetishists in practice, not in theory."[41] The fantasy of Futarchy neatly encapsulates a logical endpoint for this "practical fetishism": on an everyday level we know that markets are not natural formations but social constructs with built-in biases and prejudices; but in practice we treat the market as the only remaining neutral arbiter: the one institution exempt from the savvy skepticism directed toward other information processing institutions. Universities, political institutions, think tanks, media outlets are relegated to the realm of ideological apparatuses, but practical faith in the market as the only remaining "post-ideological" institution endures, both in practice and in neo-liberal ideology. This is the subtext of neoliberal appeals to the market as the most reliable allocator of both information and resources (and in the assimilation of the former to the latter: the circulation of money as a signaling system). Predictocracy simply seeks to generalize this practical fetishism: to subsume those deliberative realms that still carve out a space external to the market's logic. If we let markets decide important questions such as how much to compensate people for their labor, or how best to allocate goods and services, why not also let them decide policy matters ranging from education reforms to when to go to war? Viewed as both an oracular force and the sum of our otherwise uncomprehended (or unarticulated) knowledge, markets are the best way, according to this account, to present us with our "unknown knowns" – the knowledge that we don't realize we have until we run it through the prediction market. In this respect, the market takes on the role of both the social collective and the big Other. The debunking of the "big Other" and its various "grand narratives" coincides with their inevitable and disavowed persistence in the practical activity of the market. As Zizek puts it, "the big Other continues to function, in the guise of 'second nature,' of the minimally 'reified' social system which is perceived as an In-itself. Each individual perceives the market as an objective system confronting her, although there is no 'objective' market, just the interaction of the multitude of individuals – so that, although each individual knows this very well, the specter of the 'objective' market is this same individual's fact-of-experience, determining her beliefs and acts" – eventually, her decisions.[42]

The practical fetishism is strong enough to re-enter the ideological realm in the form of the market-as-social actor: it has desires, preferences, even mood-swings to which the rest of us are beholden. Fluctuations in the marketplace – usually measured by rising and falling stocks – come to be treated as insights about everything from presidential candidates to treaty agreements and health-care reform. They are offered not as a proxy measurement of public opinion, but rather as clues about the mindset of a force that operates over and against public opinion. For example, when Turks refused to let the United States use their nation as a launch pad for part of its invasion of Iraq and the Turkish stock market subsequently plummeted, this was taken by some as a sign of a policy mistake. On Fox News, Geraldo Rivera observed – after noting the market drop – that the only one happy about the decision was Saddam Hussein (overlooking the fact that 90% of the Turkish population reportedly opposed the proposed US invasion).[43] The market can be a cruel and bloodthirsty task-master. Consider, for example, the banker who told participants in a seminar in February 2003 (just before the US invasion of Iraq) that "The market wants us to go to war, and the sooner the better."[44] The fact that the market is itself the result of aggregate human activity fades into the background as it develops a will and character of its own – one that thwarts and resists the efforts of humans to tame it, and all too often seems to take a perverse pleasure in their tribulations, as when it desires bloodshed or rejoices about increasing unemployment.

In this regard, the market serves as a big Other for the post-big-Other (and post-deliberative) era. In other words, the market is the opaque organizer of the inscrutable relationship between one's actions and the system into which it is aggregated: "Although individual acts can, in a direct short-circuit of levels, affect the 'higher'-level social constellation, the way they affect it is unpredictable ... The gap between causes and effects is irreducible, and there is no 'big Other' to guarantee the harmony between the levels, to guarantee that the overall outcome of our interactions will be satisfactory."[45] The promise of futarchy is to reflexivize this opacity: if only the market can "figure out" how intentional decisions will play out at the social level, then market bets serve as the best forecasters. Such a market is not a model – an attempt to understand the logic of aggregation of individual actions – but, in the sense invoked by Bogard, a simulation. In this regard, like data mining, it moves beyond narrative accounts, interpretations, and thus symbolic efficiency. We do not turn to markets to explain outcomes to us, but simply to predict them.

As the previous two chapters indicate, the displacement of explanation by prediction is one strategy for addressing the inability of representational knowledge to keep pace with the available information. As Zizek puts it, "the problem is that not only the market, but our entire social life is determined by such reified mechanisms."[46] If markets can simulate other markets (this is, of course, the logic of futures trading and other derivatives markets), perhaps they can do something similar for other realms characterized by complex and opaque forms of interdependence. This is the wager of prediction markets, and when it turns out to be a losing proposition, the market is typically exempted from blame: it was not transparent enough, or free enough, or open enough – perhaps someone manipulated it. All of these are alibis for the alleged neutrality of the impossible ideal of a "free" market. In this regard, the prospect and promise of futarchy partakes of the form of populism described by Zizek: "for a populist, the cause of the troubles is ultimately never the system as such, but the intruder who corrupted it (financial manipulators, not capitalists as such, etc.); not a fatal flaw inscribed into the structure as such, but an element that doesn't play its role within the structure properly."[47]

We might put this the other way around: the market has become the model for contemporary populism. It champions the bottom-up "wisdom" of the people against the oppressive knowledge claims of vested elites. It is, in this regard, "truly" democratic in the sense that anyone (with the requisite cash) can participate and that the rewards flow to the most deserving, at least according to the allegedly neutral arbiter of the marketplace. The market, according to this account, speaks with the voice of the people. This populist promise is protected by the claim that market failures are not the fault of the market or the populace, but of an outside agitator or manipulator. This logic was at work in the 2010 Congressional investigation and public pillorying of Goldman Sachs in the wake of the subprime mortgage market collapse. A successful investment bank with close ties to the political establishment took on "the pseudo-concreteness of the figure that is selected as THE enemy, the singular agent behind all the threats to the people."[48] As we shall see in Chapter 7, some of the nation's most aggressively populist figures attempted to pin the collapse of the subprime market on financial terrorism – a group of outside investors deliberately attempting to crash the US economy. It is this version of populism that helps to sustain the promise of decision markets even in the face of abject market failure. The market has already hedged its bet on itself and promises to come out a winner.

GLUT INSTINCT

Body Language and Visceral Literacy

Thin-Sliced Thought

The previous two chapters explored some of the strategies for managing large amounts of data available to those with access to databases and the processing power to put them to use. This chapter examines some alternative strategies for negotiating the contemporary information landscape for those without such access. In particular, it focuses upon the resurgent interest in body language analysis and various preconscious strategies for decision-making. As in the case of data mining and predictive analytics, it argues that these strategies take shape against the background of the fate of symbolic efficiency and strategies for sidestepping the vagaries of discursive representation. If database strategies read bodies of data, the techniques contemplated in this chapter read physical bodies – our own and those of others – and tap into their alleged capacity to speak directly to us without recourse to the potentially distorting character of language. This fantasy of "immediation" – the ultimately self-deconstructing promise of bypassing mediation altogether – is far from new. John Durham Peters argues that John Locke saw words as an often imperfect medium for conveying the pre-linguistic ideas that dwell in people's heads.[1] This formulation set up the fantasy of a kind of pure communion of thoughts that sidestepped language altogether – a fantasy that has been resuscitated by Kevin Warwick's experiments in connecting different people's nervous systems with the goal of one day allowing brain impulses to cross the interpersonal divide without the need for language. According to this latter-day Lockeian, "Language is merely a tool we use to translate our thoughts. In the future, we won't need to code thoughts into language – we will uniformly send symbols and ideas and concepts without speaking ... in the future, speech will be what baby talk is today."[2] The formulation is an odd one – if language is merely a tool to translate thought (presumably imperfectly), why conserve the notion of symbols once it is obsolete? Thoughts and concepts on their own should be enough – presumably these are simply composed of nervous impulses that can be shunted through fiber optic cables, shared, stored, and retrieved at will. We will no longer have to read books or news accounts, but can simply access directly the thoughts of a philosopher or theorist – perhaps someday we might jack directly into the minds and memories of (shudder!) political figures, celebrities, and other public figures – not to mention criminal suspects (no more need for jury trials, evidence, argumentation, etc.). If symbolic efficiency poses a challenge, why not simply obviate the need for the symbolic altogether? This chapter explores some strategies for clutter-cutting that push in this direction, and then highlights their own deadlocks.

Perhaps not surprisingly, the body figures heavily in these strategies as both sensor and signaler – an allegedly extra-discursive, material guarantee of "immediation": direct access to feelings, thoughts, and desires as yet undistorted by their translation into language.

The best-selling 2005 book *Blink*, for example, relied on the evidence of palms – or, more precisely, palm perspiration – to make the case for what author Malcolm Gladwell called "thinking without thinking."[3] Describing an experiment that required test subjects to "gamble" by drawing cards from different sets of rigged decks, Gladwell noted that the participants seemed to realize which color decks indicated the safer bet before they could consciously articulate this knowledge. By the time they had drawn the tenth card, the sweat glands in the test subjects' palms revealed evidence of stress when they selected cards from the losing deck. However, it was not until the subjects had drawn about 50 cards in total that they consciously recognized their "hunch" about which deck was the safe bet, and in most cases it took 30 more cards before they could clearly articulate why.[4] The test subjects' bodies "knew" what was going on before this knowledge could be consciously articulated. Gladwell took the palm sweat as evidence of "rapid cognition," which he describes as "a system in which our brain reaches conclusions without immediately telling us that it's reaching conclusions."[5] The advantage of this form of thinking is that it allows us to make decisions about very complex data without having to consciously absorb it all.

Gladwell's book is, in part, an attempt to consciously reflect on a pre-conscious form of cognition, to think about the process of "thinking without thinking" – that is, to make conscious the forms of knowledge revealed by the palm's sweat glands. The lesson he draws from his examples is that more information-gathering and deliberation is not always better. As he put it in an online discussion of the book, "this lesson is drummed into us again and again: haste makes waste, look before you leap, stop and think. But I don't think this is true. There are lots of situations – particularly at times of high pressure and stress – when haste does not make waste, when our snap judgments and first impressions offer a much better means of making sense of the world."[6] It is a telling message for the digital era, removing some of the luster from the promise of access to unprecedented levels of information. At the very moment when more detailed and comprehensive information becomes available to a larger portion of the population, it turns out, at least according to Gladwell, that more information is not necessarily better.

Compare the role played by palms in Gladwell's interpretation of the gambling experiment with the portrayal of the role of body language in two examples from popular culture: the TV shows *The Mentalist* and *Lie to Me*. In *The Mentalist*, a show that could have been based on the insights of Gladwell's book, the lead character, Patrick Jane, is a former psychic turned police consultant with the observational and deductive power of a latter-day Sherlock Holmes (who, as further evidence of this trend, has made a comeback on *Sherlock* in the United Kingdom and *Elementary* in the United States). He channels the observational skills he developed as a fraudulent "psychic medium" into detective work with astonishingly effective results: cutting through tangled police investigations by noticing a suppressed gesture or a fleeting response that, to the trained eye, cuts through a web of lies to reveal the truth, seemingly hidden, but sitting right out there in public for those with the ability to discern it.

The "mentalist" is someone who has gotten in touch with his own rapid cognition skills. He is a master of what Gladwell, borrowing a term from psychology, calls "'the power of thin slicing" – which says that as human beings we are capable of making sense of situations based on the "thinnest slice of experience."[7] So it is perhaps not surprising that he too has an interest in palms. He watches them, feels them, and often holds them to gauge the responses of his interlocutors (sometimes he moves up to their wrists to feel their pulses, highlighting his talents as a human lie detector). As he tells the wife of one potential suspect, "I used to make a good living pretending to be a psychic. I say this because I want you to understand there is no point lying to me."[8]

In another episode, Jane grabs the hand of a reluctant suspect, using the reactions of her palm to guide him around the room to a piece of incriminating evidence she is trying to hide: a camera with digital photos used in a blackmail attempt. The attempt to interview the suspect proves futile, but Jane, seeing her nervous glances, divines the dissimulation: "There's something on this side of the room you don't want us to find. What is that?"[9] Confronted with his apparent ability to read her thoughts, the suspect insists she is hiding nothing, and invites him to search her unkempt home. "Nah, too much stuff, not very tidy," he responds, before grabbing her hand and using her as a human dowsing rod to lead him precisely to the incriminating camera. He walks her around the room, reading the responses in her palm to determine elevated stress levels that indicate when he is approaching the concealed camera. She may have been lying, but her palm unerringly conveyed the truth.

Bodily truths similarly populate Fox's *Lie to Me*, a police procedural devoted not to forensic science but to body language and allegedly based on actual deception detection research. The opening sequence of the show's pilot episode portrays the lead character, "deception expert" Dr. Cal Lightman, expressing his disdain for speech. "I don't have much faith in words myself," he says, after being told by a belligerent defense attorney that a White supremacist accused of planning to bomb a Black church "won't talk."[10] Lightman explains to the lawyer that he does not have a very high regard for speech in any case: "You know, statistically speaking the average person tells three lies per 10 minutes of conversation."[11] He goes on to discover where the suspect has concealed a bomb by gauging the reactions to his verbal probes. As he speaks, the camera gives us cues as to where Lightman's attention is directed: to tiny twitches in the suspect's lips, a tightening of the throat, a partial movement of his shoulder. When a fleeting expression lets Lightman know that he has guessed the bomb's location correctly, the lawyer objects and Lightman responds, "What do you mean? He just told me!"[12] If the suspect's words have been filled with indignant denials, lies, and misdirection, his body has been speaking the truth, however reluctantly. The next scene portrays Dr. Lightman in didactic mode, translating the suspect's gestures for an audience of law enforcement officials – and also for the show's viewers – into the emotions they express. The show's Website provides further tutorials on the "real science" on which the show is based, linking to the Website of deception detection expert Paul Ekman and his educational training videos that purport to teach anyone how to read micro-expressions – the fleeting physical gestures that give away concealed emotional responses.

Visceral Literacy

The combination of instruction and entertainment in *Lie to Me*, whose plot devices rely heavily on Ekman's research, places it in an emerging cross-genre constellation of programming devoted to what might be described as the promise of visceral literacy: the attempt to bypass the vagaries of speech in order to get directly at the true underlying emotions that speakers all too often attempt to mask. Joining *Lie to Me* in this inter-genre programming mix are reality shows that feature lie detection – perhaps most notably Court TV's *Fake Out*, in which a former FBI profiler trained contestants in the art of lie detection, and also MTV's *Exposed*, in which prospective dates are subjected to voice stress analysis. Alongside such shows we might include proliferating and recurring news analysis segments that feature "body language experts" who look behind the words to reveal what newsmakers are allegedly thinking and feeling. As the introduction to one recurring segment devoted to the 2008 US presidential campaign on CBS's *The Early Show* put it, "You heard what the candidates had to say last night during the presidential debate, but did you hear what they didn't say, did you *see* what they didn't say? There's a lot to be learned from their body language."[13] Both *The Early Show* and Fox News's Bill O'Reilly featured recurring body language segments that double as tutorials in how to carry oneself and to read the body language of others. During the 2008 and 2012 Presidential elections, every cable news outlet featured recurring segments analyzing the body language of the candidates.

I pick this range of examples to illustrate what might be described as a constellation of techniques, strategies, and technologies for "cutting through the glut" of information in an increasingly information-saturated era. It is perhaps not a coincidence that in an era when a reflexive awareness of the performative and contrived character of self-presentation is combined with media saturation that a premium would be placed on efficient and accurate information processing. *Blink* is a book of its time, one which fits neatly with a range of cultural developments related to cutting through the information glut. The recurring use of body language experts by news outlets underlined their promise to determine the *real* messages of the candidates – that which went beyond what "was conveyed in words."[14] Thanks to these news segments, and the use of body language analysis on talk shows and news magazine shows, the media coverage has helped to publicize a cottage industry of self-help books promising success in business, romance, and every other human endeavor through mastery of the power of body language in terms of both reading it and "speaking it."[15]

This chapter approaches the phenomenon of visceral literacy – the attempt to bypass the level of conscious discourse by turning to the body – as characteristic of emerging logics of surveillance associated with the mobilization of the specter of risk in a reflexively savvy era in which self-presentation is relegated to the realm of façade and speech (political speech, in particular) to that of stagecraft. It is worth noting at the outset that a paradox lies at the heart of such logics, which portray appearances as a means of moving beyond the surface to a hidden yet directly accessible "inner" state. In advocating what seems at first a radical empiricism, they simultaneously project beyond surface appearances to hidden essences. The distinction between reality and appearance gets flattened into the realm of appearances, some of which can be dismissed as misleading or inessential, others of which, at least to the initiated, allow essence to come to the surface where it can "speak" for itself.

The paradox is a familiar one that can trace its roots back through the history of the techniques of physiognomy and phrenology, which both asserted that an inner (emotional, psychological) state must find some form of direct (unmediated) physical expression that can be detected in the realm of appearance. In each case the mental is linked to the corporeal in a directly legible way.

Perhaps the clearest contemporary examples of this linkage are provided by cutting-edge neuroscience applications, including the 2008 decision by an Indian court to convict a suspect of murder based on readings from an electroencephalogram. The brain scans were processed by software that "tries to detect whether, when the crime's details are recited, the brain lights up in specific regions – the areas that, according to the technology's inventors, show measurable changes when experiences are relived, their smells and sounds summoned back to consciousness."[16] The equation here is between material traces – the electrical impulses in the brain – and memories of lived experiences. The software's designer claims that the machine can differentiate between memories of events recounted by others and those directly experienced by the subject under investigation. Highlighting the affinity between law enforcement and marketing technology, a similar equation is embraced by the developing "science" of neuromarketing (taken up in more detail in the following chapter), in which focus-group research is replaced by brain scans that measure affective response to advertising campaigns. The equation here is between blood flow in the brain and desire. As one press account of neuromarketing researchers at a company called the BrightHouse Institute put it, a "glowing yellow dot near the top of the brain ... was the magic spot – the medial prefrontal cortex. If that area is firing, a consumer isn't deliberating ... he's itching to buy."[17]

It is crucial to such accounts that the physical data are not subject to mental control – that they remain automatic, immediate, unreflexive, and thus inert from the point of self-conscious reflection; this is what might be described as the undialectical, anti-intentional framing of the relationship between bodily signification and conscious thought. Otherwise, the promised short circuit becomes subject to the same forms of reflexivity associated with conscious speech and is no longer a short circuit at all. The promise of direct access to the true emotions, impulses, and memories behind a manipulable façade is predicated on this inertness – its non-reactivity to reflection. If, for example, the drawback of focus group marketing is that consumers may not know exactly what they want and that they can be influenced by the process itself, the advantage of neuromarketing is that the short circuit provides direct access to desire: "M.R.I. scanning offers the promise of concrete facts – an unbiased glimpse at a consumer's mind in action. To an M.R.I. machine, you cannot misrepresent your responses. Your medial prefrontal cortex will start firing when you see something you adore, even if you claim not to like it."[18] Even, presumably, if you *think* you don't like it.

Generalized Suspicion

The obvious difference between the marketing and detection examples is that whereas the latter attempt to circumvent deliberate deception, the former claim access to truths about consumers that they may not know themselves. What unites these forms of monitoring is a faith in direct access to behind-the-scenes essences combined with the understanding that, for example, speech can be deceiving, either deliberately, or when caught up in forms of power or ideology of which the speaker may be unaware. This combination of generalized savvy skepticism with a seemingly naïve faith is not an unfamiliar one in the current conjuncture. In his lament on the fate of critique in a terminally savvy era, for example, Bruno Latour describes the Bourbonnais villager who treats him (the man of learning who is supposed to be savvy and informed) as a dupe for believing mainstream media accounts of the September 11 attacks rather, presumably, than the conspiracy theory outlined in Thierry Meyssan's bestseller *L'Effroyable Imposture*, which claims that the attacks were secretly orchestrated by the US government to justify invading Iraq. As Latour puts it, with a note of irony, "Remember the good old days when revisionism arrived very late, after the facts had been thoroughly established, decades after bodies of evidence had accumulated? Now we have the benefit of what can be called *instant revisionism.*"[19]

A similar combination of generalized skepticism with a willing suspension of disbelief is the stock-in-trade of right-wing publications such as *Human Events* (described by firebrand conservative pundit Ann Coulter as the "Headquarters of the Conservative Underground"), which debunks mainstream media and political narratives even as it barrages readers with get-rich-quick schemes and miracle cures. There is, at times, a tragicomic complementarity between the feature articles – which routinely ridicule social welfare programs and scientific claims about global warming – and the ads, which promise instant wealth ("If you want an opportunity to bank SAFE, annual gains of 65% while you lie on the beach in some exotic location then ... You Must Respond To This Letter NOW!") and promote miracle cures ("What if I were to tell you that a billion-dollar drug company discovered a true CURE for cancer ... and told no one?").[20]

Slavoj Zizek has described this combination of skepticism with naïveté as symptomatic of the decline of symbolic efficiency – what I have been describing in this book as a popularized and populist postmodern skepticism toward underlying truths and overarching grand narratives.[21] The result is an ersatz democratization of competing claims in which the criteria for adjudication are themselves called into question. As Zizek puts it:

> The problem is not that ... conspiracy theorists regress to a paranoiac attitude unable to accept (social) reality; the problem is that this reality itself is becoming paranoiac. Contemporary experience again and again confronts us with situations in which we are compelled to take note of how ... the "big Other" that determines what counts as normal and accepted truth, the horizon of meaning in a given society, is in no way directly grounded in "facts" as rendered by the scientific "knowledge in the real."[22]

If paranoia is not the defining mistake of conspiracy theory, he goes on to argue, category confusion is: the problem is a conflation of the hermeneutics of suspicion as "a formal methodological stance," with "the positivization of this suspicion in another all-explaining global paratheory."[23] It is this confusion that licenses the implicit message of publications such as *Human Events* and Meyssan's work: conspiracies are all the more believable precisely because they run so astoundingly counter to the received wisdom – they gain their legitimacy through the thrill of being illegitimate and their appeal to those who identify with the figure of the "non-dupe" too canny to be taken in by the official story – by *any* official story.

It is possible to trace the generalization of savvy skepticism – what Zizek describes as the subjective response to "reality itself ... becoming paranoiac" – from the micro-level of interpersonal relationships to the macro-level realm of the so-called Global War on Terror. At the interpersonal level, the forms of identity play that Sherry Turkle associated relatively early on in the Internet era with online subjectivity were complemented by the subsequent proliferation of techniques for online monitoring and background checking.[24] If the Internet helps to highlight the performative character of identity, it simultaneously spawns new techniques for background checking and verification. The online world that captivated Turkle – that of role playing in virtual fantasy worlds – has been far outstripped, suggestively, by the proliferation of social networking sites that facilitate always-on forms of mutual monitoring. If multi user domains (MUDs) allowed one college junior interviewed by Turkle to play the multiple online roles of a seductive woman, a "cowboy type," and a "rabbit of unspecified gender," Facebook makes it possible for a college student to lose his girlfriend because he listed himself online as single.[25]

Turkle's analysis suggests that the Internet thematizes an understanding of the constructed nature of representation characteristic of a population that has grown up with a reflexive understanding of media representation exemplified, for example, by meta-coverage and meta-programming (news about the constructed character of the news and television about the contrivances of TV). Stephen Coleman pushes even further in a populist direction, suggesting that perhaps the real democratizing move is to challenge elitist forms of deliberation and argumentation by championing more popular and accessible sentiments and responses. Herein resides the potential for democratic revitalization he locates in the interactive capacity of the Internet appropriated by programming formats such as *Big Brother* (that rely on viewer feedback):

> The element of performance within shows like *Big Brother* ... are also manifestations of testifying and witnessing which, at least for some people, provide a more authentic sense of accountability than parliamentary debate or political interviews. Moving from *the* political speech to everyday speech is not to abandon politics, but to mediate it in a more accessible and humane way.[26]

Reality formats, in other words, have a close affinity to the fascination evinced by Bill O'Reilly's body-language segment with the underlying emotions and interpersonal dynamics of political actors rather than with the deliberative *content* that serves merely as an occasion for accessing these responses and dynamics. The switch in registers is significant insofar as in other examples of clutter-cutting strategies discussed in this book: it directs attention away from referential content and questions of accuracy and representation toward a fascination with affective authenticity. The truth standard shifts in the direction of "affective" truths and the ways in which these can be read off of the body. Thus, for example, during the 2008 presidential election in the United States, body language analyst Tonya Reiman suggested that vice-presidential candidate Sarah Palin may have lost an important opportunity to look sympathetic when her debate opponent Joe Biden referred to becoming a single father after the death of his wife and one of their children. By comparison, Reiman gave her seal of approval to Biden's emotions: "Whenever we get very emotional, we look down. And he was. The catch in the throat, that's you know, an involuntary muscle. It just gets caught ... And that's a true emotional response."[27] However, she faulted Palin's reaction to Biden's emotional display: "instead of looking at him, making eye contact, which would have been very powerful. Instead, she chose to basically keep that smile pasted on her face and ignore that."[28] None of this had as much to do with the issues being debated as with the perceived authenticity of the candidates in their treatment of one another – and the implicit impact of these performances of sociability, witnessing, and testifying on a voting public seeking a visceral connection to the candidates.

If generalized skepticism serves as an alibi for attempts to bypass the level of discourse in the political sphere through recourse to more "direct" forms of monitoring, the generalization of surveillance in the post-9/11 era turns this logic back on the populace. One of the hallmarks of the so-called Global War on Terror declared by George Bush in the aftermath of the World Trade Center attacks is the ubiquity of potential threat: since terrorists don't clearly identify themselves, suspicion is generalized; since they use unconventional forms of warfare, virtually anything can be redoubled as either target or weapon. As Xavier Raufer, the director of the Department for the Study of the Contemporary Critical Menace at the University of Paris II, puts it, "previously clear distinctions – between attack and defense, the state and civil society, the public and private sectors, civilians and the military, war and peace, police and army, legality and illegality – are becoming blurred."[29] We might add to this list of blurred boundaries that between citizen and suspect, as evidenced by the forms of covert surveillance of the civilian population discussed in Chapter 2.

It is against this background of reflexive suspicion associated with the demise of symbolic efficiency and the generalized sense of threat associated with the discourse of the "Global War on Terrorism" that the promise of more direct forms of access via techniques for body monitoring takes shape. The turn to the body, then, might be understood as one manifestation of a more generalized attempt to circumvent the level of discourse. Other forms of information-gathering might serve a similar goal, such as, for example, the collection of patterns of interaction or movement throughout the course of the day that reveal either unconscious or disguised tendencies. The goal is to obtain information about monitored targets that is beyond their direct, deliberate, or conscious control, and which thus escapes strategies of dissimulation or self-deception. We might describe such forms of monitoring as attempts to gather useful information about potentially deceptive or misleading forms of self-representation (that is to say, *all* conscious forms of self-representation) while bypassing or sidestepping reflexively self-conscious forms of communication.

In reality, of course, such forms of monitoring are inseparable from, say, face-to-face interaction: to detect whether someone is lying according to the body language experts, you have to get them to speak. In this regard the attempt to bypass the vagaries of speech also relies upon the incitement to discourse: the more speech and gestures available, the more raw material for interpretation. The television show *Lie to Me*, for example, stages the split between conversation and body reading – it is in the space between what the words and the body say that the analyst inserts his or her interpretation. Much the same might be said of other forms of scientific psychology that ask test subjects questions not to evaluate the content of their answers but the physiological signs that accompany them. As the Website for Project Implicit, an online battery of implicit association tests that measure the response times of participants in order to detect hidden biases, puts it, "It is well known that people don't always 'speak their minds,' and it is suspected that people don't always 'know their minds.'"[30] What the tests do, in other words is sidestep self-understanding and self-representation to get at these recalcitrant minds directly. The next two sections take up the impasse of such approaches through examples from popular culture: the body language tutorials on televised poker, and the body language segments in political news coverage.

It Takes a Liar ...

Against the background of the Global War on Terror, it is possible to trace a constellation of popular culture formats that might be loosely grouped in the category of "securitainment" – a hybrid genre that provides instruction in strategies for risk management and security training alongside the entertainment content. Such cultural forms might, in turn, be considered a subgenre of "edutainment," which, in an era of ascendant neoliberalism, caters to a culture of ongoing self-training (think of those shows that teach us how to dress properly or raise our children, or video games that claim to cultivate our mental skills as we age). In the category of "securitainment" we might include such television programs as *Fake Out*, which offers instruction in lie detection from an FBI profiler, *It Takes a Thief*, which teaches viewers how to secure their homes, Australia's *Border Security: Australia's Front Line*, a reality show about customs workers, and a similarly themed American reality show, *Homeland Security USA*. What these shows have in common is not just the theme of securitization but also an instructional/informational element that caters to the interactive ethos of the digital era. If the boundaries between civilian and soldier are blurred in the war on terror, such programming reinforces this porosity: the instructional components of the show take on practical salience in an era of generalized risk.

Although it may sound like a stretch, this chapter argues that another show which partakes in the logic of securitainment is the televised version of the *World Series of Poker*, which provides tutorials in the management of (albeit contrived) risk and, especially, in strategies for reading the bodies of others who are attempting to deceive. Tournament poker serves as a metaphor for the universalization of suspicion – a microcosm of the decline of symbolic efficiency. The only guarantee at the poker table is that nothing anyone says can be trusted. This is enforced by the tournament rules, which specify that the only information a player is explicitly forbidden from sharing with other players during game play is the true content of his or her hand. In a world where everyone is expected to lie, the one form of deception ruled out is lying in the guise of truth.

The default language of the table, then, is body language. As 2004 World Champion Tim Raymer put it in an interview on the World Series of Poker, "it's about gathering data: reading tells is an important part. I like to look at the chest to see how fast they're breathing".[31] He describes the importance of monitoring the veins in his opponents' necks, following their hand movements and conversing with them not to listen to the content, but to gauge their reactions, their tone of voice, their apparent confidence levels.[32] As commentator Vince Van Patten put it when describing the chatter at the poker table, "there is a method in their madness, they are looking for some information: a few little tells, any little edge they can get".[33] Indeed, conversation at the poker table is not about what is said, but about *how* it is said. As on *Lie to Me* (which might also be the title of a poker show), speech is a ruse for eliciting somatic signals. Poker pro Phil Gordon, who has hosted a celebrity TV poker show and written a guidebook about poker strategy, claims that for the trained player, "Getting info from other players is relatively easy, you just have to know what to look for … it's not particularly the answer, but it's the style in which someone answers that gives away the strength of their hand."[34]

On *The World Series of Poker*, home viewers are schooled in the art of detecting "the tell" – spontaneous gestures that, like the "microexpressions" studied by Dr. Paul Ekman, provide information about the underlying emotional states of players. Slamming your chips into the pot aggressively, for example, is a tell. Leaning back is a tell, as is leaning forward; a show of strength means weakness, and vice versa. As *Celebrity Poker Showdown* host Phil Gordon, put it, "looking directly at your opponent is a sign of weakness. You're trying to look at your opponent to look strong; but if I have a *good* hand, why would I want to intimidate my opponent?"[35] The goal is to learn the significance of signals that are supposedly harder to control than words – to believe only your own eyes, never the other players' words. As in the case of other forms of what I am calling securitainment, the spectacle of lie detection on poker TV serves as a tutorial. "This is a lesson for the players at home," is the repeated refrain of the show's hosts, who understand that the TV episodes are advertising for a booming ancillary market in learn-to-play products, and for the tournaments whose jackpots increase in direct proportion to the number of participants they draw from the audience ranks. Instruction thus doubles as a form of recruitment.

The case for treating poker TV as a form of securitainment is based not just on the fact that it provides instruction in risk calculation and people monitoring, but in the way it relates the two. Risk is, in part, a function of the reconfiguration of discourse and the competitive conditions at the table: all are pitted against all in such a way that none can be trusted and everyone is a strategic liar. Moreover, the risk starts anew with each fresh deal since the history of the cards is obliterated with each shuffle. Walter Benjamin highlights the disjointed character of gambling, noting its affinity with the alienation of the division of labor: "Since each operation at the machine is just as screened off from the preceding operation as a coup in a game of chance is from the one that preceded it, the drudgery of the labourer is, in its own way, a counterpart to the drudgery of the gambler."[36] What Benjamin calls drudgery is the result of the alienation that makes it impossible to cognitively map any relation between subsequent instances of activity. Each deal, each cast of the dice, each turn of the wheel represents a new start – a kind of inane repetition independent of previous activity. The artifice of the gambling table is to separate risk from any historical context – even the mathematics of probability place a ban on the notion that a previous cast of the dice might influence subsequent ones. As Benjamin puts it, "This disposition (to attribute everything to chance) is promoted by betting, which is a device for giving events the character of a shock, detaching them from the context of experience."[37]

The de-historicized sense of risk parallels the mobilization of the specter of the war on terror, which in its emphasis on securitization, interrogation, and surveillance, backgrounds any attempt to, "make sense" of the threat or to situate it in its historical context. Former Homeland Security Director Tom Ridge's "readiness" campaign framed the implicitly ahistorical character of the threat by comparing terrorist attacks to natural disasters: "Families in Florida prepare themselves for the hurricane season; families in California prepare themselves for earthquakes. Every family in American should prepare itself for a terrorist attack."[38] This de-contextualization of terrorism parallels, as Rapping suggests, the de-narrativization of risk portrayed on reality shows such as *Cops*, whose twilight landscape of strip malls and trailer parks is populated by characters "that embody a proneness to random, sporadic violence that is represented as a permanent condition of human, or rather subhuman, nature. They are simply violent in ways that make no sense at all. We get no 'story' of any kind onto which we might hang a diagnosis or criminal profile."[39] The result, she argues, is what might be described as an actuarial or probabilistic approach to criminal risk resulting from a constant and irrational element of contemporary life (like the hurricane season) and justifying increasingly comprehensive forms of monitoring.

Similarly, an overview of the emerging policy-oriented literature on homeland security reveals that the risk of terror takes on the characteristic typical of Ulrich Beck's conception of reflexive risk – it is disturbing precisely because of its incalculable and unpredictable nature. Even if such risk is reflexive – directly related to human activity – any attempt to narrativize it is nonetheless foreclosed: deliberation over history and politics cannot provide access to a risk that is, by definition, at least from the recent US policy perspective, an *irrational* one. Risk management in this context relies on universal suspicion, surveillance (since everyone is potentially lying), and general mobilization (citizens must take on some of the duties of defense).

Consequently, homeland security campaigns call for the population to serve as an extension of the monitoring apparatus of the state, instructing the populace in some of the "tells" of potential terrorists (wearing unseasonably bulky coasts to conceal explosives and weapons, etc.). Life in the era of universal risk is, to put it bluntly, one big crapshoot, and survival skills include preparation, alertness, and training in the ability to read others, calculate risk, and respond accordingly. The intersection of game theory and war strategy has a storied history that entered the computer era and went mainstream in the post-World War II era scientific community. What poker adds to the risk calculation process is the cultivation of monitoring strategies associated with, as the poker wisdom puts it, playing the player and not the cards.

Despite the recurring invocation of battle and fight metaphors, it is perhaps fair to say that both poker and the war on terror share the characteristics of neoliberal forms of risk mobilization. The hallmarks of neoliberalism include the responsibilization of the citizenry in the face of an array of economic, security, social, and health risks, along with the de-differentiation of the roles of citizen, police officer, and entrepreneur. As Lupton puts it, "risk strategies and discourses are means of ordering the social and material worlds through methods of rationalization and calculation, attempts to render disorder and uncertainty more controllable. It is these strategies and discourses that bring risk into being, that select certain phenomena as being risky and therefore requiring management either by institutions or individuals."[40] Thus, at least part of the commonality between the lessons of the war on terror and those of poker

TV might be attributed to their positioning within the constellation of neo-liberal strategies for the mobilization of risk.

This commonality has not been lost on the security sector, which has not only borrowed surveillance systems from one of the leaders in the field – gambling casinos – but is funding research on the strategies of body language analysis promulgated by poker TV commentators.[41] The US Department of Homeland Security has budgeted some $3.5 million for research at Rutgers University to develop "a lie detector capable of interpreting facial expressions and body language ... scientists believe small movements such as shoulder shrugging or hand gestures can be analysed by computers to tell if someone is telling the truth."[42] *Time* magazine has reported that in the United States, "tens of millions to hundreds of millions of dollars are believed to have been poured into lie-detection techniques as diverse as infrared imagers to study the eyes, scanners to peer into the brain, sensors to spot liars from a distance, and analysts trained to scrutinize the unconscious facial flutters that often accompany a falsehood."[43] One government contractor, No Lie MRI, has announced plans for "a brain-scan lie-detection service."[44] The development of automated forms of body language measurement and analysis anticipates an era of affective computing in which devices capture, categorize, and respond not just to our intentional commands, but to our feelings and emotions.

Psychotic Politics

The political analogue of citizen tutoring in a realm of reflexive risk and savvy skepticism is the instruction in "reading" politicians provided by the analysts of political body language. If the responsible citizen needs to be ever vigilant for risk and deception, this same imperative is turned back upon the political sphere that helped to mobilize it. The result is an analysis of political discourse that attempts to reveal the true character of politicians by setting aside the content of their finely spun speech and focusing on their bodies. The combination of savvy skepticism with a desire for unmediated access to a politician's "authentic" character is symptomatic of the demise of symbolic efficiency. It is a combination that Zizek further elaborates as a form of social psychosis, referencing his interpretation of Lacanian psychoanalysis: "psychosis involves the external distance the subject maintains towards the symbolic order ... *and* the collapsing of the Symbolic into the Real (a psychotic treats 'words as things'; in his universe, words fall into things and/or things themselves start to speak)."[45] It is a world in which brain scans reveal murderers, a fleeting micro-expression can give away a lie and George W. Bush can imagine the possibility of pushing aside the curtain of language to gaze straight into Vladimir Putin's soul.

In such a world, it only makes sense that political coverage would recruit body language experts to "read" politicians the way Dr. Cal Lightman reads suspects. But when political discourse is pushed to the side, the remainders are merely broad generalities that reassert the existing common knowledge about perceived character traits. We learn whether someone seems to feel confident at particular moments, what their general disposition is toward a political rival (often, unsurprisingly, antagonistic), whether their emotional declarations are authentic or staged. When Hillary Clinton endorsed her rival in the primaries, Barack Obama, at the 2008 Democratic National Convention, we were told, for example, that she fell short on the enthusiasm scale. According to body language expert Joe Navarro, the problem lay in her hands: "we look for hand gestures to tell us what's important. So, you know, when we see them out, when we see them up, this is significant. And, you know, we saw them just a few times last night, but not enough. This was not an impassioned speech."[46] As for former vice-presidential candidate Sarah Palin, we learned perhaps unsurprisingly that she was a family person, "Well, you can see she's comfortable with her family. The family is comfortable with her. And a lot of times we – the public picks up on little subtleties. And what we can tell is that she's a loving mother, a caring mother, but a focused mother."[47] In short, we learn the kind of banalities that Hegel attributes to the soothsayers of physiognomy: "As regards their content, however, these observations are on a par with these: 'It always rains when we have our annual fair,' says the dealer; 'and every time too,' says the housewife, 'when I am drying my washing.'"[48]

Partaking of the logic of securitainment, political body language experts are framed not just as analysts, but also as tutors, providing expertise to a populace faced with the risk of possible deception. To the extent that body language analysis allows politicians to be judged on their interpersonal skills and the alleged authenticity of their emotions, the ability to discern these is readily transferable to other realms of social life. To put it somewhat differently, by setting aside its specific content, such forms of political analysis transpose political discourse into the realm of everyday social life by mediating them in what Coleman describes somewhat patronizingly as " a more accessible and humane way."[49] This notion of political authenticity is perhaps what an anonymous political consultant was relying on when he chided political reporter Ron Suskind and other critics of George W. Bush for judging the president's political competence by his apparent incuriosity and lack of detailed knowledge of the issues. The consultant suggested that what Suskind did not understand was that Bush related to his supporters on a more direct level: "They like the way he walks and the way he points, the way he exudes confidence."[50]

Since body language analysis readily defaults from political content to personal authenticity, it is a skill that transfers easily from the realm of politics to that of daily life, business, and social interaction. We are invited to train ourselves in the art of visceral literacy in order to be able to perform optimally in each of these realms. As *Today Show* host Matt Lauer puts it in one of his introductions for body language expert Joe Navarro, "So ... if it's a science, someone like you can use this in your daily life and teach others how to use it in their daily lives?" To which Navarro replies, "Absolutely."[51] As in the case of the poker shows, the expert consultants demonstrate and model literacy skills that, if audiences learn them well enough, promise to help them navigate a social landscape in which speech and appearances can all too often be deceiving. Suggestively, the realms of politics, business, and social life require the same skills, according to Lauer: "being able to decode more subtle nonverbal cues may be the secret to success in business and in love."[52]

There is a paradoxical double logic to the more direct and immediate language of the body – at least to hear the experts tell it. Just as the "speakers" – those giving off unconscious bodily cues – are not necessarily aware of the signals they are sending, so do these signals convey meanings to us in ways that we may not realize. When someone, for example, signals confidence, this confidence is apparently automatically conveyed – which is why, for example, Palin presumably lost points with her audience for not showing empathy to Biden.

As the use of body language analysts by political news shows suggests, the knowledge that these bodies conveys can turn out to be crucial for world historical events – like presidential elections. For example, according to body language expert Tonya Reiman's analysis of the notorious Charlie Gibson interview with Sarah Palin on ABC News during the 2008 Presidential campaign, Palin's body was obliging enough to tell us that she did not really believe she was qualified to be president, even though her words said otherwise.[53] Reiman unpacks a short exchange in which Gibson asks Palin whether she can "look the country in the eye and say 'I have the experience and I have the ability to be not just Vice-President but perhaps president of the United States of America.'"[54] She seizes on the moment when Palin shakes her head ever so slightly just as she says, "if we're so privileged as to be able to serve this country, we'll be ready ... I'm ready."[55] The head shake, according to Reiman, reveals the body's doubt and contradicts Palin's words: the mouth says yes, but the body says no: "She might believe that she's ready on the outside, but inside there's some turmoil going on, you can see that because she negated her own speech."[56]

Echoing the logic of "direct effects" once applied to the media, for body language analysts, to interpret a signal is simultaneously to posit its reception. Two conversations take place simultaneously at two levels: one at the level of speech that is subject to reflexive savvy skepticism, and another at the level of the body, in which signs are sent and received, exempted from reflexive forms of examination and critique. Thus, Lauer ends his segment with Navarro by noting that "if you're in social situations and you're not quite communicating what you think you're communicating, maybe stop and take a look at your body language. It might not be what you're saying; it could be what you're doing."[57]

The reflexive move – breaking the "code" of body language – collapses the difference between these two levels. The emergence of body language expertise signals the moment when this language becomes conscious of itself. Thus, the moment of interpretation signals the end of immediacy. Once we understand, as Navarro puts it, that "we're constantly transmitting. We're sort of billboards," we can attempt not just to learn the language but to turn it to our particular ends.[58] Navarro helps bring the argument full circle thanks to the fact that he analyzes both politicians and poker players. In addition to his news analysis, he serves as an instructor at the World Series of Poker Academy, which offers seminars for participants in advance of the "main event" – the tournament featured on the *World Series of Poker* television show: "I tell players I'm going to teach them what I've learned through my work in counter-intelligence, catching spies … There's no reason poker players should not be aware of why we do these things, why people behave the way they do."[59] In his poker seminars, he argues that breaking the code of body signals allows them to be put to use. Navarro's video lessons, compiled in his *Read 'Em and Reap Poker Course: A Spy-Catcher's Video Guide to Reading Tells*, advises players to cultivate an air of confidence at the table and to convey via body language the messages you want other players to receive.[60] In a segment on hand motions ("steepled" hands and hands on the table with thumb-side up project confidence), Navarro advises his viewers, "Use this information both to guard yourself, to read other people and also use it effectively in bluffing, because now you have many of the secrets that previously have been known by other people as to non-verbal behaviour."[61] What he gives with one hand, as it were – the promise of direct access to underlying emotional states – he takes away with the other by demonstrating how, once deciphered, such signals can be put to use. It is a form of self-undermining that Hegel anticipated in his critique of physiognomy: "in this appearance the inner is no doubt a visible invisible, but it is not tied to this appearance; it can be manifested just as well in another way, just as another inner can be manifested in the same appearance. Lichtenberg therefore rightly says [in his critique of physiognomy]: 'Suppose the physiognomist ever did take the measure of man, it would require only a courageous resolve on the part of the man to make himself incomprehensible again for a thousand years.'"[62]

Staying on the Surface

The analysis of body language finds itself caught in the impasse it sought to evade. In conceding the demise of symbolic efficiency, it attempted to bypass the symbolic register altogether, envisioning a direct, ostensibly unmediated form of communication. However, the attempt to repress symbolic mediation resulted, perhaps unsurprisingly, in its return: body language takes on the character of the forms of symbolic discourse it replaced. The inner depths to which access was promised have retreated once more into the recesses. Perhaps this is one of the reasons for the recourse to brain scans taken up in the following chapter: the hope that blood flow to the brain might not be amenable to reflexive forms of control.

The prospect that this too might turn out to be a vain hope is anticipated by the development of alternative monitoring strategies, including database forms of sorting and prediction described in earlier chapters. There is an affinity between these approaches insofar as both attempt to bypass the vagaries of discourse and narrative, and both see a certain kind of truth legible (or audible) on the "surface" of the body (of data or of people): just as Anderson imagines the numbers "speaking for themselves" (for those with the proper listening devices), so too do bodies do us the favor of bypassing words to tell us directly what we want to know. The attempt to stay on the surface where data speaks for itself, without having to be interpreted, neatly complements the demise of symbolic efficiency – it relies on closing the gap between sign and referent by remaining agnostic about causality and meaning. Since, as Anderson puts it, "Correlation supersedes causation" in the petabyte age, "No semantic or causal analysis is required."[63] Nothing to debunk – just patterns generated by the process of what Ian Ayres calls "super crunching" breathtakingly large amounts of data.[64] The goal here is to bypass the tricky realm of meaning by generating patterns that predict without explaining anything.

The enthusiasm for the power of super-crunching in the petabyte era is of a piece with a contemporary constellation of savvy attempts to bypass the debunked level of discourse and get "things" to speak for themselves. As I argued in Chapter 2, in the case of the database, this voice does not come from the depths of inwardness, but from the consistency of a pattern whose robustness varies directly with the comprehensiveness of the dataset. The catch, of course, is that this new form of understanding is limited to those with access to giant databanks and tremendous processing power. If practical knowledge in the petabyte era means making sense out of incomprehensibly large datasets, it is a form of knowledge destined to be monopolized by the few. In this regard it reinstates a certain asymmetry characteristic of surveillance, although it is worth considering the ways in which contemporary forms of online communication replicate the data mining perspective. Consider, for example, the emerging dynamic of Facebook, which allows users to accumulate large groups of "friends" whose actions are relayed to them and can be aggregated and sorted. Perhaps these applications can be understood as replicating the model of data-crunching at the level of interpersonal relations: the goal is not to decipher the content of a conversation, but rather to accumulate and discern patterns of information that are automatically collected and relayed to online "friends."

Moreover, the shift in models from an attempt to extract a deeper meaning – the recourse to theory and depth models – can perhaps be discerned in shifting information strategies associated with an era of information glut. Nevertheless, at least for the moment it is a shift that favors those who own and control the databases. Once again, at the moment when information becomes increasingly available to the public, the very mode of understanding allegedly shifts in ways that render it inaccessible to the populace. Body language promises to address this asymmetry: if we do not have our own server farms full of data to be mined, perhaps we can cultivate our gut instincts and our thin-slicing skills. This looks, however, like slim compensation for having to concede the demise of the power of narrative, deliberation, and explanation.

6

NEURO-GLUT

Marketing to the Brain

Chicken Soup for the Brain

When the Campbell's Soup Company embarked on a two-year project to redesign its iconic label in 2008, it took the high-tech route, presumably in an effort to ensure that if one of the best-known brands in the United States was to get a facelift, the surgeons should have the shiniest new tools available. For Campbell's, this meant bringing in the neuromarketers, who promised to sidestep the vagaries of focus groups by going straight to consumers' brains. Innerscope, the neuromarketing company that handled the Campbell's makeover, explained in its promotional material that because consumers' initial responses to advertising, "are processed below the conscious level, traditional advertising research, which relies on conscious self-report, is unable to effectively measure them."[1] Consumers, in other words, are a lot like "suspects" – they need to be examined in ways that bypass the potentially deceptive character of their conscious and controlled responses. So it is perhaps not surprising that high-tech market research overlaps with cutting-edge surveillance and interrogation techniques. For the Campbell's label redesign, then, market researchers relied on an array of monitoring techniques designed to capture somatic responses, including devices for measuring heart rate, respiration, skin conductance, facial expressions, and pupil dilation, technologies familiar to those engaged in intelligence-gathering, lie detection, and interrogation.[2]

The Campbell's re-designers also used focus groups, but that part of the project did not get the media attention generated by the neuromarketers. Indeed, the soup label redesign doubled as a promotional vehicle for the nascent practice of "neuromarketing" generating a self-stoking spiral of hype: the media fascination with neuroscience helped to promote Campbell's and the Campbell's story boosted the visibility of neuromarketing. Campbell's made itself and its consultants available to the media to discuss the role played by brain monitoring in the project redesign. In a *Wall Street Journal* article devoted to the redesign, the company's "vice president of global consumer and customer insights" said that "Campbell needed approaches that would help it understand the neurological and bodily responses to an ad rather than how people thought they'd reacted."[3]

The notion that bodies are, for marketing purposes, more truthful than the words they utter is emerging as a recurring theme in the promotion of neuromarketing, which promises to render obsolete the allegedly quaint and outdated techniques of surveys and focus groups. As Martin Lindstrom, the author of a book on neuromarketing called *Buyology*, observes, "Consumers will never, ever tell the truth … It's not because they're lying – because they're not – they're just unaware."[4] However, the recognition that words may be deceptive and self-understanding flawed does not leave market researchers suspended in a tissue of unreliable words – they can, thanks to new technologies, cut through directly to truths revealed by the brain. As social beings, Lindstrom notes, we learn techniques for staging ourselves to address the expectations of others, but at the level of brain, we are utterly sincere: "We can learn how to react and express ourselves differently … but when it comes to the brain, you really can't lie."[5]

The promise of neuromarketing, then, aligns itself with a perceived failure in conventional forms of representation and the research that relies upon them. It is a promise that, judging from its reception, has a certain appeal for marketers facing the challenge of getting their message across to an information- and advertising-saturated populace. Although estimates vary widely, the consensus is that the number of ads to which the typical person is exposed on a daily basis has increased dramatically over the past few decades, thanks in part to the multiplication of media outlets and platforms for advertising, ranging from taxi-cabs to the Internet. As the president of one marketing firm put it, "It's a non-stop blitz of advertising messages … Everywhere we turn we're saturated with advertising messages trying to get our attention … It seems like the goal of most marketers and advertisers nowadays is to cover every blank space with some kind of brand logo or a promotion or an advertisement."[6] The powerful appeal of neuromarketing, then, is the promise of an effective way for marketers to cut through a clutter of their own making.

The Neuroscientific Moment

That the "leading edge" of research on decision-making is headed straight for the brain is not surprising, given the recent surge of interest in the neurosciences. As Scott Vrecko has noted, "the brain sciences – including neurobiology, psychopharmacology, biological psychiatry, and brain imaging – are becoming increasingly prominent in a variety of cultural formations, from self-help guides and the arts to advertising and public health programmes."[7] Similarly, Francisco Ortega and Fernando Vidal have noted, "The rise since the 1990s of various 'neuro' disciplines (... neuroesthetics, neurotheology, neuroeconomics, neuroeducation and neuropsychoanalysis) that conquer ground previously occupied by the human sciences" alongside "commercial practices associated with brainhood, such as neuromarketing and the 'neurobics' [brain exercise] business."[8] Nikolas Rose has similarly explored the rise during the past two decades of discursive formations that position the neurosciences at the center of emerging ways of thinking about how subjects are governed.[9]

The neuroscientific "moment" inaugurated in the 1990s might be approached as both a cultural and a technological development – one associated with the emergence of the brain as a target of particular technologies of visibility and, thus, of management and, potentially, of governance and self-help. As Jonna Brenninkmeijer puts it, "Working on the self by working on the brain seems a logical consequence of recent developments in neuroscience which on the one hand try to unravel the mystery of the human 'mind' and on the other hand explore the prospects of the human brain." Vrecko, drawing on the work of Ian Hacking, suggests that the "flourishing" of new "neurocultural" forms – or what might be described as the increasing ubiquity of the "neuro-" prefix – is related to the ageing of the baby boomers and, thus, the "growing concern from an ageing population about cognitive decline in old age and the flourishing of new technologies which have made it possible to gain insight on the brain's sub-cellular structures and processes."[10] Surely, as Ortega and Vidal note, the development of functional magnetic resonance imaging (fMRI) technology has played a crucial role in driving "the growth of the 'neuro' fields."[11]

The (vexed) promise of fMRI scanners to show the brain at work, in real time, lent an air of scientific credibility to the promise that its mysteries can now be unpacked in physiological terms – just as the functions of other organs before it became transparent. There is something fitting about the correspondence of the promise to decode the brain with the rise of the informated world of the networked digital era. If the physical work of the organs that oxygenate, circulate, and filter the blood, that process food, or manufacture tissue have an industrial-era feel, serving as metaphors for various forms of production (and waste), the turn to the brain as the next frontier resonates with the cultural prominence of the mental and communicative forms of production associated with the rise of the information society. If, in the industrial era, the workings of the brain remained, in important ways, opaque, and therefore a matter of interpretation, the promise of the fMRI era is to render the brain visible and therefore available to the techniques of scientific management, adjustment, development, and intervention. As Ortega and Vidal put it, "Functional neuroimages seem to provide visual diagnoses, and tell us why we are the way we are."[12] They further note that even as brain imaging specialists "criticize popular presentations of fMRI, and treat images as merely visualized numbers ... they also identify the images with transparency, objectivity and progress, and personify the technique in ways that blur the distinctions between machine and image, and attribute to MRI itself the capacity to produce and express knowledge directly."[13] Neuromarketers, of course, are specialists in this form of attribution, pointing to the bright blots of color that signify brain activity as direct testimony that "does not lie."

The emergence of a new site of self-hood can, as Brenninkmeijer notes, lend itself to new forms of work upon the self: "This brain focus, combined with the unremitting quest for a better life, has resulted in a successful self-help industry for brain enhancement" – and fitness.[14] What plastic surgery and Pilates are to the bodies of aging baby boomers (amongst others), brain-enhancing elixirs and exercise are to their minds. In the interest of economic competitiveness (in the era of employment precarity associated with "flexible" capitalism), personal satisfaction, and self-maintenance, we are offered a range of devices, techniques, and substances to help counter the formerly inevitable decline of our brains associated with aging. As one brain fitness Website advises those who have managed to score a lower "Brain Age" than their actual age puts it, "Well done ... you are probably doing enough with your brain to ward off dementia."[15] There is something both satisfying and terrifying about that "probably" – an invitation to indefinite fitness training: more frenetic activity to stave off the inevitable. As a technology of self-help, brain exercise promises, as one application with the tagline "reclaim your brain" put it, to help users "do better in school, perform more effectively at work, and live a more productive life" – the trinity of self-maximization in an age dedicated to cultivation of what a 2008 report by the UK's Government Office for Science describes as "mental capital."[16] According to the report, this form of capital, when applied to members of a population, "includes their cognitive ability, how flexible and efficient they are at learning, and their 'emotional intelligence.' such as their social skills and resilience in the face of stress. It therefore conditions how well an individual is able to contribute effectively to society, and also to experience a high personal quality of life."[17] The report notes that it is "both challenging and natural" to associate the capacities of the mind with "ideas of financial capital."[18]

Certainly, it seems natural for neuromarketers to think of the mind as a potential source of economic value, although they do so in somewhat different terms than those envisioned by the promoters of mental fitness. The self-help gurus and consultants envision strategies of (self-) management that accord with those forms of neoliberal governance characterized by what Nikolas Rose has described as the injunction to envision the citizen as an "entrepreneur of him- or herself" who is "to conduct his or her life, and that of his or her family, as a kind of enterprise, seeking to enhance and capitalize on existence itself through calculated acts and investments."[19] In the throes of the recent fascination with neuroscience, we are urged to think of the work we do on our brains as an important investment in one of our most valuable resources – one that surely has the potential to be realized in other forms of capital. We are enjoined to maximize our mental capital in accordance with the guidance provided by those with appropriate forms of neuroscientific expertise – in the name of our own self-interest. It is the combination of the structuring of self-help guidelines with economic (in the double sense of the term) strategies for guiding people's conduct that results in what Rose calls forms of governing "'at a distance" ... by shaping the ways they understand and enact their own freedom."[20]

By contrast, neuromarketers are interested in more direct forms of influence – in particular, those that bypass conscious reflection on the part of consumers. As the CEO of the Danish advertising group Bark put it when explaining the company's investment in neuromarketing, "As marketers, we know that emotions rule thoughts, and thoughts rule consumer behavior ... By using Mindmetic's new neuromarketing technology, we will be able to better understand consumer reactions and create messages that result in the desired consumer response."[21] Similarly, the advertising consortium DraftFCB described its neuromarketing initiative as a means of taking "further steps to enhance its ability to influence consumer behavior" by focusing on "instinctual" forms of decision-making: precisely those that sidestep the forms of reflexivity associated with the "conduct of conduct" and the forms of expert guidance upon which this form of governance relies.[22] As we shall see, the promise of neuromarketing is tailored, in a sense, to a context characterized by a knowing skepticism toward expertise – one in which the grounds for "expert advice" are called into question in the name of a reactionary populism. First, however, it is worth exploring in a bit more detail the promise of neuromarketing.

Brain Whispering and Somatic Markers

In the simplest terms, neuromarketing is the application of recent developments in brain research to marketing. As one marketer puts it, neuromarketing refers to "studying the brain to help advertisers tap into people's unarticulated [responses] needs, drives and desires."[23] Companies including Google, Intel, DaimlerChrysler, and Microsoft have all incorporated neuromarketing into their market research strategies, at least on a trial basis, and the AC Nielsen company, internationally known for its media ratings services, recently acquired Berkeley-based NeuroFocus to supplement its market research offerings, literally buying into the claim that "Great advertising strikes a responsive chord with consumers where it matters most: the subconscious. Only neurological testing can make the 'deep dive' required to access that level of the brain and discover how it responds to all forms of advertising, in every medium."[24]

From a somewhat different perspective, we might describe neuromarketing as a particular way of thinking about individuals as what Fernando Vidal calls "cerebral subjects" – entities whose very essence as subjects is defined by their brain. As Vidal puts it, "the neuroscientific hype highlights the ascendancy, throughout industrialized and highly medicalized societies, of a certain view of the human being ... As a 'cerebral subject', the human being is specified by the property of 'brainhood,' i.e. the property or quality of *being*, rather than simply *having*, a brain."[25] It is easy to trace this understanding of the subject in neuromarketing discourses, which invoke the brain metonymically to refer to consumers of all kinds. NeuroFocus's promotional literature, for example, observes that "Great entertainment engages and delights the brain with content that is new, exciting, relevant, and memorable. Neurological testing allows producers to develop material the brain loves and remembers."[26]

The company's founder, A. K. Pradeep, describes his book on neuro-marketing as being about "how and why brains buy" – not *people* or *consumers*, but *brains*. Thanks to advances in technique and technology we find ourselves, or so the neuromarketers claim, in direct conversation with brains, sidestepping the all-too-unreliable mouths to which they happen to be connected. As Pradeep observes in his description of techniques for monitoring the brain's responses to marketing appeals: "Measurements at this deep level of the sub-conscious are essential for companies to understand fully how consumers truly respond to their products, their packaging, their brands, their marketing, and the in-store shopping experience. The brain whispers those truths, and we listen."[27]

Neuromarketers themselves tend to trace the emergence of their field to the crossover publications on the nature of decision-making by neuroscientist Antonio Damasio during the 1990s. For them, Damasio's work represents two important turning points in the so-called science of marketing. The first is a reconfiguration of the relationship between emotion and rationality in the decision-making process; the second is the claim that elements of this process can be studied and measured scientifically, thanks to recent technological developments.

Damasio's theory of "somatic markers" countered previous understandings of the relationship between reason and emotion by suggesting that emotion is not antithetical to rationality, but an integral part of reasoning and decision-making. In the conventional view – which Damasio describes as "the high-reason" view of decision making – the assumption is that reason operates in a realm aloof from (if occasionally overwhelmed by) the passions associated with emotion. The hope is that "Formal logic will, by itself, get us to the best available solution for any problem. An important aspect of the rationalist conception is that to obtain the best results, emotions must be kept *out*. Rational processing must be unencumbered by passion."[28] This is not to say that emotions do not interfere in the decision-making process – but rather that they are to be understood as just that – a form of interference in, or contamination of, the operation of pure reason. The corollary to this view is that reason is at its most powerful, efficient, and effective when freed from emotional encumbrance. By contrast, Damasio argues that reason cannot function properly without the assistance of emotion. The "delicate mechanism" of reasoning is actually impaired by the loss of signals hailing from the neural machinery that underlies emotion. Reason without emotion is, in a very practical sense, indeterminate. Imagine trying to make a truly complete list of all of the potential "pros" and "cons" of even a relatively simple decision: "if this strategy is the only one you have available, rationality … is not going to work. At best your decision will take an inordinately long time … At worst, you may not even end up with a decision at all because you will get lost in the byways of your calculation."[29]

Damasio illustrates this reconfiguration of the relationship of reason and emotion with the case of a patient he called Eliot who had lost a portion of the frontal lobe of his brain when a sizeable benign tumor was removed. Eliot, who had been a successful professional, seemed largely unchanged by the surgery – at least according to a battery of intelligence and IQ tests. He nevertheless suffered a debilitating consequence of the damage: he had become all but incapable of making decisions, fixating for long periods of time on tiny details, seemingly paralyzed by the infinite amount of information that needed to be weighed before a decision could be made. Elliot became an embodied example of the impasse of what Damasio calls "high reason," caught up in an endless series of rational calculations. As Jonah Lehrer's account of Damasio's work puts it, "Routine tasks that should have taken ten minutes now required several hours. Elliot endlessly deliberated over routine details, like whether to use a blue or black pen, what radio station to listen to and where to park his car. When he chose where to eat lunch, Elliot carefully considered each restaurant's menu, seating plan, and lighting scheme, and then drove to each place to see how busy it was. But he still couldn't decide where to eat."[30]

Damasio noted that Elliot seemed singularly devoid of emotional response – dispassionate and uninvolved, even when it came to discussing the devastating impact his disability was having upon his personal and professional life, including the loss of his job and the breakup of his marriage. At one point Elliot told Damasio that his own feelings had changed from before his illness: he could sense that topics which had once evoked a strong emotion no longer caused any reaction, positive or negative. Damasio summarized Elliot's predicament as follows: "to know, but not to feel."[31] Furthermore, it turned out that the ability to feel was an integral part of the decision-making process: without it, reason was paralyzed. Emotion did not interfere with reason, but enabled it.

What emerged from these and similar findings was the notion that the role of emotional response in the process of cognition was, in a sense, to cut through the clutter of information by summarizing past experience in the form of emotional shorthand. Damasio describes the emotional responses that facilitate the decision-making process as "somatic markers" that play an invaluable role in the process of *rational* deliberation. These visceral responses, as Damasio puts it, "have been connected, by learning, to predicted future outcomes of certain scenarios."[32] Our body stores these links in the forms of embodied responses that can intervene in the deliberation process, helping to point us toward particular decision and away from others: "imagine that before you apply any kind of cost/benefit analysis to the premises [of a particular decision], and before you reason toward the solution of the problem, something quite important happens: When the bad outcome connected with a given response option comes into mind, however fleetingly, you experience an unpleasant gut feeling."[33] The somatic marker hypothesis envisions a form of embodied cognition whereby responses are recorded, stored, and replayed subconsciously so as to skirt the impasse of "pure" reason. Drawing on the work of Joseph LeDoux, Lerner puts it this way: "every feeling is really a summary of data, a visceral response to all of the information that can't be accessed directly – feelings are an accurate shortcut, a concise expression of decades worth of experience."[34]

Somatic markers can also work much more rapidly, accurately summarizing and responding to a situation more efficiently than conscious forms of cognition, according to the gambling experiment described in the previous chapter – an experiment that Damasio helped to design. As Lerner puts it, "The emotions knew which decks were dangerous. The subject's feelings figured out the game first."[35] In this regard, Damasio provides one explanation for the operation of what Gladwell calls "rapid cognition" or "thinking without thinking": "a system in which the brain reaches conclusions without immediately telling us that it's reaching conclusions."[36] Gladwell's entire book is about the effectiveness of thinking without thought. It is, in keeping with the times, a treatise on the dangers of thinking too much, deliberating too much, and collecting too much information.

Clutter-Cutting in an Era of Information Glut

The promise of these forms of thoughtless thought is to cut through the morass of a data-drenched world. In this regard, it is possible to situate the appeal of neuromarketing, writ large, within the broader constellation of strategies for managing information overload or short-circuiting indeterminacy. Body literacy, like neuromarketing, promises access to truths otherwise obscured by the vagaries of discourse and the perceived futility of attempts to obtain accurate, unbiased representations. In this regard, it is suited to a culture that has become reflexively savvy about the constructed, incomplete, and perspectival character of representation.

The combination of savvy skepticism toward discursive forms of representation with a seemingly naïve faith in the direct evidence of the body (and the brain) is perhaps not as counter-intuitive or unfamiliar as it might at first seem.

It is, in a sense, a popularized version of the impasse of "high reason" described by Damasio. In a world where more information is available to more people more easily than at any other time in human history, a reflexive skepticism based on the perceived indeterminacy of evidence-based decision-making goes mainstream. As I argued in Chapter 1, the palpable information overload associated with the digital, multichannel era has made us aware in significant and novel ways of the impasses of representation, in part by directly staging it for us in the form of the proliferation of media content readily available to a growing number of people. The World Wide Web, for example, provides a ready portrait of information futility in the sheer vastness of the expanse of information it arrays before us, combined with its ability to house multiplying and competing narratives. The short notification at the top of each Internet browser search window reminds us how many millions of pages we have managed to conjure up with the simplest of queries, and how impossible it would be to read them all.

Thanks to the proliferation of narratives and counter-narratives, of evidence and counter-evidence in online forums, the process of navigating the Web to arrive at a determinate decision recalls the pathologies of Elliot's frontal lobe damage. Anyone who wanted to assess the entire body of evidence on a controversial issue – including the critiques and rejoinders of the received wisdom or the apparent consensus – would have to suspend judgment indefinitely. Against such a background it is not hard to discern the appeal of "thinking without thought" as a survival skill for the digital era. It is, perhaps unsurprisingly, a skill that is invoked by a resurgent conservative populist critique of expertise in the United States – a critique licensed by a savvy mistrust of representation.

Consider, for example, the response to global warming – one in which the scientific evidence is pitted against both commonsense and gut reaction. When a Berkeley-based scientist who had expressed skepticism toward global warming announced in late 2011 that his assessment of the evidence, financed in part by right-wing climate deniers (who presumably thought his preconceptions would shape his findings), was that global warming is real, this was taken by the right not as an invitation to reconsider the evidence, but as further confirmation of the corrupt and unreliable character of scientific research. One Republican consultant and Fox News commentator responded by claiming that "scientists are scamming the American people right and left for their own financial gain."[37] And how did the commentator, who is not a climate scientist, know that she was right and the scientific community was wrong? Pure gut instinct – the triumph of thoughtless thought over the intricacies of scientific reason and the deluge of so-called data. "I think if every American really thought about it, they would have a gut feeling that some of these numbers that the scientists are putting out are not right."[38] Notice the shift in register here: *really* deep thought, in the end, defaults to a feeling. Best of all, this kind of thought is "democratic" in the reductionist sense that it is available not just to the commentator but to anyone, since it relies so little on the *other* kind of thought – the sort that depends on the cultivation of forms of expertise, upon the mobilization and assessment of evidence, and the exercise of reason: the form of thought, in short, once upon a time associated with knowledge.

Although Gladwell would surely balk at the commentator's use of "thin-sliced" thought to assess climate science, his critique of the dangers of over-thinking and the inefficiencies of deliberation align themselves with Damasio's critique of the deadlock of "high reason." It takes a further step, however, to get from the notion that gut reactions can be efficient forms of decision-making to the collapse of knowing into feeling. This is the step that I have been describing in terms of the demise of symbolic efficiency. The reflexive recognition of the partial character of representation is accompanied by an almost indignant savviness: "do you think I'm dumb enough to take this incomplete representation, this partial, perspectival, and potentially misleading portrayal for a substantial, palpable *reality*?" Dominant narratives and the truths they underwrite are relegated to the realm of dupe fodder, while evidentiary claims and narrative arguments seem to lose their purchase. As I will argue in the following chapter, critique collapses into conspiracy theory in a disturbing refutation of the promise of the digital information era. The proliferation of information and the forms of representation that convey it, however, threatens to render itself useless: a data-rich morass to be escaped, bypassed, and overleapt.

The Appeal of Affect

It would be overstating the case to assert the final triumph of symbolic inefficacy, or the complete collapse of critique, but such assessments perhaps help to describe tendencies in contemporary political and media culture. New Yorker columnist Hendrik Hertzberg made a similar observation about the popularity of Newt Gingrich amongst Christian fundamentalists during the 2012 presidential campaign.[39] Gingrich's appeal to this group of voters was difficult to explain logically – after all, Gingrich was famous for his serial adultery and his occasional outright opposition to pet right-wing causes, including, notoriously his belief that global warming exists and his (occasional) critique of Republican plans to shift more of the tax burden away from the wealthy onto the middle class – a plan he denigrated as "right-wing social engineering."[40] Rather, Hertzberg speculated, his appeal stemmed "less from his vaunted 'big ideas' than from his long-cultivated unparalleled talent for contempt" – that is, his affective charge.[41]

The notion that the appeal to affect, understood as an efficacious intensity that circulates below the realm of consciousness, is warranted by the short-comings of representation marks the link between neuroscience and affect theory noted by Ruth Leys.[42] The affect theorists whom she critiques invoke something very similar to the impasse of "high reason" identified by Damasio: "These theorists are gripped by the notion that most philosophers and critics in the past (Kantians, neo-Kantians, Habermasians) have overvalued the role of reason and rationality in politics ... The claim is that we human beings are corporeal creatures imbued with subliminal affective intensities and resonances that so decisively influence or condition our political and other beliefs that we ignore these affective intensities at our peril."[43] Affect theory's fascination with neuroscience, according to this account, derives from the ways in which the latter promises to monitor, measure, and assess these influences – to replace analysis and critique that take place at the level of representation and ideology with techniques for accessing the influence of subliminal affective intensities. The notion of affect at work here is somewhat different from that of somatic markers outlined by Damasio, but both serve the purpose of addressing the impasses of reason and the deadlock of representation. In other words, both "turns" – one to affect and the other to neuroscience (and neuromarketing) address the so-called demise of symbolic efficiency not by rehabilitating the efficacy of representation, but by short-circuiting it.

The claim that the appeal of affect neatly slices the Gordian knot of data glut recalls the promise of neuromarketing: to avail itself of the power of direct, subconscious appeals that bypass the demobilizing welter of information and argument. From a marketing perspective, information clutter is a recurring concern. DraftFCB, one of the world's largest global advertising agency networks, announced in 2010 its plans to create a research arm called the "Institute of Decision Making" that would focus on cutting-edge research in neuroscience and behavioral economics. The institute's new director defined one of the institute's central challenges as finding ways to influence consumers in an era of multi-tasking and media saturation: "We believe that with less time and more information, heuristics will only become more important. The instinctual side of decision-making is better understood every day, and we want to work with those who are at the leading edge of this exploration."[44]

From Causation to Correlation

If, once upon a time, marketing to consumers meant tapping into deep subconscious desires, selling to brains ends up being something a bit more physiological. Neuromarketing treats consumers as bundles of nerve centers that respond to various stimuli forming triggerable pathways as a result. As one account in *The Wall Street Journal* put it, "Years ago, Revlon founder Charles Revson drily observed that 'in the factory, we make perfume; in the store we sell hope,' Neuromarketing can now pinpoint where in our brain such hope is triggered and tell a marketer which ad campaign will send the most blood there."[45] If marketing to consumers is an uncertain business, going directly to their nerve centers promises to be less so. Viewed through the lens of neuromarketing, these bundles of nerves become, as marketing guru Martin Lindstrom puts it, the core of "our truest selves": the part of us that yields up the truth of our desire more accurately and objectively than consciously articulated thoughts or psychological interpretations.[46]

Neuromarketing promises not simply to provide clues about how best to directly influence the emotional triggers that allegedly shape subconscious consumer cognition, but also to allow marketers to bypass the welter of potentially inaccurate research data (including our own misleading accounts of our preferences) that threatens to conceal our *truest* selves from them. The paradox of savvy reflexivity recurs in this formulation, which pairs a deep mistrust of mediation with a seemingly naïve faith in that most mediated of artifacts: the red blot on the fMRI scan. As Zizek puts it, the paradox of the decline of symbolic efficiency results in a version of what he calls a resurgent fundamentalism: "what is foreclosed in the symbolic (belief) returns in the Real (of a direct knowledge). A fundamentalist does not believe, he *knows* directly."[47] This formulation sums up the attitude of "gut" knowledge: "don't bother me with your so-called facts, I already understand at a level that they cannot touch."

It turns out that, according to neuromarketers, the primary threat to such unadulterated and direct forms of knowledge is posed by sociality and, consequently, language and consciousness: those layers that build upon the allegedly primary subjectivity of the brain.

For example, NeuroFocus founder A. K. Pradeep claims that language too often mistranslates the impulses of our truest selves: "Neuroscience has demonstrated that the accuracy of conventional marketing research and surveys is often compromised by an exclusive focus on articulated responses. By contrast, NeuroFocus measures at the deep subconscious level, where perceptions are formed, unaffected by the multitude of factors that influence and distort articulated responses."[48] If, on this account, consciousness is the realm of illusion and delusion and sociality that of distortion, then neuromarketing captures the essence of desire before it is released into the world, while it is still locked up, in its essential form. As Pradeep puts it:

> When you ask someone about how they felt or what they thought or what they remember about something, in the process of replying their brain actually changes the original information it recorded. In contrast, when you measure at the subconscious, precognitive level of the brain, you're accessing the original information immediately following its reception, before it can be distorted by all the factors that can influence articulated responses, from cultural and language differences to education levels and many more.[49]

According to neuromarketers, the problem with people – as opposed to their brains – is that they are notoriously unreliable. They may not want to expose the truth of their feelings; they may not even know how they really feel; or they may be influenced by interviewers, the presence of others, social norms, and so on. It's not hard to detect a certain note of resentment toward the stubborn opacity of humans in these formulations. Steven Quartz, a researcher who joined the neuromarketing bandwagon early on, noted that his test subjects were often surprised by how their brains responded – but they were willing to defer to the allegedly objective truth of the scans: "they are surprised, they maybe don't want to admit that they find an action hero attractive, but you can see it directly in their brain."[50]

Although this language of neuromarketing seems to recapitulate a logic of depth – the ability to excavate below the surface of discourse into the recesses of the reptilian brain – this formulation turns out to be self-misreading on the part of neuromarketers. Far from providing underlying explanations for the functioning of emotional forms of cognition (in the register of psychoanalysis) or even of the brain's inner workings (in the register of structural physiology), neuromarketing research invokes the power of correlation – an increasingly familiar one in the data-driven world of contemporary market research.

Consider, for example, research about the role of neuromarketing in the recording industry. In 2006, researchers at Emory University scanned the brains of 27 teenagers while they listened to short clips of more than 100 then-unknown songs. They then ranked the songs according to those which lit up what they described as regions of the brain associated with pleasure and reward. Several years later, they returned to the research and discovered that half of the songs on their neural top-10 list had gone on to become hits. The findings led a Stanford marketing professor to proclaim the triumph of neuromarketing: "brain activation is able to predict what music is going to become popular two or three years from now."[51] The study said nothing about the psychological or aesthetic appeal of the songs or even about why these songs might have yielded scans indicating activity in certain parts of the brain. Nor did the findings reveal whether those who were scanned had gone on to purchase the songs to which their brains had apparently responded. The key finding in this instance was purely correlational. A neuro-economist, who worked on the project at Emory's Center for Neuropolicy, noted that, even though the researchers couldn't explain why, "The punch line is that brain responses correlated with units sold," making the nucleus accumbens "an effective focus group" – a focus group whose predictions were more robust than the information provided by the teens' stated preferences.[52]

For the purposes of marketers, this type of correlation is, in the end, all that is needed. If Vance Packard, writing in the heyday of psychological approaches to marketing in *The Hidden Persuaders*, described the activities of those who were "known in the trade as the 'depth boys',"[53] we might describe the new generation of neuromarketers as the "correlation kids" or the "data diviners." The promise of neuromarketing devices is, in a sense, to black-box the problem of causality: who cares why a particular blend of colors or sounds "activates" a consumer's brain, what matters is that it *does* – and that this correlation has predictive power (allegedly). This approach to neuromarketing was driven home to me during a visit to a company called MindSign, which boasted, at the time, the only freestanding (non-institutionally affiliated) fMRI machine in the United States. The entrepreneurs at MindSign were working on a variety of projects, including using the fMRI machine to test viewers' responses to movies and the use of fMRI technology for lie detection. At the time of my visit, however, they were in the process of conducting an experiment to see whether they could use brain response to predict short-term consumption behavior. This meant exposing test subjects to particular brand images and then checking back later to see whether they had purchased the products in question. Once they had the data about actual purchases, they could search the fMRI record to see if there was any consistent relationship between areas of brain activation and consumption activity. The goal was not to explain, but merely to predict, based on pure induction of data patterns.

Neuro-promises

The promise of neuromarketing can be situated within the broader context of the impasses of representation it promises to resolve. If we are confronted by our own awareness of the practical and theoretical limitations of representation in a self-consciously savvy era, these are ostensibly addressed by defaulting to "thinking without thought," on the one hand, and, on the other, to an appeal to the technology for direct access to the brain. Neuromarketing does not attempt to work through the impasse of representation in order to come out the other side, but purports to sidestep it entirely by circumventing the vagaries of language and social life to gain direct access to the seat of selfhood and its desires: the brain. Encapsulated in the promise of neuromarketing is a set of vexed assumptions and a repressed paradox. The first have to do with the nature of desire and self-hood, and they assume an understanding of subjective essence as pre-social insofar as language and sociality are portrayed as distorting and obscuring the true nature of desire. The notion of truth invoked by neuromarketers is a purely pragmatic, non-correspondence one: it does not attempt to match representations to underlying realities, but correlates measured responses to monitored activity. Even as neuromarketers seemingly recapitulate a Lockeian commitment to the primacy of the individual brain as the pre-social seat of meanings and desires, they sidestep the shortcomings of this formulation by focusing on correlation and prediction. This strategy, whether deliberately or not, addresses the suppressed paradox of neuromarketing: the attempt to bypass mediation with more mediation. Brain scans do not provide direct "glimpses" into the recesses of authentic selves, but instead offer up highly mediated images subject to the same vagaries and impasses they purportedly avoid. The promise of direct access to our "true selves" relies on the faith in representation debunked by the forms of skepticism that underwrote the turn to neuro-marketing in the first place.

The reliance on correlation transforms the promise of neuromarketing from that of direct access to individual desires to the prediction of the behavior of populations. Moreover, the claim to be able to influence consumers at the subconscious level shifts strategies of influence from the level of ideology to that of affect. Framed in these terms, neuromarketing aligns itself with those strategies that Patricia Clough identifies with emerging practices of social control described in Chapter 3: the shift in probabilistic measuring techniques from "representing populations, even making populations, to modulating or manipulating the population's affective capacities."[54] If ideology functions in the realm of symbolic efficiency, alternative strategies such as neuromarketing claim to withstand its so-called demise. According to the neuromarketers, we are on the threshold of being able to engage in direct recording and manipulation of emotional response that compensates for the demise of symbolic efficiency at the level of representation. In the end, the knowledge that neuromarketers seek aligns itself with that of data-miners in the digital era: a predictive version in which a gesture toward interior truths may be retained, but is simultaneously displaced by the goal of prediction.

7

THEORY GLUT

From Critique to Conspiracy

Real-izing the "Big Other"

Not long ago, during the course of a graduate seminar in media theory I was teaching, a student asked if I had seen the movie *Zeitgeist*. When the class learned I had not even heard of the movie, they offered to lend me a copy. I was much surprised, upon skimming through the movie, to discover that it was a classic conspiracy-theory pseudo-documentary that assembled a highlight reel of hackneyed conspiracies ranging from the manipulation of religion by secret cabals to the claim that the World Trade Center was brought down not by terrorist planes but by controlled detonation. To my mind, the class I had been teaching – which focused on the ways in which corporations were using the Internet to collect detailed information about people in order to more effectively advertise and market to them – had little in common with classic conspiracy theory, which left me mulling over the question as to why the students thought I'd be part of the target demographic for a movie like *Zeitgeist*. In fact, this was the *only* thing interesting to me about the movie: the fact that the students saw some kind of connection between what I thought was an accurate, albeit critical, description of the workings of the online economy and an assemblage of well-worn inaccuracies, distortions, and half-truths calculated to provide a particular kind of "what if it were true" thrill and little more.

At least part of the apparent connection, I'm assuming – since I didn't ask the students outright – was the aura of critique. In both cases, the students apparently discerned the account of a potentially pernicious power at work, and in both cases a related form of unveiling: a narrative of debunkery meant to be at odds with the dominant received narrative. I had been telling a tale about the emergence of new media technologies which called into question celebratory accounts of the digital era by exploring the new forms of surveillance and social sorting that characterize it. I was asking students to think beyond the limits of the accounts they had been offered by publicists of the digital economy to consider how such accounts worked to the advantage of particular groups, and to the detriment of others. *Zeitgeist* similarly appealed to savvy, skeptical viewers by inviting them to quit the ranks of the "duped" and gain some insight into the "real" behind-the-scenes forces that shape human history (apparently a cabal of bankers and secret societies who orchestrate costly wars in order to justify the forms of government borrowing and spending that enrich them at the expense of the populace).

Both stories were about something wrong going on behind the scenes or below the surface; perhaps more importantly both were accounts of the concentration of hidden or non-obvious power and the forms of dissimulation or ignorance that enable its operation. Both, in this regard, might even be considered critical in a populist vein insofar as they seem to take the side of the misled or under-informed masses against the powerful few. In an era of generalized savviness and reflexive debunkery – one characterized by the popularization of a hermeneutics of suspicion in the Internet era – critique becomes indistinguishable from conspiracy. This form of cultural convergence, whereby social critique is assimilated to (and thereby relegated to the realm of) conspiracy theory invokes the challenge critical thought faces in an era of information glut.

Slavoj Zizek identifies this convergence – the default of critique to conspiracy – as one of the symptoms of the demise of symbolic efficiency. As he puts it, "The paradoxical result of the mutation in the nonexistence of the big Other – or the growing collapse of symbolic efficiency – is thus the proliferation of different versions of a big Other that actually exists, in the Real, not merely as a symbolic fiction."[1] This is the "short circuit" between the imaginary and the real – what I have described as the attempt to achieve "immediation" – that is, to bypass the realm of symbolic representation altogether and gain direct access to the real. As Zizek points out, however, "The belief in the big Other which exists in the Real is, of course, the most succinct definition of paranoia; for this reason, two features which characterize today's ideological stance – cynical distance and full reliance on paranoiac fantasy – are strictly co-dependent: the typical subject today is the one who, while displaying cynical distrust of any public ideology, indulges without restraint in paranoiac fantasies about conspiracies, threats, and excessive forms of enjoyment of the Other."[2] The allegedly critical stance that debunks the ideological alibi of power, insofar as it embraces the demise of symbolic efficiency, also embraces the default to conspiracy: "The distrust of the big Other (the order of symbolic fictions), the subject's refusal to 'take it seriously,' relies on the belief that there is an 'Other of the Other', that a secret invisible, and all-powerful agent actually 'pulls the strings' and runs the show; behind the visible, public Power there is another obscene, invisible, power structure."[3] This is, as we shall see, an almost verbatim description, *avant la letter*, of the rise of radio talk-jock and former TV host Glenn Beck and the Tea Party movement for which he serves as figurehead and avatar.

The rise of Beck reflects and epitomizes the dissolution of the distinction between accounts that adhered to evidentiary norms of rational critical debate (and the Enlightenment-derived claims of rationality and universality upon which they rely) and those that invoke the thrill of a secret and un-debunkable conspiracy. In an era in which the shared grounds for adjudicating between multiplying competing narratives is undermined, allowing each of these to fragment into idiosyncratic and incompatible knowledge sets (or mutually untranslatable "language games"), critique becomes, in a sense, a sub-genre of conspiracy theory – and conspiracy theory endows itself with the affective and political charge of critique.

This convergence can be traced through the realms of both high theory and low culture. The theoretical work devoted to highlighting the ways in which knowledge is imbricated with power – and, in particular, with the reproduction of dominant narratives that underwrite prevailing power relations – calls into question the notion that rational critical debate can live up to its claim as neutral arbiter between legitimate and illegitimate knowledge. The related challenge posed to expertise in an era in which the forms of symbolic efficiency that underwrite it (including the evidentiary claims of science, established criteria for evaluation and performance, symbolic forms of authority, and so on) are called into question similarly undermines familiar standards of adjudication: why trust the journalists, the experts, or the scientists? It is not enough to point out how often the experts are wrong (or under the influence of vested interests) – this leaves intact an implicit standard of adjudication. What is really called into question, as the previous chapter argues, is the very notion of expertise itself (otherwise the problem could be addressed by simply replacing the wrong experts with the "right" ones).

If the hallmark of a conspiracy is the co-optation or complicity of the so-called experts, that of conspiracy theory is a knowing and allegedly democratizing mistrust of expertise *per se*. In current political parlance, expertise is simply another form of self-deluded and patronizing elitism (remember Hillary Clinton's dismissive refusal to cast her lot with the "experts" who opposed her populist appeal for short-term gas tax relief). The result has been, in many instances, a slide down the rabbit hole into the zany world of contemporary US politics, in which familiar debates over practical issues of taxation and regulation find themselves rubbing shoulders with a throng of wacky newcomers: suspicions that Barack Obama is a covert Muslim socialist, that his administration is running guns to Mexican drug cartels to terrorize

Americans into supporting gun control laws that undermine Second Amendment rights, that his friends and advisors are America-haters hell bent on pursuing a drastically radical agenda revealed only by occasional slipups (including the Department of Defense's redesign of the Missile Defense Agency's logo to include a covert reference to an Islamic crescent and star). Once again a relentlessly savvy and cynical attitude toward appearances is coupled with a mind-numbingly naïve default to faith in gut-level access to a more authentic hidden agenda: the "Other of the Other" pulling the strings behind the scenes.

This is not to deny that expertise continues to matter and therefore to function in a variety of contexts. However, its populist dismissal situates it within the broader context of information overload with which this book is concerned. A landscape in which the sheer volume of available information highlights the impasse of representation – not just the difficulty of gaining a complete picture, but the apparent failure of those systems that were supposed to help us adjudicate between rival accounts – provides fertile ground for the rehabilitation and reconfiguration of conspiracy theory. We might note, in this regard, the high-profile political role of conspiracy theory in the past decade or so: its mainstreaming alongside the rise of cable TV and the rapid expansion of the Internet. The stories remain monotonously similar, but their position in the public realm has shifted to the point that someone as seemingly "out there" as the famed conspiracy theorist Glenn Beck can get a prime slot on the top-rated cable news network (at least for a while) and build a multi-media empire. From one perspective there's nothing particularly new about Beck's conspiracy mongering, which is a pastiche of fringe theorists ranging from Cleon Skousen to erstwhile stalwarts of the John Birch Society. Unlike those figures, however, Beck has managed to parlay his act into a nationally syndicated radio show, two cable TV shows, a high-priced road show, and books that have reached #1 on the *New York Times* Bestseller List in *four* different categories. Beck has earned a fortune, staged a mass rally on the National Mall, and launched his own multi-media production company. In the figure of Glenn Beck, the mainstreaming of conspiracy theory has come into its own.

Conspiracy Redux

In a review essay on studies of conspiracy theory, Jodi Dean outlines several theories for explaining the contemporary "prevalence" of conspiracy as evidenced by its migration into the political mainstream in the era of the Tea Party, the spread of the so-called "birther" movement, and the prominence of figures such as Glenn Beck and Minnesota Congresswoman Michelle Bachmann. Dean cites with some approval George Marcus's assertion of conspiracy theory's relation to the "crisis of representation often denoted as postmodernism" – an account that aligns itself with what this book describes in Zizek's terms as the demise of symbolic efficiency.[4] In the same volume, as Dean notes, Kathleen Stewart makes the connection to digital media technology: "The Internet was made for conspiracy theory: it *is* a conspiracy theory: one thing leads to another, always another link leading you deeper into no thing and no place."[5]

A reflexive awareness of information overload – of the futility of gathering *all* the evidence in order to adjudicate between multiplying competing accounts – marks the collapse of a residual faith in the promise of the Enlightenment project. As Jodi Dean puts it, "bringing every relevant and available fact into the conversation, as the Habermasians like to say, may well entangle us in a clouded, occluded nightmare of obfuscation."[6] As I will argue in the following chapter, this is not the only way to think about the fate of information in the digital era or the role of the Internet, but it is this occluded nightmare that undermines the distinction between conspiracy and critique, allowing a right-wing conspiracy huckster such as Glenn Beck to portray himself as the populist hero of the new millennium.

It seems strangely fitting that Beck's most reviled target is the Progressive era and its long outdated populism of a pre-postmodern era in which the muckraking media took as their targets the barons of the Gilded Age and the kingpins of the industrial era. A century later, during a period whose level of economic inequality has led some economists to liken it to the Gilded Age, Beck looms as a kind of parody of those he mocks: a critic of the critics of postmodern finance capital who apes the gestures of the investigative reporter, the prophet and the truth-seer – making up for the shoddy randomness of his "research" with the affective intensity of highly emotional performances that lurch abruptly from snarky and snotty to somber and tearful (and back again).[7] Beck positions himself much as the muckrakers did: a people's champion, one of the few willing to expose the entrenched forms of power that are corrupting the nation; but he does so from the opposite side: a champion of *laissez-faire* capitalism as the apotheosis of freedom, he lumps together any and all critics of unfettered capitalism (ranging from unions to religious leaders) as complicit with an overarching radical plan to subvert the nation. If commercial populism in the first decade of the 20th century aligned itself with the working class and the labor movement, its 21st-century reincarnation has made an about-face: for Beck, the labor unions are a mix of agitators forwarding the interests of the "shadow government" and their unwitting dupes. I draw on the example of Beck in order to argue that his brand of conspiracy is symptomatic of the collapse of critique into conspiracy theory associated with the demise of symbolic efficiency. The result is far from politically progressive or empowering – what once seemed critical has headed off in a reactionary direction that marks the reinforcement rather than the undermining of existing power relations.

Theorizing Conspiracy

Not all theories about conspiracy are conspiracy theories. Indeed, the term conspiracy theory is, in this respect, a misnomer – the various incompatible and at times incoherent understandings of the world it advances are not theories, in the conventional sense of the term, because they cannot be falsified. Consider an example that I have taken up elsewhere in the book: that of the "birthers" who believe that Barack Obama was not really born in the United States and is not really a US citizen but a covert foreign national and a Muslim infiltrator intent on fundamentally transforming the United States in accordance with his covert socialist/Islamist agenda. The key (missing) piece of evidence that confirmed this theory, according to birthers, was Obama's "long-form" birth certificate. The fact that he had produced a version of his birth certificate – one that had served as proof of identity for all government purposes for his entire adult life – did not sway them. They wanted to see his elusive "long-form" birth certificate, and the fact that he had not produced it proved to them that something suspicious was going on. However, when Obama finally *did* release the much talked about long-form birth certificate, shortly after real estate mogul and media personality Donald Trump announced that he had sent his own team of private investigators to Hawaii to research Obama's background (resulting in Trump's well-publicized, coyly provocative claim to the press that "they cannot believe what they are finding"), it made hardly a dent on the birther move-ment.[8] Longtime right-wing provocateur and propagandist Jerome Corsi announced that he was unfazed by the release of the birth certificate, even though he was about to release a book called *Where's the Birth Certificate: The Case That Barack Obama is not Eligible to be President*. Not only did Corsi stand behind the book, he took the release as good publicity for it: "Public pressure finally forced Obama to do what he did today. Now the game begins."[9] When could it ever end?

After clamoring for years for Obama to just release the long-form version of his birth certificate, claiming that it was the only piece of evidence that could be used to accurately judge whether the president was, indeed, a "natural-born" United States citizen (and therefore eligible to rule the nation), the "birthers" rapidly downgraded this evidence to the status of previously debunked proof – one more piece of deception alongside the official short-form certificate. The necessarily mediated character of the evidence had rendered it perpetually suspect.

This response defines conspiracy theory: even the most compelling forms of counter-evidence serve simply to illustrate the depth of the conspiracy and the power of the conspirators. In this regard, conspiracy theory is, as Mark Fenster puts it, "a machinic assemblage, devouring all that comes in its path, articulating all new, seemingly random, and often contradictory elements within the expansive framework of the conspiracy, doing so at remarkable speed and velocity across time as well as geographic and cognitive maps of meaning and power."[10] The fact that there were published announcements of Barack Obama's birth in Hawaiian newspapers, for example, serves only to illustrate how far back in time the tentacles of conspiracy can reach: either by creating fake articles (can anyone prove that the copies in the library are authentic?) or by tracing its roots to a well-thought-out, long-term plan to eventually place a recently born baby in the White House.

One of the symptoms of what I have been describing as the demise of symbolic efficiency – the erosion not just in the basis for belief in "grand narratives" and the truths to which they have recourse, but in the basis for adjudicating between competing and multiplying narratives – is the refusal to mark the distinction between theories of conspiracy and conspiracy theories. For example, in his discussion of conspiracy theory with author Mark Fenster, Jack Bratich highlights the apparent affinity between competing conspiracy-themed accounts of the causes of the 9/11 attacks: "the dominant account of 9/11 is considered by many in the 9/11 Truth Movement to itself be a conspiracy theory (small group of plotters, hidden in secret locations, making conscious decision to cause great harm, with world-historical consequences) ... So, the question becomes Nietzschean: 'which one?'"[11] Why not understand the dominant narrative, in other words, as itself a conspiracy theory since it seems to incorporate elements of conspiracy? Such an observation nudges even further in the direction of leveling the distinction between rival accounts: why accept the dominant conspiracy narrative (that a small group of people led by a terrorist mastermind in a cave on the other side of the planet conspired to bring down the World Trade Center to forward its political agenda) over the opposed conspiracy narrative (that a small group of people in Washington, DC, conspired to bring down the World Trade Center in order to justify its political agenda). The real question lurking here, of course, is why accede to accepted standards of evidence and deliberation, or, somewhat recursively, why not turn these against themselves?

This gesture pushes an acknowledgment of the entwinement of power and knowledge in the direction of a perhaps overly simplistic maxim: if dominant forms of knowledge are simply artifacts of power, then challenges to them have subversive tendencies and potentials. Anyone who has spent any time reviewing journal articles in the humanities in recent years has come to recognize the ready invocation of "subversion" as a taken-for-granted politically progressive goal. In an era in which there remain a few "dominant narratives" that still underwrite progressive commitments and concerns, the automatic equation of savvy debunkery with a kind of romanticized rebellion has been embraced by the far right for all too regressive purposes. It is this ready equation that leads Tea Partiers to imagine in some distorted way that they represent the legacy of the civil rights movement; it is what yields the ironic spectacle of an ultra-regressive right-wing politician such as Paul Ryan working out in the

Congressional gym with *Rage Against the Machine* playing on his iPod as he plots the dismantling of those "dominant narratives" that curtailed the excesses of big business and justified the creation of a social safety net.

This chapter pushes against the overly fast assimilation of conspiracy theory to critique, drawing on the example of Glenn Beck to argue that conspiracy theory is, in its structure and political import, far from subversive in any progressive sense of the term. Rather, it tends toward a political quietism tantamount to conservatism. Although I will be considering what amounts to conspiracy theories on the political right, much the same argument can be made about such theories on the left.

First, however, it is worth clarifying what we mean when we talk about conspiracy theory. Cass Sunstein and Adrian Vermeule propose an "intuitive" definition that strikes me as worse than useless: "*an effort to explain some event or practice by reference to the machinations of powerful people, who have also managed to conceal their role.*"[12] According to this definition, my students would certainly have been right to consider me a conspiracy theorist – along with anyone else who has any knowledge of history, replete as it is with examples of powerful actors attempting to conceal their influence on events or practices. Presumably a prosecutor accusing companies of price fixing, for example, would be a conspiracy theorist, as would anyone who imagines that world leaders do not disclose the ways in which they conspire to influence world events. The belief that conspiracies may actually exist does not make one a conspiracy theorist, but a realist.

But if simply positing a conspiracy is not enough, then what constitutes a "conspiracy theory" proper? Jodi Dean has noted that when it comes to identifying conspiracy theory, "some focus on its style, others on its preoccupation with plot, still others on its pathological motivations."[13] Conspiracy theories are accused of being irrational or overly detailed and systematic, of being "too complicated or too simple."[14] The plots they outline are either too all-encompassing or too fragmentary and incoherent and the theorists themselves are falsely relegated to the realm of "outsider" status – as if members of political and social elites do not also indulge in conspiracy. All of these critiques of conspiracy are useful insofar as they go, but for the purposes of this chapter, Dean's definition of conspiracy theory as an "information assemblage linking lines of power … and possibilities for agency … along the axis publicity/ secrecy" invites further clarification.[15]

The salient characteristics of conspiracy theory, as I understand the term, include the following: non-debunkability (non-falsifiability); the displacement of accounts of systemic or structural forms of conflict with tales of deliberate, intentional machinations (what might be described as the "subjectivization" of structure); and, finally, a populist tendency to "other" the alleged conspirators. In this regard, to relegate a theory to the realm of conspiracy is not simply to identify formal characteristics of the "theory" itself (that it posits a small group of covert conspirators, and so on), but also to posit something about the subject position of those who espouse it. The pathology of conspiracy theory lies not in the content of the theory, the form of subordinated, alternative, or even false "knowledge" to which it lays claim, but in the subjective investment that renders it, among other things, non-falsifiable. According to this formulation, even the truth content of a theory about conspiracy does not exempt it from entering into the realm of conspiracy theory proper.

We might imagine a world (not our own) in which the "birthers" turn out to be right: fighting valiantly against the scorn of the mainstream media and Obama's Islamo-socialist minions, they manage to reveal the disturbing truth that he really is a "Kenyan candidate," ineligible to rule the United States. If this could be proven it would be an example of a "subjugated" knowledge jumping leagues, as it were, in order to enter the realm of accepted mainstream narrative. Wouldn't this (hypothetical) outcome demonstrate that conspiracy theory has the potential to transition into the realm of proven fact? And wouldn't this, in turn, force us to approach any and all such theories as possibly true and thus as potentially destabilizing forms of critique? Transitioning from the realm of the highly hypothetical to that of history, we could point to similar instances in which accounts once dismissed as conspiracy theory were eventually accepted as fact: the claim that the second Gulf of Tonkin "incident" was a fake; the fact that the United States conducted human experiments in Guatemala in which people were deliberately infected with syphilis, and so on; the fact, in short, that governments and corporations have frequently and systematically attempted to cover up awful things that they have done either intentionally or accidentally. That claims once relegated to the realm of conspiracy have subsequently proven to be true, in other words, opens up the field of possibilities: how can we be sure that the same thing will not happen to allegations currently dismissed and denigrated as conspiracy. Shouldn't historical awareness prevent us from being too quick to accept mainstream dismissals of seemingly outlandish plots?

How, then, to meaningfully distinguish between conspiracy theory, on the one hand, and subjugated or suppressed knowledge, on the other, that has been deliberately discredited to protect vested interests? The truth content of a claim is probably not sufficient: a conspiracy theory can turn out to be true without absolving it of what might be described as the pathology of conspiracy. The fact that conspiracy theorists might have arrived, somehow, at the truth does not undo the ways in which their forms of theorizing reject – in spirit, if not in form – the evidence-based deliberation and standards of argumentation that might, in some cases, end up legitimating their claims. In this regard, the conspiracy theorist has something in common with the jealous husband invoked by Zizek: "Lacan's outrageous statement that even if what a [pathologically] jealous husband claims about his wife (that she sleeps around with other men) is all true, his jealousy is still pathological."[16] In other words, it represses the true reason the husband *needs* the fantasy of the cheating wife to "stitch up the inconsistency" in his own ideological edifice.[17]

Much the same might be said of the "birthers": even if it turned out that Obama were a foreign national working to subvert the US government from the inside, this would not diminish the pathology of their forms of theorizing – of the intense need to blame the instances of economic malaise and internal tension that permeate the experience of life in contemporary America on an implacable, racialized "other." In this regard, like the jealous husband, conspiracy theorists might conceivably turn out to be objectively "right" about particular facts (although obviously not in the case of the Keyan candidate), but still wrong (in their misdiagnosis of their subjective investment in their own conspiracies, and the ideological role played by their theories). In ideological terms, conspiracy theory does the work of projecting pathologies inherent to the system and enacted by those who operate within it upon the figure of the corrupting interloper, the "outside agitator," the secret cabal. In so doing, they paper over social contradictions and tensions with the promise that these would evaporate if only the nefarious interference could be eliminated. In the absence of the outside agitator – the implacable and inscrutable other – the system itself could run smoothly and in the best interests of all concerned (save the outside "others" who do not count). Structural conflicts and antagonisms would disappear because they do not really exist – they are simply the ideological ruses fomented by outsiders to divide an otherwise harmonious (once purified) whole. For the conspiracy theory-inclined portion of the populace, Barack Obama figures as the paradigmatic outsider responsible for fomenting class warfare, promulgating racial and class tensions where there really ought to be none.

The persistence of this fantasy in the face of relentlessly hostile facts goes hand-in-hand with the un-falsifiable character of conspiracy theory. The theory *must* be true – truer than the facts – if any engagement with the causes of social conflict and contradiction is to remain endlessly deferred. And this deferral, in turn, underwrites what Fenster describes as the productivity of conspiracy theory: "The history of twentieth-century conspiracy theories ... demonstrates that the interpretive practice does not in fact end but continues to engage in the search for more connections in the present and past ... The future, when the secret will be revealed, never arrives."[18] In this regard, as Jodi Dean observes, the logic of conspiracy theory fits neatly with that of the online information environment in which we are overwhelmed by a flood of information which suggests that our knowledge is always incomplete, that there perpetually remains a layer behind the scenes that eludes us: "These two ideas, that things are not as they seem and everything is connected, are primary components of how we think about and experience the information age. They are also the guiding impulses of conspiracy theory."[19]

To recap, the fact that a form of theorizing posits a conspiracy does not automatically make it a "conspiracy theory" – it is possible to assert the existence of a conspiracy in ways that are amenable to the forms of evidentiary claims and deliberation that render it debunkable. Moreover, the fact that conspiracy theorizing might turn out to be right does not mean that it is has cast off the mantle of "conspiracy theory." It is possible to be factually right, but still to partake of the logic of conspiracy theory that replicates the symptoms of the decline of symbolic efficiency. Glenn Beck repeatedly and gleefully pointed out on his show that he was right about the devaluation of the US dollar, but even if he had turned out to be completely wrong, this fact would not have had any impact upon his theories about the nefarious forces working to undermine the United States and end the "Western way of life" (and the fact that he was right about the devaluation of the dollar does not provide the vindication he imagines).

If, in some cultural studies circles, the mantra of the "active reader" or the "active viewer" tends to underwrite the notion that the content of a media text is for all practical purposes immaterial because it can be creatively reinterpreted (overtly sexist texts, for example, might be reinterpreted or reappropriated in "oppositional" and "empowering" ways), conspiracy theory represents the somewhat disconcerting triumph of the "active" reader. The facts themselves become immaterial because they can be interpreted in ways that fit the predilections of the interpreter – "reality," such as it is, provides little in the way of resistance (as Karl Rove suggested in his famously scornful dismissal of the "reality-based community"). Beck, in this regard, might be described as a postmodern populist. He is not particularly original in this regard: the disintegration of textual authority and the dismantling of Enlightenment-derived norms of rational-critical deliberation long predate Beck's ascent to the pinnacle of media success. But his approach comes into its own when these tendencies work their way out of various rarefied theoretical circles and – in somewhat altered form – into the mainstream.

The conservatism of conspiracy theories follows from their reliance on the demise of symbolic efficiency: their embrace of a generalized savvy skepticism according to which all representations are suspect, combined with a default to gut instinct that gives one the courage of one's preconceptions and prejudices. If the *power* of symbolic efficiency is to allow one to think beyond what one "sees with one's own eyes" (what we already think we directly know), its demise results in a kind of demobilizing hermeticism. We know what we know, but have a hard time finding ways of getting from our individual preconceptions to shared, social, collective understandings (these are, of course, implicitly dismissed by the individualization of meaning and the critique of "dependent" reasoning discussed in the previous chapter). Not only is it impossible to imagine that arguments might have some type of purchase on preconceptions (other than to confirm what people already "know"), but it seems equally difficult to use communication to break out of one's own individual horizon: one either connects with another in advance or discovers that other to be an outsider: someone who doesn't get it (who's not *in on* the conspiracy).

The dismantling of the purchase of representation explains why, as Fenster puts it, "the basic unit of investigation in the discursive practices of conspiracy is the individual who is distrustful of the collective."[20] In political terms, the result is that "imagining a collectivity based on conspiracy theory is virtually impossible."[21] Conspiracy theory is not necessarily conservative at the level of content – indeed, it is just as easy for a conspiracy theorist to target, say, the billionaire, right-wing Koch brothers as Barack Obama or the Trilateral Commission; but it is deeply conservative at the *formal* level, insofar as it discredits the grounds for collective political action while simultaneously positing the futility of change at the systemic level. Conspiracy theory may sound political, but its implications are politically demobilizing. As Fenster puts it, "conspiracy theory ultimately fails as a political and cultural practice."[22] Failure here refers to the ability to serve as the basis for social change – not the ability to generate publicity, sell t-shirts or books, or capture the cultural limelight, however fleetingly.

If one inhabits the perspective that embraces the notion that standards of rational deliberation and evidentiary logic are simply ruses of power – little more than outdated Enlightenment delusions – then much of the analysis here will have little purchase. This would be the perspective that asserts (somewhat incoherently) the truth of the demise of symbolic efficiency. However, it is difficult to push this position to its logical conclusion without foundering in a sea of paradoxes. As I shall argue in the conclusion, one of the ways to address the symptoms of the demise of symbolic efficiency is to discern in them the repressed horizon of truth they fail to transcend, despite their best efforts. If, once upon a time in the era of perceived information scarcity, the subversive gesture was to point out the ways in which seemingly settled claims about the world relied upon forms of closure that could be excavated and reopened, in the era of information glut, by contrast, the complementary (subversive?) gesture is to point out how even seemingly settled forms of relativism and "vernacular postmodernism" conserve a commitment to the notions of truth and reason they ostensibly undermine.

The Pastiche of Reason

The failure to work through these seeming contradictions results in a strange pastiche of deliberation: the persistence of what looks like reasoned discourse and evidentiary claims in the absence of any commitment to their substance. The formal adherence to the *appearance* of discussion and deliberation about an actually existing world no longer serves the interests of a debunked set of Enlightenment claims about evidence, rationality, and truth. Rather, it is retained for its affective charge: for the way it looks and comes across – for its performative power. Fenster invokes Lawrence Grossberg's notion of "mood politics" to describe the result: "scandal replaces debates, and emotional confessions become the dominant form of political self-definition … politics is relocated from the realm of social conditions to that of the affective and scandalous."[23]

Glenn Beck, whose rise to media prominence will be discussed in more detail in this and the following sections, is one of the master performance artists of "mood politics" and the pastiche of reason – and not just in his physical appearance, though his media persona invokes the well-worn stereotype of the tweedy, elbow-patched, bespectacled professor. This character is one of the multiple personae that populated Beck's one-man performance piece on Fox News, joining the ranks of the weepy televangelist, the sarcastic shock jock, and the aggrieved but unbowed messianic victim of the vast left-wing media con-spiracy. Often eschewing the high-tech graphics that have become the staple of cable news shows, Beck relied on antique-looking blackboards and the occasional pile of ponderous well-worn books as set props. He donned wire-rimmed spectacles and wandered the studio – sometimes with an unlit pipe – making it hard to determine whether he was engaged in a form of mockery or homage. Beck prides himself on being a self-taught visionary, but, at the same time, adopts a "who me?" attitude of humility, repeatedly qualifying his outrageous claims with a disarming "what-do-I-know" shrug and making a show of urging viewers not to trust him, but to go out and verify for themselves the accuracy of his pronouncements. He portrays himself, as the educational jargon puts it, not as the "sage on the stage," but as the simple "guide on the side" who can educate us in the Socratic sense by helping us to find the truth for ourselves.

It is a strange posture, given that anyone who attempts to verify Beck's most sensational claims can easily determine them to be not simply unverifiable but demonstrably false, including assertions (to name just a few) that the government could seize control of the computer of anyone who used its "cash for clunkers" Website; that Obama's director of science and technology policy supported forced abortions and imposed sterility to control population growth; that labor leader Andy Stern was the most frequent visitor to the Obama White House; and so on. Intriguingly, in his notorious week-long takedown of bil-lionaire financier George Soros, the alleged "puppet master" of the new world order, Beck assured viewers that everything he was telling them about Soros could be found in Soros's own writings: "It is right out in the open … do your own research, go to his own books."[24] At the same time, Beck portrays himself as the revealer of the big secret: the one person who can penetrate the carefully crafted public persona of George Soros to reveal him as the mastermind behind a devious plan to destroy capitalism (presumably from deep inside), dismantle the United States' power, and create a one-world government.

Beck claims that this secret project has been both publicized openly in Soros's own books and carefully concealed from a distracted and uninformed public: "What he's doing was never meant to be published [despite the fact that it is "all out in the open" in Soros's own books], but we're not playing your game."[25] The challenge of holding together these two thoughts – the hidden nature of the conspiracy, and the fact that it is all out there in the open to be seen by anyone who opens their eyes – is a recurring one in Beck's performances. The double logic recalls the savvy subject who uses the power of gut instinct to cut through the tangled web of discourse: the truth is hidden in plain sight – available to be grasped by anyone who can avoid the misleading cues of representation in order to rely on what one already knows to be true, regardless of the facts. This might be described as the conspiracy theorists' version of "thinking without thought" – or, in homage to George W. Bush, one of its most prominent and prolific practitioners – a gut instinct that can directly see truths that are only available to the initiated (the true nature of Putin's soul, etc.).

Once you cross over to the place where these truths can be seen, the conspiracy becomes obvious (more or less): Soros, who bent the capitalist system to his own ends in order to enrich himself through currency arbitrage and hedge funds ("is it a coincidence that everything under the sun is targeted for regulation by Congress. Except for hedge funds?"[26]), is bent on destroying the capitalist system along with a crew of unlikely bedfellows (including "Radicals, Islamists, communists and socialists"[27]) in order to impose a new world order that will either take the form of a caliphate or global communism. The script is not entirely clear on the endgame: at times Beck suggests that the final goal of the revolutionaries is an Islamist caliphate ("I believe the communists are being used quite frankly" he says – presumably by the Islamists), at other times the apparent goal is a New World Order presided over by George Soros and his minions.[28] The result is a free-verse mash-up of dystopian anxieties: "Ok. There is a world view – that has been allowed to fester and it is anything other than a republic. There is an open society and look how many people are swarming around in an open society with George Soros. There is the United Nations. And there are so many people in the United Nations. There's a caliphate. There's communism. They all want global domination."[29]

On the one hand, as Fenster puts it, the conspiracy is all-encompassing, "devouring all that comes in its path, articulating new, seemingly random, and often contradictory elements within the expansive framework of the conspiracy, doing so at remarkable speed and velocity across time as well as geographic and cognitive maps of meaning and power."[30] On the other, it remains impressionistic and highly variable, riven with contradictions (the arch-capitalist wants to destroy capitalism ... the Islamists are making common cause with the communists *and* the arch-capitalist). Perhaps the most challenging task is to make *everything* fit. Suggestively – and reflexively – one of the ways in which Beck achieves this is by highlighting and sarcastically mocking the critique of the "patterns" he unearths. Rather than saying everything fits, in other words, he suggests that the very fact that mainstream politicians and pundits feel the need to forcefully deny the conspiracies he weaves proves they are real – that he must be on to something.

For someone who is not already tuned into Beck's wavelength, the presentation style can be a disconcerting mix of innuendo, seemingly random association, and sarcasm, with only sporadic (and impressionistic) bursts of actual explanation. Here, for example, is Beck explaining how US Middle East policy is part of a larger (secret) pattern designed to overthrow the Western way of life: "Now, our president encouraged the youth to rise up in revolt all across the Middle East ... yet he did nothing to help the Iranian people with their revolt against Mahmoud Ahmadinejdad. Then the president went into Libya to 'help and protect' because [Samantha] Power said, 'we've got to do it.' Yes. And then they even armed the rebels with ties to al Qaeda and some with ties to GITMO who were directly fighting against our troops in Iraq or Afghanistan. And he's also backing the extremist Muslim president in the Ivory Coast who last weekend had 1,000 people killed."[31]

Within this creative interpretation of an apparently inconsistent and at times self-defeating policy, Beck discerns a pattern – or at least he mocks those who do not: "So, I just find this interesting – [sarcastically] those are just all noticeable events that are all completely disconnected and unrelated and have nothing to do with anything else in the world. Just a noticeable moment that as we've launched a third war against a Muslim nation, further inflaming the radicals, the president has decided it's OK to try the Muslims at GITMO, something that he said we couldn't do because it would inflame the Islamic world. But don't worry, none of those things are connected ... ."[32] The alternatively self-deprecating and viciously mocking approach relieves Beck of the burden of providing a coherent narrative account: everyone knows that narratives are always partial anyway. The result is something a bit different from Fredric Jameson's description of conspiracy theory as "the poor person's cognitive mapping in the postmodern age ... a degraded figure of the total logic of late capitalism."[33] It is perhaps more accurately the poor person's *affective* mapping of this logic: not so much a description that attempts to make sense of an underlying reality, but a feeling tone that links up with the fears and anxieties of the audience.

The aggressively non-cognitive aspect of the web of affects he weaves got Beck into trouble the one time he tried to quiz his viewers on what they learned from watching his show. They respond to his emotional display – the affective symphony of hate, fear, anger, resentment, snark, and sentimentality he orchestrates – but he nonetheless imagines they are making sense of his impassioned ramblings. So he seems slightly taken aback when they are unable to replicate the logic of his theories when he tries to get them, like good students, to repeat back to him his conspiracy catechism, starting with his antipathy toward Obama advisor Samantha Power (wife of Beck's imagined nemesis, the legal scholar Cass Sunstein):

Beck: Sam Power ... why is she ... why is she scary?
[Audience member] Josephine: She has Obama's ear, she's right next to him.

Beck: She's next to him. And what is she encouraging him to do. What was her big policy?

[Audience member] Barbara: She is a big threat. She is a big threat against Israel.

Beck: OK, why?

Barbara: She's pushing ... I can't ... .

Beck: "The responsibility to protect" [one of his bugbears] ... OK, what is that? Anybody know? See, this is why it's so hard. You guys are an informed group of people.

Male audience member: I got it like halfway.[34]

It is not easy to reconstruct Beck's worldview in narrative terms; he does not operate in the mode of shared logic or evidentiary appeal, but in the register of affective modulation. What sets him apart from fellow right-wing outrage-jocks such as Rush Limbaugh, Bill O'Reilly, and Sean Hannity is not just his messianic zeal, his desire to be a latter-day radio prophet – not simply a ratings magnet, but the founder of a movement – but also his highly emotionally labile performance, his revivalist preacher's ability to swerve from sarcasm to outrage to tears. As Alexander Zaitchik puts it in his critical profile of Beck:

> If people know one thing about Glenn Beck, it is that he cries. He is the Crying Conservative. Alone among cable news and talk-radio personalities, he frequently chokes up, quivers his lips, wipes his eye and holds tortured misty pauses until he can hold them no more. For more than a decade, Beck has been crying on the radio, on television, on stage, in interviews, and even in scripted commercials.[35]

Pat Gray, Beck's onetime morning-radio partner, provided a gendered analysis of his emotional performances in a public endorsement at one of Beck's public rallies: "He's the same person you know and love ... He's honest, caring, open, sensitive. I used to wonder if Glenn was a woman. I tell people there are two women in my life: my wife and Glenn."[36]

This framing of Beck's presentation style portrays his emotionally charged performances not simply as a marker of authenticity, but as the avenue whereby he connects with his audiences. As with the heart of Bush and the soul of Putin, the sincerity of Beck is visceral – a matter of gut instinct rather than the ability to unravel the tangled web of conspiracy he weaves. In this regard, it is worth recalling the words of Bush's senior advisor responding to *New York Times* reporter Ron Susskind about how reporters view Bush:

> You think he's an idiot, don't you ... all of you do, up and down the West Coast, the East Coast ... Let me clue you in. We don't care.

You see, you're outnumbered 2 to 1 by folks in the big, wide middle of America, busy working people who don't read *The New York Times* or *Washington Post* or The *L.A. Times*. And you know what they like? They like the way he walks and the way he points, the way he exudes confidence.[37]

It is tempting to say something similar about Beck to academics and other left/ liberal types: "You think he's an idiot, don't you? With his rambling, allusive, style, his factual errors, his manufactured outrage, and his implied slurs. But there's a whole world of viewers out there who like the way he smirks and rants and whines. They like his fear and his outrage, his indignation and his wacky combination of hubris and humility. They don't need to understand him, they *feel* him." As Beck put it one afternoon on his Fox show, "I want you to know this is an opinion show … I only have my gut and my opinion on this, but I believe I should tell you my opinion."[38]

The characterization of Beck as the "crying conservative" is calculated to emphasize his emotional sensitivity and his intuitive side. The gendered comparison is, in this regard, not coincidental. The disturbing result is that he partakes of the right-wing appropriation of the postmodern critique of the relationship between patriarchy and reason. The invocation of Beck's "feminine" side recalls the rise of female right-wing figureheads on the far right, including political figures such as Sarah Palin, Michele Bachmann, Betsy McCaughey, and Christine O'Donnell and pundits such as Michele Malkin, Ann Coulter, Laura Ingraham, and Megyn Kelly. The increasing visibility of such figures represents a significant shift from the male-dominated public image of the political right (prefigured, perhaps, by Phyllis Schlafly and Anita Bryant, but without the foreground emphasis on the "women's place is in the home" backlash of the 1970s). Interestingly, such figures are also at the forefront of the postmodern/"Tea Party" right, its split with the patrician, intellectual conservatism of the George Wills and William F. Buckleys, its scorn for the "lamestream" media and its embrace of the power of gut feeling in the face of the facts. Sarah Palin is, of course, famous for her death panel meme (which amplified false charges popularized by both McCaughey and Ingraham): her false claim that Obama's healthcare plan would create panels of bureaucrats to decide which Americans were worthy of receiving medical treatment based on their "level of productivity in society."[39] Michele Bachmann is a full-bore conspiracy theorist whose most recent diatribes are focused on the claim that the Muslim Brotherhood has infiltrated the US government. All of these conspiracy theories are rehashed by right-wing commentators both male and female, but figures such as Palin and Bachmann take the lead as darlings of Tea Party movement. The result is a kind of post-feminist populism that avails itself of the co-optation (and oversimplification) of the feminist critique of the gendered character of Enlightenment norms of rationality and deliberation. The emphasis upon Beck's sensitivity and intuition, his gut-level knowledge, his ability to *relate* rather than to explain (or to explain *by* relating), aligns him with this version of faux-feminist populism.

If, in other words, as Jung puts it, in modernity, "privileging and valorizing the autonomy and authority of reason" wound up excluding and suppressing "(reason's) Other, whether it be body, woman, nature, or Orient,"[40] the post-modern right takes the critique to its illogical extreme by simply, and simplisti-cally, dispensing with the "authority of reason" altogether. Against the background of the critique of the gendered character of Enlightenment ration-ality, reason's "Other" can be figured as subversive and empowering insofar as it challenges reason's autonomy and authority. This, of course, is an ersatz form of the critique mobilized by feminism and other critics of the gendered character of Enlightenment rationality – its implicit appropriation for strategic political purposes: namely, a dismissal not simply of the "elitist" experts and the forms of evidence-based deliberation that supposedly underpin their claims, but also of their allegedly arrogant challenge to the commonsense understandings of the people.

The challenge faced by Beck is to portray himself simultaneously as a genius and a man of the people – a giant amongst the non-elites – which explains his constant refrain of "hey, what do I know," offered up both as a sign of humility and as a sarcastic rejoinder to those who just don't get it. Beck summed up this approach in the final episode of his show on Fox News – his departure from his television show (but not from radio, the bestseller list, or the Internet): "I'm no smarter than you," he humbly reminded his audience – even though he presumably "gets it" at a gut level better than anyone else.[41] The accompanying admonition is not to trust anything he says, but to go out and verify it for yourself.

Perhaps he is so confident in offering up the familiar challenge to viewers not to simply trust him, but to do the work to find out for themselves because, in the end, he understands that the gut feelings he caters to are unde-bunkable, even if the facts are not. If, for example, climate scientists, in Beck's world, are driven by some combination of resentment toward the free enterprise system born of their own pseudo-socialist commitments and an instrumental desire to fan the flames of anxiety in order to free up more research money, there is no point in even trying to make sense of their arguments. If there is no need to trust the alleged experts, then we are absolved of the responsibility of trying to understand what they might be saying and are thrown back upon our commonsense resources, our pre-conceptions and our predispositions. Consider, for example, Beck's exchange with right-wing Senator Rick Santorum on the topic of the global warming "hoax":

Beck: What about global warming?

Santorum: There is no such thing as global warming. It is, in my opinion, you have hundreds of factors that cause the earth to warm and cool and a trace gas of which human participation in this trace gas is –
Beck: Seals the deal for me. Does it seal the deal for – whatever, whatever, I got enough.[42]

This is not even a rebuttal – it is, rather, a near total (and totally incoherent) retreat from the frontier of argument back to the secure homestead of one's preconceptions. The pastiche of argument echoes Beck's parody of the professor, which does the double duty of invoking the figure of the subject who has "done the detailed research" – presumably by poring over the dusty tomes occasionally stacked up beside him – and mocking the elitist pretensions of any such figure.

Precursors?

The somewhat disorienting combination of parodic irony, snide sarcasm, professed bewilderment, and tears sets Beck apart from some of the precursors who have been assigned to him by his critics, perhaps most notably the figure of Father Charles Coughlin, the populist demagogue who created a hate- and fear-based media empire in the 1930s, and at times sympathetically portrayed Nazism as an understandable response to Communism, which he described as the result of a Jewish conspiracy. But listening to Father Coughlin recalls a very different era – pre-ironic and pre-information glut: yes, there is emotional manipulation, but it takes place in the form of sonorous tones and serious-sounding explanation. Coughlin traded on the authority of his elegant voice and turn of phrase to elaborate clearly articulated, if false and misleading accounts. He operated in the register of pre-postmodern propaganda, and he never, ever cried on air. His rhetoric still retained traces of the concern about capitalism mobilized by the muckraking critiques of the early 20th century – including his support for greater economic equality – and he was, early on, a supporter of the New Deal. Beck's version of conservative populism, by contrast, incorporates the Christian right's embrace of the unfettered free market, regressive taxation, and the wholesale dismantling of the social safety net. Its villains are those who would seek to smooth the brutally rough edges of capitalism and thereby, as he puts it, end the "Western way of life" as we know it.

The Other of the Other

Beck's version of populism illustrates the philosopher Slavoj Zizek's description of its defining attribute: "In populism, the enemy is externalized or reified into a positive ontological entity (even if this entity is spectral) whose annihilation would restore balance and justice."[43] If one of the targets of the progressive reformers and the muckrakers was unregulated capitalism (and its depredations), for Beck the system itself is not at fault – and therefore there is no need of reform. In this respect, the logic of populism and that of conspiracy theory overlap: they both displace any diagnosis of structural or systemic problems with the assertion of a shadowy presence wreaking havoc from behind the scenes. Thus, for Beck, the apparent crises of capitalism, including the sub-prime lending scandal, are the result of the machinations of agents of the Islamo-Anarcho-Communist, One World Government cabal. As he put it, referring to a speculative report by a Pentagon sub-contractor, "terrorists and other financial enemies were likely responsible for the U.S. financial collapse in 2008."[44] The "good news" is that there's no need to re-regulate the banking sector or to rein in the rampant short-termism that characterized the speculative boom of the new millennium. The somewhat more disturbing news is that an external enemy has managed to infiltrate the system and turn it to their own ends. As Zizek observes, "for a populist, the cause of the troubles is ultimately never the system as such but the intruder who corrupted it ... not a fatal flaw inscribed into the structure as such."[45] He also provides an inadvertently apt description of the role played by George Soros in Beck's fervid theories as the concrete embodiment of the shadowy and imprecise figure of the conspiratorial cabal: "In populism proper, however, this 'abstract' character is always supplemented by the pseudo-concreteness of the figure that is selected as the enemy, the singular agent behind all threats to the people."[46]

The intersection of conspiracy theory with populism suggests an explanation for Jodi Dean's observation that conspiracy theory "seems to be enjoying a particularly strong popularity today."[47] Structural forms of critique – those that focus on social, economic, and political systems in order to transform or replace them – are reliant on two conditions: first, the ability to construct a shared understanding of the targeted formation as a system; and, second, the ability to envision an alternative system (and the collectivity that might bring it into being). This book discerns a failure on both of these levels. One of the characteristic pathologies of an era of information glut explored in previous chapters is the lack of any effective argumentative purchase of symbolic representations of our shared social world. It is this lack that worries Cass Sunstein in his account of the demise of general interest intermediaries: how do people act upon their shared social world if they have no shared vision of it? One possible answer might be overlapping consensus: that they can agree on a shared course of action for a variety of different, probably contradictory, reasons. But even such action requires some sense of closure on the part of those involved: the belief that they have gained a sufficiently clear picture of their world to act upon it. However, both conspiracy theory and the savvy reflexive attitude symptomatic of the decline of symbolic efficiency render this basis for action problematic. Conspiracy theory is not about action – it is about the endless project of interpretation and the imagined power of the conspiracy to fold even resistance into itself. The paradox of conspiracy theory is that it is both totalizing and indefinite. Perhaps most tellingly it captures the sense of paranoia and alienation associated with the hermetic version of the subject that emerges in the wake of the decline of symbolic efficiency. When the other's words are always suspect, when language is stripped of its deliberative purchase, we are left somewhat helplessly stranded within the horizon of our own unchangeable preconceptions. As Jodi Dean, invoking the work of Slavoj Zizek, puts it, the demise of the guarantee of symbolic efficiency – a guarantee necessary to give language its effective power, "might suggest a new setting of complete openness and freedom," but the actual result is "unbearable, suffocating closure."[48]

As for the second condition for political action – the ability to envision an alternative social structure – conspiracy theory fits neatly with the post-Cold War triumph of global capitalism. One of the features of a familiar, superficial, and popularized post-structuralist criticism is the promulgation of a taboo on totalization (that can, in the wrong hands, have the paradoxical effect of enacting what it sought to avoid). In practice, the political failure to imagine an alternative to capitalism leads to a similar result: henceforth all forms of social change must take place within the unsurpassable horizon of capital. The eclipse of the possibility of systemic change lends itself to forms of critique that eschew an analysis of social structure in order to focus on the ghostly conspiracy that haunts the machine. We needn't worry about being stuck within the horizon of capitalism if we know that the system itself is not the problem: everything would work just fine if we could only free the system from the clutches of George Soros and his Islamic/anarchist/communist minions. In this respect, conspiracy theory is post-political and populist in the sense outlined by Zizek:

> … populism is emerging as the inherent shadowy double of institution-alized postpolitics … Its basic gesture is to refuse to confront the complexity of the situation, to reduce it to a clear struggle with a pseudoconcrete enemy figure … Populism is thus by definition a negative phenomenon, a phenomenon grounded in a refusal, even an implicit admission of impotence.[49]

In the conspiratorial form it takes in Beck's version of critique, populism is profoundly conservative both in theory (because it rules out any attempt to address systemic issues) and in practice (because it undermines the basis for shared, collective, political action). As Fenster puts it, from the perspective of the conspiracy theorist, the political route is foreclosed not simply because it is always already captured by the conspirators, but because of the challenges posed to shared action by the ideology of conspiracy (which renders all collectivities and any possible ally suspect): "Nor is political engagement considered to be a possible realm of activity; it has been abandoned as a site of endemic disappointment."[50]

In this regard, conspiracy theory, despite its infinite productivity, remains a failure of the imagination that corresponds to the inability to think, in the current instance, outside the horizon of capitalism. To put it somewhat differently, if capitalism is taken as an unsurpassable social given in the form of the naturally ideal social order, and if, in practice, it fails to live up to its promise, then this failure must be the result of sabotage by powerful forces external to the system that have managed to infiltrate it. Thus, it turns out that the true foe of the Western way of life is the *uber*-capitalist (but ultimately still foreign) figure of George Soros; that the US president is actually a Kenyan nationalist; that top aides to political insiders are covert Islamists working to impose Sharia law on the nation; and so on. Such contortions are a form of sense-making, paradoxically enough, in a context in which the possibility of thinking the structural contradictions and pathologies of capitalism is foreclosed. In the terms that this book has been developing, the deadlock of representation doesn't simply foreclose the purchase of shared social representations, it simultaneously frees up the field for the proliferation of imagined narratives and counter-narratives. The result is a kind of bestiary of the imaginary: a familiarly disturbing world in which claims once relegated to the political margins start to mingle with those once considered serious and credible. It is a world populated by death panels, in which providing healthcare and welfare is one step away from the Nazi death camp, in which foes of abortion claim that women's bodies naturally protect them from being impregnated by rape, in which centrist Democrats are pursuing a covert agenda of euthanasia and eugenics. Once upon a time, the thorough debunking of all dominant narratives would have been taken as a form of liberation – doesn't it free up the field, after all, for "subjugated" knowledges? The answer is yes, but only at the cost of their efficacy. In a world in which the shifting strands of discourse lose their purchase, the two-way relationship between power and knowledge is, in a sense, severed.

Correlational Thought

If Beck is a specialist in the art of choosing his gut instincts over the potentially deceptive words of others – especially those of the academic "elites," researchers, historians, and scientists dismissed with a knowing aside – he also operates, unsurprisingly, at the level of pure correlation: unearthing patterns largely divorced from any connection to underlying meaning or surrounding context and attaching profound significance to them. The results come across as a kind of parody of the notion that unstructured data can generate useful connections. It is almost as if Beck is embracing the dis-embedded post-referential logic described by Chris Anderson in his discussion of the big data era – except Beck is no super-computer, and the data he processes is far from "big" – rather, it tends to be limited, selective, and skewed. The results of his scattered "research" come across as borderline nonsensical – like a parody of pattern-based reasoning. Put somewhat differently, they partake of the kind of logic that emerges when meaning no longer matters. Consider, for example, Beck's description of the link between George Soros and Osama bin Laden: "So let's see if we have this right: Israel and the U.S. are an obstacle to what he [Soros] and his groups believe should happen. Huh! You know who else thinks that? Osama bin Laden. And, oh, I know, how about, like Iran."[51] And there you have it, a kind of nonsensical chain of equivalence: Soros is, in his intentions, complicit with Osama bin Laden, and let's throw Iran in there, too, since they all fall within the embrace of the master category of evil. Of course, Beck does not say outright Soros is a Nazi (Soros is a Hungarian Jew who had to take on a fake identity while his family went into hiding during the Nazi occupation) – he merely makes a chain of equivalence in his, "I'm-just-sayin' … " mode.

When it comes to Soros, the fact that he made a fortune by betting on the devaluation of the British pound and that he backed pro-democracy movements in Eastern Europe are strung together as proof of a pattern of sub-verting nation states in order to destroy the "Western way of life." Of course, currency arbitrage is a prime example of the capitalist way of life Soros is ostensibly out to destroy – and the opposition movements he supported in Central and Eastern Europe were pro-democracy groups challenging authoritarian regimes. None of this matters at all to Beck – it remains entirely absent from his discussions of Soros – who was the topic of a multi-day exposé on Beck's Fox News show that described the financier as "The Puppet Master." As in the case of the marketing patterns described in previous chapters, the goal of Beck's exposé was not so much to understand as to unearth correlations. Beck does not care to understand the story behind the correlations; rather, he treats dis-embedded anecdotes, observations, and out-of-context facts as so many dots to be connected in order to trace nonsense pictures designed to inspire fear and anxiety.

This is what might be described as post-referential, correlational, (pseudo-) thinking – but without, of course, the statistical basis that such thinking draws upon in the context of data mining and predictive analytics. Such post-referential incantations assume either a basic lack of contextual knowledge on the part of the audience, or, perhaps more likely, a willingness to consider any such knowledge irrelevant in the face of a truth that goes much deeper than any actual facts can reach. In an era in which contexts and histories are considered to be not just incomplete but indeterminate, their content is functionally irrelevant. What matters is not the referential accuracy of Beck's implications, but their ability to tap into and reinforce existing preconceptions, prejudices, and anxieties. This is why it is difficult for even the most hardcore of Beck's fans to replicate his "arguments" – they are simply strings of correlations that carry an affective charge. The ability to reverse engineer, to assess the evidence, to craft an argument – these are, in Beck-world, the tools of a kind of elitist obscurantism: an attempt to suppress one's visceral commonsense reactions. The tone is captured by the parody news show *The Daily Show*, which included the following exchange with conservative talk radio host Wayne Allyn Root about his allegations that President Barak Obama is a socialist:

> Interviewer: Do you have proof?
> Root: Listen, I can only guess, but I'm watching it every day.
> Interviewer: So you can kind of feel it.
> Root: Yeah, it's a feel, there's no physical proof.
> Interviewer: In today's day and age, having no proof is good enough for me.[52]

Post-Enlightenment Legacies

In tracing the relationship between knowledge and power, Michel Foucault characterized critique as "the movement by which a subject gives himself the right to question truth on its effects of power and question power on its discourses of truth."[53] It is a formulation that assumes linkages that are, however, called into question by the apparent demise of symbolic efficiency. In particular, this formulation posits a constitutive and potentially constructive relationship between truth and power. In this regard, as Judith Butler notes, Foucault's work exhibits a certain continuity with the aims of the Enlightenment, both in content and, arguably, in approach.[54] There is, in Foucault, the evidence-based argumentation of the happy positivist – the conserved understanding that it is possible, with enough evidence, to intervene in the functioning of established truths and the power that promulgates them. As Butler puts it, "The categories by which social life are ordered produce a certain incoherence or entire realms of unspeakability. And it is from this condition … that the practice of critique emerges."[55] Nevertheless, the critical apparatus invoked in this formulation depends upon the argumentative purchase of such evidentiary claims – even if these are, in a sense, reflexive: knowledge claims about the nature of knowledge claims. To trace the constitution of a particular way of knowing, the critic is compelled to rely upon a conserved and shared symbolic efficacy. The whole critical apparatus breaks down when this once-removed horizon (for the excavation of horizons of knowledge) dissipates.

Put in slightly different terms that will be taken up in more detail in the following chapter, there is a not yet recognized or acknowledged impossibility to the demise of symbolic efficiency. In the current pre-recognitive era (prior to realizing the impossibility of completing this decline altogether), strange and futile miscommunications come to characterize realms of public discourse, critique collapses into conspiracy, and Glenn Beck wins a $100-million a year payday. One of the most obvious disconnects is between those who continue to operate in what might be described as the realm of symbolic efficiency and thus who have shrugged it off: on the one hand, scientists assembling their evidence of global warming and fact-checkers picking through the tapestries of correlation woven by Glenn Beck; on the other, the gut-check thinkers without thought.

8

CUTTING THROUGH THE GLUT

Knowledge Small Enough to Know

Fact-Checking the Fact-Checkers

Perhaps the most memorable line of the 2012 Presidential election in the United States was uttered by a pollster for Mitt Romney's campaign, summing up the attitude of the consummate insider in a post-referential era: "We're not going to let our campaign be dictated by fact-checkers."[1] A telling argumentative abyss opened up around the comment as various commentators and pundits attempted to fact-check the role of fact-checking in journalism, political and otherwise. A columnist for the right-wing editorial page of Rupert Murdoch's *Wall Street Journal* described the newfound affection for fact-checking as further evidence that "The political season brings out the worst in many."[2] However pure the intentions of fact-checkers may once have been – and the column cast more than a few shades of doubt on this purity – the author claims that fact-checking "has morphed into a technique for supposedly nonpartisan journalists to present opinion as 'facts.'"[3] The column went on to quote another pundit's observation that "Fact checkers often don't know what they're talking about" – a double-edged claim when wielded by a fact-check checker.[4] The "bad infinity" that opens up under such claims is, perhaps, the desired result of a column like the one that appeared in the *Wall Street Journal*. With one hand, the column seems to gesture in the direction of a kind of rehabilitation of symbolic efficiency: the reality principle is preserved even as the facts themselves are subject to perpetual challenge. But with the other, the author performs a disconcerting bit of sleight-of-hand to make this principle itself disappear: if the checkers of the fact-checkers need to be checked, then, of course, it's nothing but fact-checkers all the way down. Reality recedes infinitely toward the horizon, always one step ahead of the checkers.

The psychoanalytic relationship between desire and drive, as described by Jodi Dean (following the work of Zizek and Lacan) is invoked by this infinite recession. Desire, according to her account, is about constant pursuit and disillusion – the endless attempt to catch an ever elusive object. With each gesture of capture, the obtained object is revealed not to be *it* – the true object of desire – and the chase begins anew. By contrast, the logic of drive reflexivizes the process, conceding the impossibility of ever catching up with the infinitely deferred object, although "conceding" isn't the right term – enjoying or "getting off on" this impossibility might be a better way to put it: "Drive circulates, round and round, producing satisfaction even as it misses its aim, even as it emerges in the plastic network of the decline of symbolic efficiency."[5] There is a self-satisfied gesture of the "non-duped" in this reflexive recognition – a certain glee in "getting" what the dupes do not. But there is also something altogether too facile about this recognition insofar as it imagines in its reflexive wisdom that it has captured a bit of truth about truth – in this regard, it is not quite reflexive enough. As Alenka Zupancic puts it, "If we simply keep repeating that all our knowledge is subjectively mediated and necessarily partial, we have said nothing of importance."[6]

Echoes of the perverse enjoyment of the drive resonate in the right-wing embrace of what the comedian Stephen Colbert famously dubbed "truthiness" (a "zeitgeisty" term, according to the *New York Times*): a cynical and ultimately conservative realism that concedes the demise of symbolic efficiency while continuing to rely upon it.[7] Consider the example of a vexed exchange about the details of Obama's health care plan between CNN anchor Soledad O'Brien and Republican mouthpiece John Sununu during the 2012 US Presidential campaign:

> O'Brien: I'm telling you what factcheck.com [sic] tells you, I'm telling you what the CBO says, I'm telling you what CNN's independent analysis says ... There is independent analysis that details what this is about ....
>
> Sununu: No there isn't!
>
> O'Brien: Yes there is!
>
> Sununu: [shouting] No, there's Democratic analysis ... there's Democratic analysis![8]

The very attempt to appeal to a notion of independent analysis or objective fact is aggressively (and somewhat gleefully) debunked. On its face, this dynamic might seem an instance of the logic of desire: the ongoing attempt to capture an infinitely receding piece of the real – as if a more accurate, better constructed analysis might reveal the true impact of policy in question. However, such a formulation doesn't capture Sununu's position, which is not "you need better analysis," but the post-reality-based community assertion that "*your* analysis can never catch up with *my* (affective) facts." The assertion is a self-undermining gesture for pundits and commentators insofar as it highlights the futility of analysis altogether (at least insofar as its purported goal of clarification and explication is concerned), and yet the endless loops of analysis proliferate on 25-hour cable news, blogs, and Websites. To point out, as one systematic study did,[9] that a coin-flip is more accurate than the predictions of expert commentators and analysts is to miss the point: in a post-deferential era, analysis is simply more "word clouds": "elements that reinforce the collapse of meaning and argument and thus hinder argument and opposition."[10]

The fact-checking cottage industry is a legacy of the journalism of the 1980s and 1990s, which replaced an ostensibly outdated commitment to "objectivity" with the convention of balance – a convention that was so badly abused by skilled public relations strategies and spokespeople that some news outlets felt compelled to revive the notion of objectivity as a separate division, like the *Tampa Bay Times*'s Politifact.com, to which reporters could have recourse as one more "source." This kind of sock puppetry along with the occasional willingness of a mainstream media outlet to identify a politician's blatant lie has been greeted in some circles as a welcome exercise in "shucking the old he-said-she-said formulation and directly declaring that some claims are false."[11] But the damage might run too deep for the occasional invocation of a truth claim to heal. As the *Atlantic* put it in a hand-wringing piece on the fate of political campaigning triggered by a misleading ad run by the Romney campaign: "But what if it turns out that when the press calls a lie a lie, nobody cares? The bottom line, of course, is that the ad is continuing to run. It is continuing to run because the Romney campaign's polling shows it to be effective."[12]

This is a familiar claim in the context of post-referential tactics that privilege an instrumental pragmatism over representation and understanding. In this instance, the effectiveness of the ad is contingent upon its imagined reception by an audience that has decided not just to consume information that reinforces its preconceptions, but one that has adopted a worldview in which the attempt to capture and ground facts in something other than a Web of bias and partiality is fruitless. Similarly, the post-reality-based world envisioned by Karl Rove has not given ground in the face of the "facts" that seemed to discredit it (that no weapons of mass destruction were found in Iraq, that the deregulated market imploded, that cutting taxes on the wealthy failed to boost government revenues, and on and on).

By the time of the 2012 Presidential election, the postmodern right had adopted a set of new strategies to challenge those "realities" that did not accord with its worldview. For example, when President Barack Obama continued to increase his lead over rival Mitt Romney shortly before the election, poll "truthers" started to insist that the mainstream polls oversampled Democrats. As right-wing talk show host Rush Limbaugh put it, "I think they're trying to get this election finished and in the can by suppressing your vote and depressing you so that you just don't think there's any reason to vote, that it's hopeless."[13] Shortly afterward, when the non-partisan Bureau of Labor Statistics announced that the economy had added enough jobs to lower the unemployment rate, right-wingers claimed the numbers were rigged. Former General Electric CEO Jack Welch expressed his disbelief on Twitter: "Unbelievable jobs numbers ... these Chicago guys will do anything ... Can't debate so change numbers."[14] *The Atlantic* characterized the advent of the jobs-report truthers as a "bleak demonstration of a post-truth politics in which people steadfastly refuse to believe the facts."[15]

There is nothing particularly new about people dismissing evidence that does not accord with their commitments and beliefs – or finding ways of rationalizing and explaining the discrepancy through recourse to the very logics they have discredited. However, this book makes the broader case that such practices are mainstreamed in the form of a savvy critique of representation associated with a reflexive culture of information abundance. The previous chapters have explored the interlocking relationship between the advent of information "glut," the demise of symbolic efficiency, and a renewed focus on the role of affect and emotion as alternative modalities for thinking about the role of communication in a post-referential era. The emergence of techniques for detecting sentiment, for "directly" accessing emotional intensities, and for predicting rather than comprehending directly addresses what Jodi Dean has described as the displacement of content by affective intensity – the emergence of "representation without understanding."[16] It is the combination of these developments and their relationship to one another that this book approaches as a unique contemporary formation: the way in which a reflexive awareness of the partiality of narrative accounts coincides with their mediated proliferation and the development of technologies and strategies that directly address this combination. The preceding chapters attempt to think together the marketing industry's "turn to affect," the popularization of a facile (and conservative) debunking of symbolic efficiency, and the computer-inspired drive to process data independently of the attempt to understand it.

However, it is important to acknowledge that the trappings of comprehension and narrative explication have not fallen by the wayside. The reality-based community persists in various guises, including the parody version explored in the previous chapter. Glenn Beck serves as an example of a figure engaged in a communication practice that amounts to a post-narratival communication of affective intensities in which questions of referentiality and comprehension are relegated to the background. The show's invitation is not to understand what Beck is saying or to reproduce his logic – when pressed, even his most avid followers find it difficult to reconstruct his arguments – but to "get" where he's coming from intuitively, to feel alongside him the range of emotional intensities he traverses during the course of his show. By the same token, techniques such as sentiment analysis and neuromarketing do not attempt to understand what particular viewers are thinking, but to register their emotional intensities and to correlate these with future outcomes and behavior. In this respect, the book describes an alternative informational architecture from that of narrative deliberation and symbolic representation. In their stead, what emerges is a model in which correlation takes the place of correspondence (between symbolic representation and that which is represented) and affective intensity comes to stand in for and displace referential "truth," authenticity, and factual evidence. The point in marking these distinctions is not to re-inscribe a set of binary oppositions (truth–appearance; intellect–affect; and so on) and the privileged terms with which they are associated. The book is not a call for the rehabilitation of a surpassed Enlightenment fascination with the clear delineation between rational truth, perceptual experience, and emotional intensity. On the contrary, it argues that the very attempt to *privilege* the post-referential modality of correlation and affect constitutes a re-inscription of what it promises to surpass. If the "recuperative" movement of rationality's self-critique was to explore the undervalued, abjected categories whose suppression marked reason's triumph, the import of the preceding chapters is that the need for recuperation may itself have shifted. When power adopts "infoglut" strategies, reflexive debunkery becomes its ally and the attempt to trace the suppressed but inescapable horizon of truth its foe. In this respect, I am sympathetic to Nicholas Brown and Imre Szeman's (Adorno-inflected) plea for the recuperation of a dialectical thought that eschews teleology:

> The Universal, in the name of which an oppressive particularity came to dominate the globe, suddenly seems the last bastion against a neoliberal world order that is happy enough to maintain differences … as long as they are subsumed without resistance within the global market. A notion of subjective authenticity that had seemed to justify the worst sort of complacent self-privilege … tempts us once again with the offer of protection against the most corrosive and cynical ironies of commodity culture. The aesthetic, which was so plainly the property and instrument of an elite defending its prerogatives, may yet turn out to be the last subjective vestige of utopian possibility. Totality, which was once surely an alibi for a will to power, may be our only tool for grasping the new functioning of global Capital.[17]

The authors recognize and attempt to sidestep the reactionary tendencies of such a plea: "In a lapsarian mode, this would be globalization imagined by John Gray or Samuel Huntington – the decline and necessary return of tradition and of 'values,' an essentially conservative stance."[18] The forced choice they confront and their own self-consciousness about clinging to the "bad objects" of contemporary critique is testimony to the triumph of an anti-dialectical, ahistorical mode of thought – the totalizing critique of totality.

In retrospect, it is not difficult to trace the emergence of this critique: Horkheimer and Adorno did so in their account of the "Dialectic of Enlightenment," where reason embarks on what Simon Jarvis describes as an excursion of "ever-increasing skepticism about any claims for access to a 'transcendent' concept or meaning ... All invocations of anything which might transcend thought in this way are progressively regarded as being mere poetry, thought's own fictions. In this way, thought turns itself into a 'context of pure immanence,' pure inside-ness, in which 'Nothing at all may remain outside.'"[19] What they describe as the reversion of enlightenment to myth (understood not as a distinct historical period, but as "a series of related intellectual and practical operations which are presented as demythologizing, secularizing or disenchanting"[20]) enacts the dismantling of a particular grand narrative – that of the triumph of an autonomous reason that seeks to install itself in the place of the master narratives it displaced: "Mythology itself set in motion the endless process of enlightenment by which, with ineluctable necessity, every definite theoretical view is subject to the annihilating criticism that it is only a belief, until even the concepts of mind, truth, and, indeed, enlightenment itself have been reduced to an animistic magic."[21]

The Agency of Things

We might regard the current fascination with the post-human as a culmination of this self-cannibalizing logic: there is something mystical, transcendent, all-too-metaphysical about notions such as human subjectivity, creativity, desire, and so on. A countervailing emphasis upon the agency of things and the thing-hood of agents (humans emphatically included) fits neatly with what I have been describing as the paradigm of "post-comprehension" forms of knowledge in several respects. First, post-comprehension refers to a reconfigured concept of agency in which questions of desire, motivation, and intention, are bracketed. Similarly, one of the recurring themes of post-human approaches is the reconfiguration of the notion of agency such that "the efficacy or effectivity to which that term has traditionally referred becomes distributed across an ontologically heterogeneous field, rather than being a capacity localized in a human body or in a collective produced (only) by human efforts."[22]

This view of agency comes close to aligning itself with the post-narratival and post-intentional logic of the forms of data mining and predictive analytics described in Chapter 2 and the displacement of causality by correlation. Post-comprehension monitoring eschews narrativized questions of motivation and "hidden" desires. It does not seek to tell a tale, as it were, about a suspect, but rather to unearth patterns with predictive power. In this sense it escapes what one data analyst has described as the "tyranny of the anecdotal": "the terrible tendency of people to use anecdotes and stories to make decisions."[23] The fact that a police patrol might be diverted to a particular garage at a particular time of day has less to do with the "anecdotal" life stories of the individuals subsequently picked up on outstanding warrants than on patterns of past activity correlated with a wide range of potential variables: weather, temperature, economic indicators, and whatever else can be folded into the algorithm. The range of pertinent "actants" extends far beyond the human suspects to encompass the range of variables (non-suspects) captured by the algorithm: in the place of a story of subjective intention, we find an assemblage of actants that converge on, for example, a garage in Santa Cruz: the heat and humidity, the rhythm of the work day, the chemistry of crystal meth, perhaps eventually a wide range of variables with no clear explanatory link to automobile break-ins (the behavior of soybean futures, ground tremors, solar flares – anything that can be monitored, measured, tracked). The version of "vital materialism" advocated by Jane Bennett seeks to continue to tell stories about these broader collectives of objects, influences, and actants – but the scope of such stories rapidly expands the reach of narrative. How would it be possible to take into account the full range of influences on even the smallest of decisions? For that, we have the database.

This rapidly expanding scope of relevant variables – a scope that soon becomes "too big to know" – leads to a second dimension of "post-comprehension" knowledge: the emergence of patterns that cannot be modeled and, in this respect, are inexplicable – patterns that simply emerge from the database and can be neither anticipated nor explained once they emerge. This is knowledge that has operational efficacy but no descriptive, explanatory, or even causal purchase. Horkheimer and Adorno discerned relatively early on the turn to this kind of knowledge in their diagnosis of the fate of enlightenment: "On their way toward modern science human beings have discarded meaning. The concept is replaced by the formula, the cause by rules and probability."[24] Perhaps what marks the gulf between Adorno and contemporary strands of post-human theory is the valence associated with this diagnosis – from an indictment predicated on a sense of loss (of meaning, substance, experience) to a celebration of the possibilities revealed by a "wider distribution of agency" and the chastening of "fantasies of human mastery."[25] This gulf is marked by a historical/theoretical shift: the discrediting of the dialectic. If Adorno, still within the horizon of a reconfigured conception of the dialectic, retains the hope that the Enlightenment might become enlightened about itself, post-humanism seeks to step out beyond its horizon. If Adorno's critique is what might be described as allopathic (the attempt to temper subject-centered reason with an injection of a sense of irreducible otherness), there is an element of homeopathy to the post-human critique which confronts (and mirrors) the autonomous subject of liberal pluralism with the disaggregated actants of a post-human pluralism. Bennett concedes this point when she notes that one disadvantage of what she calls "thing-power" – the agentic capacity and vibrancy of things (as actants) – is "its latent individualism, by which I mean the way in which the figure of the 'thing' lends itself to an atomistic rather than a con-gregational [collective?] understanding of agency."[26] One consequence is a rather neat fit with the logic of contemporary neoliberalism which, similarly, operates as a kind of self-described demystification and defetishization machine when it comes to notions of collective goods and agency. All such notions are dismissed from the perspective of neoliberalism as symptoms of top-down regulation – as opposed to the spontaneous forms of aggregation and ordering resulting from ostensibly "free" (deregulated) markets composed of the combined but otherwise disarticulated actions of individual actors.

The free market in such accounts emerges as the "assemblage" *par excellence* – the mechanism that coordinates an unpredictable and undirectable outcome derived from a range of influences including both human and non-human "participants." Any one individual may attempt to act in accordance with a particular intention, but this attempt becomes caught up in, captured by, and ultimately reconfigured by the myriad forces of the marketplace. As Bennett puts it in her discussion of the logic of assemblages: "an intention is like a pebble thrown into a pond or an electrical current sent through a wire or network: it vibrates and merges with other currents, to affect and be affected."[27] Such a formulation does not simply disperse or distribute agency, it also reassembles it in the form of the "agentic capacity" of the assemblage – what Bennett describes as "the dynamic force emanating from a spatio-temporal configuration rather than from any particular element in it."[28]

This emergent dynamic recalls the logic of the database/algorithm – another assemblage – and its ability to generate new, unpredictable, and hitherto "unknown" patterns. With this in mind, we might trace a chain of equivalence that marks a distinctly neoliberal post-humanism that treats the market as both assemblage and algorithm: an information-processing machine that takes on its own dynamic force. Translated back into Zizek's formulation of symbolic efficiency, we might describe this as the combination of the debunking of a particular version of subjective agency and its simultaneous reincarnation in a transposed register. As Zizek puts it:

> The deadlock is here deeper than it may appear ... the problem is that the big Other continues to function in the guise of the "second nature", of the minimally-reified social system which is perceived as an In-itself ... although each individual knows very well that there is no objective market, just the interaction of individuals, the specter of the "objective" market is this same individual's fact-of-experience ... Not only the market, but our entire social life is determined by such reified mechanisms.[29]

The television show *Person of Interest* (CBS) neatly captures this double logic of de-subjectification and reification in its portrayal of an imagined all-seeing surveillant assemblage comprised of the totality of existing databases, sensors, and cameras. On the one hand, the monitored humans are reduced to inter-acting atoms whose actions can be predicted in advance as easily as the trajectory of a billiard ball – at least from the perspective of the all-seeing assemblage. On the other, this assemblage emerges as a distinct para-human intelligence, animated by its attempts to prevent future crime by directing its own billiard balls (its human assistants) into the fray. As the series progresses, the sub-jectification of the assemblage unfolds: first it simply spits out the social security numbers of people related to an impending murder. Over time, however, we learn about its development (its "childhood") and its early "conversations" with its creator. Eventually, one of the main characters starts to speak to it – directly addressing surveillance cameras on the street that, in turn, respond via cryptic messages delivered (somewhat anachronistically) by nearby payphones. What emerges is a subjectivized version of "ubiquitous computing": the entire communication and information network has become sentient and can communicate through its countless extensions: its CCTV and Webcam eyes and its microphone ears. Wherever the network reaches it can watch, listen, and communicate with us.

Once upon a time we might have discerned a disturbing sense of alienation in this emergence of (the return of our own) agentive force in the form of an inscrutable meta-agent beyond our control. Now we call it realism – or perhaps a new materialism – and, oddly enough, endow it with the force of ahistorical, naturalized truth: now it can finally be realized *this* is really the way it is between us and the world of things we (who are also things) inhabit. We might note here the commonality between the hermetic conception of the asubjective (and alinguistic) agency of things and the antipathy to notions of collective agency enshrined in both prediction markets and conspiracy theory. In this regard, we confront another iteration of the demise of symbolic efficiency, one that attempts to eschew the "fetishes" of the "the subject, the image, the word."[30] This worldview neatly accords with the triumph of the algorithm as an organizing social principle: one in which the rhythms of our daily lives create patterns beyond our comprehension and our predictive abilities (but not that of the database) – patterns that are turned back upon us for the purposes of sorting, exclusion, management, and modulation. We fuel the algorithmic assemblage – we even create the algorithms (or at least the para-meters according to which they develop) – only to face the prospect of finding ourselves at its mercy: subject to distributed and unaccountable decisions that affect our life chances and access to goods and services. In our algorithmic future there may be no way to truly know why the algorithm has curtailed our mobility, denied us a job, loan, or health insurance – or, on the other hand, promoted us, passed us, admitted us into a particular institution. As in Jorge Luis Borges's parable of the Lottery in Babylon, which comes to control all aspects of life (not just wealth) and eventually fades into the background, merging with the chance occurrences of daily life, the opaque decision-making of the database – the fruit of our own efforts – may come to look to us like a second nature.[31] As we become more reliant on complex algorithmic decision-making, it becomes harder to access the reasoning behind individual decisions; these start to look like aspects of an implacable fate or, alternatively, the oracular whim of the database. The algorithm "launders" our collective behavior, turning it into a force beyond our reach: the machine may say "no" or "yes," but there is no clear causal explanation – it simply detected a pattern that intersected with its operators' priorities in order to generate a denial or an approval. What is implicitly foreclosed, as Zizek suggests, is the notion that "humanity, as a collective subject, has the capacity to somehow limit impersonal and anonymous socio-historic development, to steer it in a desired direction. Today, such a notion is quickly dismissed as 'ideological' and/or 'totalitarian': the social process is again perceived as dominated by an anonymous Fate beyond social control. The rise of global capitalism is presented to us as such a Fate."[32] The database has the capacity to reinforce this ideological message.

The result is a disturbing affinity between an account of, say, global warming that embraces the logic of what Bennett calls "thing power" and a seemingly demobilizing critique of environmental activism as a fetishization of human agency. The spirit of Bennett's account pushes in the opposite direction: her hope is that an anthropomorphizing tendency that cultivates a sensitivity to the call of matter (seen as having some form of agency, *just like us*) might curtail the inflated sense of self-importance that fuels a destructive sense of human entitlement. However, her logic runs the risk of heading off in another direction altogether: one according to which the very notion that global warming is the result of human agents and activity is yet another symptom of an overweening anthropocentrism. A "thing-power" approach unintentionally approaches the right-wing critique of global warming in its emphasis on the fact that there are multiple "actants" involved that render the situation much more complex than a simple story of human meddling. The fact that there is a complex and virtually limitless set of interactions at work means it is not entirely clear that humans are uniquely responsible or that their intentional intervention will have the desired results – this is also the familiar refrain of the unwitting post-humanists on the far right. Consequently, it is not evident that this form of de-anthropocentrism is progressive rather than demobilizing – especially when it comes to the attempt to foment change through collective action. It is not difficult to portray climate change deniers as what Bennett calls "vital materialists" *avant la lettre*: humans are just one participant, and perhaps not a very significant one, in the grand scheme of climatological history. There are many other actants at work, from solar activity to the natural rhythm of the ice ages, meteorite strikes, volcanic activity, and changes in the distribution of water vapor in the atmosphere. Viewed from the perspective of geological time, we might not want to even think of humans as central actors in the development of the environment. As Bennett puts it, "In the long and slow time of evolution, then, mineral material appears as the mover and shaker, the active power, and the human beings, with their much-lauded capacity for self-directed action as its product."[33] Perhaps global warming is simply another example of "mineral agency" at work, enlisting humans as convenient mediators. In its smack-down of the hubris of human agency, such a position is not as far as it might seem from that of fundamentalist Christian right-wingers such as US Senator James Inhofe, who famously dismissed the notion of human-caused climate change as blasphemous hubris: "God's still up there. The arrogance of people to think that we, human beings, would be able to change what He is doing in the climate is to me outrageous." Who are we to think that we can intervene in the greater scheme of God – or, alternatively, the slow but deliberate grind of "mineral power"?

By the same token, the attempt to ameliorate climate change may be well intentioned, but it cannot possibly take into account all of the ways in which humanity's best efforts will become caught up in an assemblage of interactions and feedback effects (in the mineral assemblage?) that may render them not just ineffective but potentially counter-productive. In practical terms, one potential danger of the hyper-diffusion of "agency" envisioned by Bennett's brand of vital materialism is the parallel dissolution of responsibility (as one more anthropocentric fallacy?). Zizek diagnoses this impasse as follows: "The problem is that, although our (sometimes even individual) acts can have catastrophic (ecological, etc.) consequences, we continue to perceive such consequences as anonymous/systemic; as something for which we are not responsible, for which there is no clear agent."[34] Bennett's "vital materialism" runs the risk of embracing this outcome in the name of de-fetishization: the undermining of the sovereign subject and the forms of domination and oppression that it has underwritten. In this regard, the critical purchase of such a position seems at best questionable against the background of the diagnosis of the demise of symbolic efficiency described in previous chapters.

The Demise and Resurrection of Symbolic Efficiency

What, then, might it mean to rehabilitate the efficacy of the symbolic in the face of its ostensible demise? This seems to me to be the challenge posed by the impasses of the (admittedly incoherent) attempt to move beyond the horizon of symbolic representation outlined in the preceding chapters: to dispense with the need for representation by constructing a fantasy of "immediation" that takes the shape of either direct access to knowledge in the real (neuromarketing, body language analysis) or by sidestepping the need for comprehension altogether (predictive analytics, decision markets, sentiment analysis). Correlational forms of knowledge generated by the database defer referentiality, leaving the body of data to speak directly for itself. I consider the task of the rehabilitation of symbolic efficiency to be an "immanent" one in the sense that these post-representational approaches inevitably rely upon the forms of symbolic efficiency they disavow. Thus, for example, body language analysis turns out to be caught up in the level of discourse it ostensibly surpassed – not just in the trivial sense that it circulates in discursive form, but in the default of allegedly involuntary signals to symbols that can be mobilized at will as a deliberate form of manipulation and deception. We might say something similar about neuromarketing, insofar as the promise of immediate access results in a paradigmatic example of mediation: the red blot as signifier of excitation, desire, fear, or anxiety.

By contrast, the promise of algorithmic models of information processing to bypass the deadlock of representation seems somewhat more robust. Yes, they rely on anchor points in the form of recorded events, but they discern patterns that do not correspond to any model-able reality. The ideological fiction of algorithmic models of information processing is that they are allegedly content-agnostic and naturally neutral. In actuality, as Shoshana Magnet has neatly illustrated in her work on biometric technologies, biases, preconceptions, and prejudices get baked into the code – where they continue to operate in opaque ways. Magnet explores, for example, how debunked conceptions of race are incorporated within facial recognition technology: "As these scientists label the images according to their understanding of their own biological race and gender identities, preconceptions about gender and race are codified into the biometric scanners from the beginning."[35] Expertise makes its suppressed return in the realms of data mining and predictive analytics, which, at least for the moment, rely upon domain knowledge to assist in structuring the data and developing algorithms. As one IBM primer puts it, "in most cases, we should and do use expert knowledge and data-driven knowledge together."[36]

The difficulty in predicting very rare and exceptional occurrences (such as events like the 9/11 attacks or the Colorado shootings) is that there is, by definition, a lot less historical data available, which brings the "crutch" of expertise into play to help identify key indicators and to craft search algorithms. Perhaps machine learning will allow the guided evolution of algorithms to eventually displace expertise altogether – but it is unlikely to be able to develop its own imperatives, its unique goals. (This was always the constitutive fantasy of the "rise-of-the-sentient-machines" genre of science fiction: that desire could enter the realm of thing-hood. Unsurprisingly, it is typically the human desire for domination of external nature – including humans – that is projected back upon the machines.) These goals and imperatives will be set by those who own and control the monitoring apparatus.

Digital Incarnations of the Big Other

A world in which preconceptions, biases, and prejudices are coded into the decision-making infrastructure poses new challenges for attempts to intervene, symbolically as it were, in the network of shared meanings. We might describe this outcome in terms of the autonomization of the symbolic order: it is allowed to retain its efficacy even as those caught up in it are free to adopt the subjective position of savvy debunkery. Because the symbolic processing power has migrated into the form of the algorithm that effectively shapes the decisions of everyday life (who gets hired or approved for a loan, who can cross the border and who cannot, who will be targeted, monitored, included or excluded in a variety of contexts), we are free to imagine that we have somehow moved beyond the constructed assumptions, prejudices, biases, and "truths" that shape its operation. We embrace an external relationship to symbolic efficiency – disavowing it in daily life while it continues to do its work behind the curtain of the interface.

Slavoj Zizek uses the example of a gesture interface system developed by the Massachusetts Institute of Technology's (MIT's) Media Lab to consider the implications of the automatic writing of the big Other. The "SixthSense" system allows users to see information about the external world projected upon it (this was also the initial promise of Google Glass): when we look at the landscape around us we can query it to see, for example, reviews and ratings superimposed on a nearby restaurant, or even attributes of particular individuals superimposed upon them (if our computer recognizes them). The network of shared knowledge that shapes our understanding of the world around us is directly superimposed upon it for us to see. Imagine the ways in which such devices might be used by, say, police (or anyone else in the era of "War 4.0" in which the distinction between civilian and soldier, suspect and spy becomes blurred): forms of background profiling might be incorporated into the system in order to impose a threat level rating on each individual as he or she walks by. The result is the automation of the "big Other" at work, demonstrating how we never see the world around us directly but always through the lens of the system of meanings that endow it with significance for us. Zizek imagines that this direct staging has the potential to open up a space for critique: instead of relying on the largely unrecognized internalization of such knowledge, we see it explicitly displayed for us as it is projected upon our environment. The world around us becomes visibly overlaid with the information and preconceptions we have about it. As Zizek puts it:

> The first thing to note here is that SixthSense does not really represent a radical break with our everyday experience; rather, it openly stages what was always the case. That is to say, in our everyday experience of reality, the "big Other" – the thick symbolic texture of knowledge, expectations, prejudices, and so on – continuously fills in the gaps in our perception ... This is why SixthSense presents us with another case of ideology at work in technology: the device imitates and materializes the ideological mechanism of (mis)recognition which overdetermines our

everyday perceptions and interactions. The question is to what extent the open staging of this mechanism might undermine its efficiency.[37]

Perhaps once we externalize this knowledge, we can distance ourselves from it and intervene in it – such is the hope forwarded by Zizek in this example.

The world of data mining and predictive analytics, however, is much less transparent: the knowledge it generates is not projected onto the world for all to see, but is embedded in the background of the interactions it structures. To take just a trivial example, consider the customization of search results by a commercial search engine such as Google: if we have been paying attention we might know, somewhere in the back of our minds, that the results we get in response to our queries are tailored to what Google already knows about us (including, if we happen to be logged in, all of the information it has gathered about us from its suite of services). In practice, we tend not to dwell on the fact that our results are tailored and not to inquire as to why a particular result may have come up first for us. Sometimes it is not difficult to discern the operation of the algorithm behind the scenes, as in the case of obvious forms of targeting based on our past behavior.

In other contexts, the algorithm is made transparent for us – as in the case of Amazon.com's book recommendations, which allow us to see which past purchases or searches have resulted in a particular book being suggested for us. For the most part, however, the workings of the algorithm are opaque and are likely to become increasingly so for two reasons. First, the advent of "big data" mining, as I have noted in previous chapters, results in algorithms whose results defy referential explanations. Someone who purchased a particular car in a particular place and buys a certain brand of toothpaste may be more likely to be late paying off credit card debt – but there is no clear underlying explanation as to why this constellation of demographic details resulted in that prediction: the pattern is a purely correlational one. Second, as this example suggests, those who control the database and the algorithm have little incentive to make the basis of algorithmic decision-making available, not least because this would entail revealing the increasingly powerful forms of monitoring and surveillance upon which they are based. Moreover, from the perspective of both marketing and policing, the incentive is to allow the algorithms to operate behind the scenes in order to protect their efficacy. Recall the example of Target's attempt to identify expectant mothers: the company did not want customers to realize the extent of the targeting, and so concealed the fact that pregnant women had been singled out by creating targeted mailers in which baby-related products were embedded alongside unrelated items. These are relatively trivial examples, but they suggest that when even more significant issues are at stake, the decision-making process may be equally opaque. In contrast to the model of SixthSense described by Zizek, the algorithmic decision-making process is not one in which the externalization of the "big Other," in the form of implicit sets of assumptions, biases, and preconceptions, opens them up for examination. Rather, these remain operative but largely invisible, inscrutable, and perhaps even incomprehensible: the uncanny persistence of symbolic efficiency in the wake of its alleged demise.

Something similar can be said about prediction markets in which the market, with its embedded set of values and presuppositions, plays a role analogous to that of the algorithm. As the concern about "dependent decision-making" – otherwise known as collective action – suggests, the market incorporates a naturalized understanding of what constitutes the rational economic actor: atomistic, competitive, and profit-maximizing. Decision markets cannot work unless there are losers – they are a clear example of a zero-sum game: nothing is produced and money merely changes hands between winners and losers. For such markets to work there has to be a large and diverse enough pool of participants to attract the "stupid" or "uninformed" money that generates profits for the winners. There have to be enough people willing to take the losing side of the bet: "According to economists, this requires a certain alchemy of expertise and stupidity … forecasting also needs more so-called noise traders, who do business with almost no information. Noise traders boost accuracy by increasing volume and the potential profits of informed traders."[38]

For a prediction market to form, a particular event has to be considered realistic enough to draw traders – that is to say, the pre-existing biases of conventional wisdom intervene prior to the formation of a market. As in the case of predictive analytics, one-off, rare events – precisely those that predictive strategies for national security seek to anticipate – are the least likely to draw active trading, even at very long odds. As Surowiecki puts it in his discussion of prediction markets, "One open question is whether they are good at forecasting genuinely discontinuous innovations or leaps. Or do they work very well only when the range of variables you are basing a forecast on is relatively well defined?"[39] The "conventional wisdom" has already inserted itself as a conserved set of assumptions into the very formation of the market. As the author of the book *Future Savvy* puts it, "while prediction markets sort out probabilities between known likelihoods, they are not adequate to the task of investigating complex situations where we cannot frame the likely outcomes, or at least can't know if we've framed them right."[40] To prevent an "underwear bomber" a market would first have to conceive of this possibility.

Similarly, prediction markets have a short-term bias when it comes to forecasting, thanks in part to the diminished expected value of anticipated winnings in the distant future. Since speech not backed up by money is explicitly discounted by advocates of prediction markets, those with the greatest wealth (and the highest tolerance of risk – at least in the short run) are, unsurprisingly, those with the greatest voice in a "predictocracy." Subsidized and non-money markets have been proposed to level the playing field; but these both run counter to the recurring argument in favor of such markets: that talk not backed up by money is, literally, cheap. If the whole point of prediction markets is that they more effectively capture public knowledge and sentiment precisely because they require people to "put their money where their mouth is," such "fixes" neutralize one of the central claims for the efficacy of such markets.

The Return of the Repressed

Although portrayed as a neutral mechanism, then, markets, like algorithms, smuggle in a wide range of conserved biases and constructions. They similarly come to function as a stand-in for the "big Other" in the wake of its alleged demise: they remain the one object of faith that withstands the all-encompassing embrace of savvy debunkery. This pattern recurs throughout the examples considered in the previous chapters of the book: in the face of ongoing assaults and critiques, symbolic efficiency persists – albeit often in a disavowed, unacknowledged, or opaque form. To put it somewhat differently, the range of examples of clutter-cutting strategies are meant to trace a portrait – albeit in negative form – of the impossibility of dispensing with symbolic efficiency, representation, and comprehension.

If, once upon a time, the political task taken on by critical theory was to challenge dominant discourses, naturalized truths, and the power relations they sustained, transformed political and historical conditions suggests a new task: that of contesting the "post-truth" politics of the political right. This task poses the challenge not of unmasking every truth claim as a ruse of power, but rather of extracting some kernels of truth from power's latest ruse. It is a task that enjoins reflexivity to get reflexive about itself. When Cary Wolfe summarizes the achievements of 20th-century critical theory, he echoes the Frankfurt scholars who predate the theorists he invokes: "the first lesson of both Derrida and Luhmann … is that Enlightenment rationality is not, as it were, rational enough, because it stops short of applying its own protocols and commitments to itself."[41] The reflexivization of Enlightenment rationality is not, however, a discrete, one-time gesture (this is the oft-overlooked lesson of Hegel). To simply turn reason back upon itself – as one more target of the corrosive power of debunkery – is to enact the default of enlightenment to myth. What differentiates the vernacular postmodernism critiqued in previous chapters from the more philosophically sophisticated versions of deconstruction and post-structuralism is, for lack of a more elegant formulation, the reflexivization of reflexivization. At the most basic level, this refers to the recognition of the conditioned character of the claim that all thought is conditioned – as well as to the excavation of the truth claims at work in the critique of truth claims. It is much more difficult to develop the implications of the reflexivization of reflexivization (as something other than an infinite regress) than to locate those moments where the reflexive gesture stops short, limiting itself to a simple, discrete, and incoherent self-critique. Recall, for example,

Jacques Derrida's exchange with John Searle, in which the former confronts the latter's accusation that since deconstruction undermines any attempt to impose a dominant reading of a text, Derrida has no right to accuse anyone of misinterpreting his own texts. Searle accuses Derrida of making the reflexive gesture that fails to reflect upon itself. Derrida's response is suitably scathing:

> Let it be said in passing how surprised I have often been, how amused or discouraged, depending on my humor, by the use or abuse of the following argument: Since the deconstructionist (which is to say, isn't it, the skeptic-relativist-nihilist!) is supposed not to believe in truth, stability, or the unity of meaning, in intention or "meaning-to-say," how can he demand of us that we read him with pertinence, precision, rigor? How can he demand that his own text be interpreted correctly? ... The answer is simple enough: this definition of the deconstructionist is false (that's right: false, not true) and feeble; it supposes a bad (that's right: bad, not good) and feeble reading of numerous texts, first of all mine.[42]

By the same token, Michel Foucault clearly traced the way in which power manifested itself in the formation of bodies of knowledge and the discursive regularities with which they are associated. But he also invoked the possibility that knowledge might have some purchase back upon the exercise of power – that, in other words, one was not purely reducible to the other. Indeed, he locates some political potential in what he describes as subjugated knowledges: "I also believe that it is through the re-emergence of these low-ranking knowledges, these unqualified, even directly disqualified knowledges (such as that of the psychiatric patient, of the ill person, of the nurse, of the doctor – parallel and marginal as they are to the knowledge of medicine – that of the delinquent etc.) ... that it is through the re-appearance of this knowledge, of these local popular knowledges, these disqualified knowledges, that criticism performs its work."[43] This is not quite the same thing as ideology critique – and yet there is a kinship, a Foucauldian reworking of critique whereby "disqualified" forms of knowing can emerge to challenge or denaturalize established relationships between knowledge and power, and thereby disrupt the latter's operation.

In their reliance on a specific version of the symbolic efficiency of knowledge as critique, both figures remain indebted to the Enlightenment project. However, the popularized uptake of the dismantling of symbolic efficiency looks entirely different: more like an individualized return to tradition than an attempt to engage in reflection upon knowledge practices. The result is a paradoxically rootless resurgence of faith in the absence of the organic, historical community upon which it was grounded: a pastiche of tradition in which the ostensible celebration of "traditional values" takes on a highly individualized and hermetic cast: there is an appeal to an unquestioning, un-interrogated commitment to an idiosyncratic formulation of tradition. Freedom consists of choosing one's own invented version of history invoked for the purposes of defending the individuating logic of market competition. The unsurprising result is the dismantling of symbolic efficiency in the historical realm.

Glenn Beck and other figures on the "Tea Party" right, for example, have embraced the revisionist historical writings of Republican activist David Barton that suggest the nation's founding fathers wanted to create a Christian state. Erstwhile presidential candidate Mike Huckabee went so far as to say that the nation would be better off if all Americans were "forced – at gunpoint, no less – to listen to every David Barton message."[44] When Barton's subsequent book (about Thomas Jefferson) was pulled from the shelves by its Christian publisher, which had "lost confidence in the book's details," Barton's deputy responded with a familiar denunciation of expertise as unprincipled elitism, and evidence-based deliberation as a form of tyranny tantamount to Nazism.[45] The comments supporting Barton's struggle to contest dominant discourses read like a pastiche of Foucault's account of subjugated knowledges.

The critical concern raised by this example is not simply that the dismantling of symbolic efficiency can be used by left and right alike or that right-wing Christian fundamentalists have adopted an ersatz Foucauldianism, but that this strategy's consequences are fundamentally conservative insofar as it works more than anything else to dismantle critique (in the guise of embracing it). Although Beck and Barton adopt a critical pose, they are engaged in something else altogether: a parodic imitation that works to absorb and disable the strategies they blame for challenges to their convictions: a massively homeopathic attack that challenges rational critical deliberation not by opposing it to faith but by drowning it in its own discourses. There is little point in attempting to ignore their uptake of critical reason's reflective turn. Resuscitating critique – and differentiating it from conspiracy theory – will require moving beyond their gesture rather than ignoring it. If, once upon a time, the progressive political gesture was to locate the fulcrum for dismantling dominant narratives, contemporary developments require a different response: an exploration of the inability to shake off entirely and definitively the language of truth and, by the same token, an interrogation of the limits on the attempt to push the demise of symbolic efficiency to its logical extreme. More specifically, and in the terms outlined in previous chapters, this means thinking through – and beyond – the affect–intellect divide reinforced by neuromarketing and sentiment analysis; it means excavating the as yet unsurpassed horizon of symbolic efficiency, and thereby excavating the grounds for a resuscitated critique of the political economy of the database.

The Impasses of the Critique of Representation

The claim that data is "the new oil" may reveal more than it intends. Obviously this formulation suggests that data is a new and important source of value, and that those who learn how to properly extract and refine it will gain an economic advantage. But there is a somewhat bleaker subtext – one that is worth taking seriously: that the concentration of control over data is a form of power and control, one that differentiates the haves from the have-nots and thereby undergirds new forms of hierarchy and inequality. One of the central themes of this book has been the challenge posed to democratic ideals of citizenship and participation by new techniques for using data – and the changing ways of thinking about information with which these are associated. In a hypothetical world in which knowledge claims and the forms of evidence and argumentation upon which they rely have been relegated, across the board, to the status of local language games, the result is a leveling pluralism. These disparate perspectives do not connect with one another in any meaningful sense other than a pragmatics of competition.

However, if a new form of knowledge practice emerges amidst this disjointed landscape – one that promises to surpass the pluralism of competing language games (Christian fundamentalism versus scientific discourses versus new age obscurantism, and so on) because it operates in a different register, then the potential emerges for shifting power relations dramatically. This is another way of describing what Chris Anderson refers to as "the end of theory": the power of petabyte crunching to leap over the terrain on which various competing models fight it out – surpassing the need for modeling altogether. Data mining and predictive analytics operate in the register of prediction, correlation, and modulation even as the status of other types of knowledge claims is called into question by the apparent demise of symbolic efficiency.

At its most dystopian, the resulting information landscape is one in which those with access to the database can derive practical, if probabilistic ("post-comprehension"), knowledge about how best to influence populations while members of these population are left with an outmoded set of critical tools that, in practice, can be pitted against one another's worldview, but which have little purchase on the forms of knowledge turned back upon them by database-driven apparatuses of influence. In somewhat more concrete terms, this dystopia would be one in which political parties, for example, might use giant databases to exert influence in the affective register (by determining which appeals result in triggering desired voting behavior), overleaping the tangle of "reality-based" policy analysis, verification, and so on. This asymmetry would free up politicians to engage in "infoglut" strategies in the discursive register (promulgating reports that contradict themselves endlessly, pitting "expert" analysts against one another in an indeterminate struggle that does little more than fill air time, or perhaps reinforce preconceptions) while simultaneously developing new strategies for influence in the affective register. Fact-checkers would continue to struggle to hold politicians accountable based on detailed investigations of their claims, arguments, and evidence, while politicians would use data-mining algorithms to develop impulse- or anxiety-triggering messages with defined probabilities of success – what Shouse has described in more positive terms as the power of the media that lies "not so much in their ideological effects, but in their ability to create affective resonances independent of content or meaning."[46] Such power is predicated on the split that this book has repeatedly targeted: between, on the one hand, the savvy debunkery of ideology and, on the other, the recourse to gut reaction, thinking without thought, and the modulation of affect. The subject associated with this split is similarly divided between an impotent, comprehension-based form of rationality (like Damasio's patient who could not make even the smallest of decisions without getting bogged down in the attempt to weigh all of the possible outcomes) and a reflexive, affective set of responses that are given the leading role in the decision-making process.

Revisiting Affect

In her ongoing critique of the turn to affect, Ruth Leys describes this split as the "presumed separation between the affect system on the one hand and signification or meaning or intention on the other"[47] It is a presumption she characterizes as a mistake not least because it smuggles in the very binaries these theorists imaged they had surpassed: "in spite of their explicit hostility to dualism, many of the new affect theorists succumb to a false dichotomy between mind and body."[48] This dualism is characteristic of "post-comprehension" strategies of influence and "literacy" (brain reading and body reading) taken up in previous chapters. The "mind" (intentional, conscious, available for rational cognition) may have gotten much of the attention when it comes to information processing and communication, but the *body*'s language is more trustworthy. By the same token, the mind may think it is deciding, but what look like before-the-fact analyses are, in actuality, after-the-fact rationalizations: the mind always arrives too late and then takes credit for what has already been decided. Viewed from the perspective of influence, ideology (which targets the mind in the mode of language and narrative: comprehension) is trumped by affective modulation, which directly affects populations in the form of asubjective intensities and preconscious impulses. As Leys puts it, affect is figured as "prior to ideology": "an inhuman, nonsignifying force that operates below the threshold of intention, consciousness, and signification."[49]

The turn to affect is thus framed as a (re)turn to the body, and in this sense as consonant with contemporary reformulations of materialism insofar as it takes into account "the way that political attitudes and statements are partly conditioned by intense autonomic bodily reactions that do not simply reproduce the trace of a political intention and cannot be wholly recuperated within an ideological regime of truth."[50] This model of communication as immediate physical influence – the direct communication of force in the classical sense – is rehabilitated not least in the strategies of neuromarketers and the sentiment analysts. Although data mining is agnostic about this split, allegedly eschewing models of causation and explanation, in this very refusal it has already taken sides.

In theory, there may be an element of political promise in the turn to the autonomic, bodily version of affect, perhaps because it opens up new possibilities for political practice freed from the constraints of a one-dimensional rationalism (Leys relegates this promise to the province of the "usual homilies on the emancipatory value of affect").[51] In practice, however, it may end up being more demobilizing than liberating, as the examples considered in this book suggest. The critique offered by Ruth Leys – which contests the interpretation of the scientific experiments upon which the affect theories she challenges rely – looks more politically promising, not least because it addresses the symptoms of the demise of symbolic efficiency. As she puts it, one price paid by those who ascribe to "a radical separation between affect and reason" is "to make disagreement about meaning, or ideological dispute, irrelevant to cultural analysis."[52] This is a familiar gesture in the database era of "the end of theory" – one which fits neatly with the operational imperatives of machine-readable data: the displacement of narrative by the word cloud. Ostensibly, cutting-edge theories of bodily affect align themselves neatly with the conservative tendencies of post-truth, post-narrative, and post-comprehension politics. Leys acknowledges this default in her observation that the moment one abandons the "radical separation between affect and reason," "one finds oneself forced to provide thick descriptions of life experiences of the kind that are familiar to anthropologists and novelists, but are widely held to be inimical to science."[53]

The privileging of a hermetic system of affects sealed off from the realms of reason and cognition lends itself to database-driven machinic modulations – sentiment analysis and neuromarketing – and to post-narratival forms of "knowing" that align themselves with the demise of symbolic efficiency. The reflexive critique of rationality and symbolic efficiency associated with an era of information overload and the perceived deadlocks of representation should be added to the list of "complex institutional, intellectual, and social factors" that contributed to the success of what Leys describes as the "anti-intentionalist" paradigm (in which affective response occurs prior to and independently of conscious intention). Leys usefully opens up avenues for critiquing anti-intentionalism by reinterpreting some of the experimental findings embraced by its advocates and by tracing alternative scientific genealogies of the emotions, particularly findings in the early 1960s that "claim to demonstrate that affect and cognition are indissociable."[54]

There is also a rich philosophical tradition to draw upon in this regard: a dialectical one that is largely antithetical to the theoretical commitments of those who embrace the turn to affect. This is not necessarily a bad thing, given the political stakes in mounting a critique of the embrace of symbolic efficiency's demise. The appeal of the affective turn and associated versions of anti-intentionalism is predicated on their challenge to the domineering Enlightenment subject – hence the interest in various forms of neo-materialism and critical realism in leveling relations between humans and things. There is a *realist* thrust to these accounts that challenges the implied Enlightenment delusion of constitutive subjectivity. According to this account, a preoccupation with deliberation, evidence, cognition, and rationality is misguided because it misses the fact that as interacting social beings we are not driven (solely or, in some cases, at all) by these faculties. We are a lot closer to the object world than we like to imagine: buffeted by forces to which we respond in automatic ways. Our conscious cognitive faculties provide us with the opportunity to imagine ways of intervening in these forces, and thereby indirectly on our responses – but not directly or intentionally as the familiar model in which our intentions are sovereign would have it. There is also a *critical* thrust to such accounts insofar as they seek to address the forms of political manipulation that operate in the affective register: "we ignore those affective intensities and resonances at our peril, not only because doing so leads us to underestimate the political harm that the deliberate manipulation of our affective lives can do but also because we will otherwise miss the potential for ethical creativity and transformation that 'technologies of the self' designed to work on our embodied being can help bring about."[55]

On their face, such claims seem compelling, but the version of subjectivity they posit – and here I am referring to the anti-intentionalism described by Leys – poses some theoretical challenges, including the difficulty of holding together the notion that intentionality arrives after the fact and that it can simultaneously be enlisted (intentionally, how else?) to modulate the forces exerted upon our embodied being for ends salutary and otherwise. This difficulty is an artifact of the entwinement of the demise of symbolic efficiency with the critique of a constitutive Enlightenment subjectivity that seeks to reduce external reality to itself.

By contrast, the dialectical critique of constitutive subjectivity identifies similar targets: the pathologies of identity thinking and the domination it underwrites (of nature, the self, and others). However, it slices things somewhat differently: the split is not between affect and reason (bodily response and mental cognition) but is internal to a speculatively expanded version of reason. Moreover, the split is not an absolute biological one, but a thoroughly historical one that carries within it the capability to be experienced as such: as a divide or diremption. This is the import of Adorno's theory of "mimesis": that reason can be turned back upon itself not in order to liquidate itself (or to relegate itself to a realm of secondary importance, an after-the-fact rationalization), but to reveal its partial character, its incompleteness, and thus to gesture, albeit negatively, in the direction of a reconciled reason that would incorporate its suppressed mimetic capability. For Adorno – who draws his inspiration from Walter Benjamin's discussion of "the mimetic faculty," mimesis is a thwarted form of reason, unrecognizable as such within the coordinates set out by instrumental reason – but a rational form of cognition nonetheless.[56] Mimesis is the disavowed foundation of instrumental reason insofar as the latter attempts to obliterate in the abstraction of the concept the recognition of the sensuous particularity upon which reason necessarily relies. The emergence of an instrumental, domineering, and necessarily partial or incomplete (or un-self-aware) reason takes shape against the background of the suppression of this particularity. This mimetic aspect of reason comes to be sequestered in the "irrational" realm of aesthetics to allow identity thinking to pursue its course un-harassed. Hence, the significance of art and aesthetic theory in Adorno's critique of instrumental reason – a critique in which the term aesthetic should be understood both in the historical sense of a particular understanding of autonomous art characteristic of capitalist modernity, and in its etymological sense referring to embodied forms of sense perception. Adorno's approach figures the realm of the aesthetic as a cognitive experiential realm in which knowledge of particularity and non-identity is not obtained through the subsumption of particulars to their appropriate concepts, but through a non-dominating and embodied form of cognition. Historian Martin Jay provides a useful gloss on Adorno's notion of mimesis:

> Mimesis ... involves a more sympathetic, compassionate, and non-coercive relationship of affinity between nonidentical particulars. ... Rather than producing a hierarchical subsumption under a subjectively generated category, it preserves the rough equality of the subject and object involved. More precisely, it assimilates the latter to the former in such a way that the unposited, unintended object implicitly predominates, thwarting the imperialist gesture of subjective control and constitution that is the hallmark of philosophical idealism.[57]

This formulation conserves Benjamin's understanding of the embodied character of the mimetic faculty, which first expresses itself in attempts not to know the object, but to become it. As Shierry Weber-Nicholsen puts it, "This perspective on mimesis is linked with his interest in occult experience which signifies for him an identification of perception with its objects, a kind of continuity or affinity between subject and object, psyche and matter, macrocosm and microcosm."[58]

There is a similar interest in "attending to the object" in the recent resuscitation of a post-Marxist materialism in Jane Bennett's theory of "thing power" and "vibrant materiality" which emphasizes the object-character of humans in order to challenge the depredations of anthropocentrism. Bennett hopes to cultivate a constructive anthropomorphism that tempers the privileging of humans over things – a misguided sense of privilege that licenses (among other things) "human hubris and our earth-destroying fantasies of conquest and consumption."[59] Bennett's project is more of a poetic project than a theoretical one insofar as it attempts to model a sensibility that acknowledges its own conceptual impasses. The imaginative/perceptual leap she describes is one that manages, fleetingly, to slip the bonds of the situated human subject to capture a glimpse of things in their independent vibrancy, radiating their "thing power" – her term for an inhuman agentic capacity.[60] She describes a moment when this ecstatic vision of mundane objects is triggered by the glint of the sun on a black plastic glove lying in the gutter: "In this assemblage, objects appeared as things, that is, as vivid entities not entirely reducible to the contexts in which (human) subjects set them."[61] To borrow Adorno's language, the moment she so vividly describes eludes the grip of the subsumptive regard of subjective reason. In comparing her own thinking to that of Adorno, Bennett observes that "a philosophy of non-identity [Adorno's] and a vital materialism [Bennett's] share an urge to cultivate a more careful attentiveness to the outside," which, in her lexicon, refers to "in irreducibly strange dimension of matter … That which refuses to dissolve completely into the milieu of human knowledge."[62]

It is telling that Bennett's account of Adorno relies heavily on his *Negative Dialectics* and elides entirely his account of mimesis (developed in his work on art, and especially in *Aesthetic Theory*). This account drives a further wedge between a negative dialectic and vital materialism, highlighting the form of "identity thinking" that characterizes the latter. For Bennett, the possibility of recognizing the vibrancy of matter is predicated on a reconfiguration of the relationship between humans and objects that allows them to approach one another as like to like: human subjectivity is backgrounded in order to assert a version of agency that can be assimilated to the "agentic" capacity of objects. The virtue of anthropomorphism for Bennett is that it might foster a greater sense of empathy toward the non-human – likeness becomes the basis for the ethical claim of recognition: "One moral of the story is we are also non-human and that things too are vital players [like us] in the world."[63] This is a slippery and potentially self-undermining reconceptualization of recognition insofar as it pushes in the direction of what J. M. Bernstein, following Adorno, describes as "the universal fungibility of particulars."[64]

Bennett's push in this direction is, admittedly, qualified insofar as she adopts the ironic strategy of embracing a quasi-post-human perspective in the service of ultimately humanist ends: relinquishing our narcissistic anthropocentrism might allow us to create a better world for ourselves (and not, say, for organisms that thrive in a post-apocalyptic landscape devoid of humans). Other variants of neo-realism, such as Object-Oriented Ontology, push further in the direction of this universal fungibility. As Ian Bogost puts it, Object-Oriented Ontology takes the position that, "nothing has special status, but that everything exists equally – plumbers, DVD players, cotton, bonobos, sandstone, and Harry Potter, for example. In particular, OOO rejects the claims that human experience rests at the center of philosophy, and that things can be understood by how they appear to us."[65] This egalitarianism of things should recall the omnivorous appetite of the database – which casts an equal regard on all objects of data collection. With just a few tweaks, we get a formulation that shares the sensibility described by Bogost: the database is interested in all data equally, whether it is about people, earthquakes, flea populations, the shifting migrations of birds, meteorite showers, or best seller lists. The non-human, decentered, and flat perspective imagined by Bogost replicates the "view from nowhere" of the surveillant assemblage in *Person of Interest*: everything before the sensors is, at least initially, equally embraced by its blank gaze – the tap dripping in the sink, the assault taking place in the subway car, the explosion at the electrical plant, someone tying their shoe in the library, the puddle in the corn field, and so on. If, as Slavoj Zizek observes, the true formula for materialism is "not that the world exists outside our mind [the version that gets the attention of the critical and vital materialists], but that our mind does not exist outside the world,"[66] we might describe the contemporary idealist gesture as the embrace of a "mindless" perspective. Paradoxically, this apparently compelling version of realism conserves the idealism it seeks to surpass. As Zizek puts it, "the idea that outside of our reflections there is an objective reality presupposes that our mind, which reflects reality, functions as a gaze somehow external to this reality": how else to sustain the perspective of the view from nowhere?[67]

Post-Subjective Idealism

The view from everywhere/nowhere is the contemporary avatar of a post-subjective idealism that subsumes the external world to the universal medium of digital, storable, sortable, data. Adorno was concerned with *subjective* idealism when he wrote that "The system is belly turned mind, and rage is the mark of each and every idealism."[68] He saw subject-centered reason as voraciously omnivorous, seeking to digest the totality of external reality by reducing it to its own concepts. The target of the critique of idealism has since shifted: it is not the eradication of otherness via the reduction of sensuous particularity to the subject's concepts, but, on the contrary, the liquidation of the subject (in structure if not in name). These are correlative moves – both subsume difference to identity, the latter through the "university fungible of particulars"; both align themselves with instrumental reason. Even the vital materialist's assertion of matter's vibrancy arrives too late for an era in which the celebrants of predictive analytics envision data that "speaks for itself." The cultivation of an attentiveness to the call of things may be a novelty for those who dwell in the realm of arguments and theory – a stubborn hangover of the Enlightenment's subject-centered binge; but this faculty is already well established amongst those sifting through the signals collected from a growing array of sensors that track humans, plants, and things alike. Aren't the real post-humanists the ones who no longer view crime through the lens of motive and intent, but through a crowd of "actants" that include meteorological readings, economic indicators, code violations, traffic patterns, color schemes, and so on?

When the Procrustean concept wielded by subject-centered reason has been displaced by the algorithm "and the cause by rules and probability," the subject takes on a renewed salience, not as primary target of critique, but as that which, re-construed, might provide a purchase point for a critique of post-subjective idealism. Recall Zizek's formulation of materialism as radically perspectival: "The only consistent materialist position is that the world does not exist – in the Kantian sense of the term, as a self-enclosed whole." He opposes this to the idealist position (associated with a familiar positivism): "The notion of the world as a positive universe presupposes an external observer, an observer not caught in it."[69] This latter version of wholeness recalls the asubjective, post-human perspective – one in which there is no subjective distortion because the subject is simply one more object. This formulation helps to explain the fascination with the attempt to liquidate the subject position – that familiar, finite culprit responsible for the partial character of all representation – evinced by the post-comprehension version of post-human knowledge. As Alenka Zupancic puts it, "This fantasy of wholeness clearly indicates that the 'subjective gaze' is regarded as something that distorts the image of the object *from the outside*, being in no way inherently related to the object."[70] Reclaiming the object means abstracting away from this gaze – leaving it behind, liquidating the subjective perspective. In describing this approach to reality as a fantasy, Zupancic embraces the materialist position described by Zizek: "if we take the thesis that the subjective gaze is inscribed in the object seriously, then it follows from this that the object is necessarily non-whole."[71] This partiality is not simply an artifact of the finite subject's own limitations; that is to say, it is not epistemological but ontological, according to Zupancic. By contrast, it is the perspective that invokes the notion of a complete thing "in itself" that is the purely subjective artifact, and not the partial or perspectival realm of appearances.

For Zupancic, it is not by refuting perspectivalism that one excavates a conserved but suppressed attachment to truth, but by thinking through it: "There is a perspective on things that emerges only when one shifts perspectives. It does not exist as a separate perspective with its own point of view; yet it is a perspective."[72] The real question, in other words, is how is it that the very notion of perspective can persist in this situation? If there are nothing but myriad perspectives (the claim that underwrites the vernacular postmodernism diagnosed in previous chapters), then the very notion of perspective cancels itself out. Zupancic continues in this vein: "How is it possible to formulate the thesis about all truths being perspective truths without this statement being a meta-statement, exempt from the situation it describes? The answer is: the point from which it is possible to formulate this thesis is the point of disjunction introduced into the reality of a given situation by the shift of perspective."[73] As Zizek repeatedly emphasizes, if the Kantian move is to posit an external relationship between the thing-in-itself and its phenomenal appearance – a split that continues to haunt the largely unsurpassed horizon of Kant – the Hegelian materialist response is to reflexivize and internalize this split: "what appears to us as our inability to know the thing indicates a crack in the thing itself, so that our very failure to reach the full truth is the indicator of truth."[74]

By contrast, attempts to liquidate the subject are revealed as strategies for eliminating the experience of this crack (of appearance *qua* appearance). In this regard, there is a strong affinity between Zizek's materialist Hegelianism and that of Adorno. As J. M. Bernstein, one of Adorno's most astute contemporary interpreters, puts it, "In raising ourselves above it, in making the world an object of representational knowing in which, ideally, even the perspective of the knower would disappear (or, what amounts to the same, become just another item within the object world), all subjective response to the world, and thus the world as it appears to human subjects, disappears."[75] Drawing on Adorno and Walter Benjamin, he describes this perspective as (an attempt at) the liquidation of experience: "we no longer directly experience the diremption of subject from object, universal from particular. There has been a 'withering of experience.' The disproportion between the all-powerful reality and the powerless subject creates a situation where reality becomes unreal because the experience of reality is beyond the grasp of the subject."[76] This is perhaps the most succinct way of describing what I have rather awkwardly tried to get at with the notions of "post-comprehension" (too-big-to-know) knowledge, post-truth politics, and post-referential forms of "meaning." Similarly, my attempt to trace the inadequacy of various strategies for addressing the alleged demise of symbolic efficiency is meant to tap into those moments that help to resuscitate the experience of diremption *as* diremption – for example, to experience the attempt to hold apart affect and rational cognition, the sensory and the cognitive, as an imposed separation, a social pathology rather than a truth of nature.

This theory detour is meant to get at the following point: that the liquidation of the subjective moment goes hand-in-hand with the withering and not the heightening of experience. The goal of critique at such a conjuncture is (in awkwardly negative terms) to unearth the experience of the withering of experience itself. My further intention is to highlight the ways in which recent theoretical developments that focus on "things" – objects liberated from the human contexts in which they are embedded and, thus, ostensibly, from human ways of knowing – align themselves with the "post-comprehension" forms of knowledge associated with the instrumental pragmatics of the database. I understand there is wonderful potential for good in the big data era and I anticipate that the forms of unknowable knowledge generated by predictive analytics and other forms of data mining will provide many useful advances that improve our lives in important ways. I think there is also peril that needs to be recognized before we leap headlong into the realm of generalized database-driven decision-making (or "Futarchy," for that matter). Of greatest concern is the notion that the proliferation of data means we can leave behind the challenges associated with representational forms of knowledge, narrative, and deliberation rather than working through the impasses they currently confront.

Revisiting Alienation

The attempt to resuscitate the critical purchase of the subject opens a further avenue for a critique of the political economy of big data: that of the role played by alienation. I start from the premise that if data is the "new oil," the wholesale capture of a growing range of information about everything that users do in networked digital environments might be described as a digital era version of "primitive accumulation." In this regard, I concur with Alistair Croll's claim that "Big data is our generation's civil rights issue, and we don't [yet] know it."[77] As he argues, data capture is not so much a matter of privacy as one of power – and this power is structured in familiar ways: by ownership and control over the material infrastructure for our breathtakingly powerful and convenient new information and communication practices.

Strikingly, one of the recurring marketing strategies mobilized by the companies that control this infrastructure can be construed as the promise of the end of alienation: from one another, from the product of our labor (as suggested by the neologism "prosumer"), and even from ourselves (new avenues for self-expression provide new forms of self-knowledge). If the implicit invocation of critiques of alienation is ready-to-hand for advertisers, the same is not true, oddly enough, of critical theorists. The same critique of the subject that licenses what I have described as post-subjective idealism threatens the critical purchase of the notion of alienation. In somewhat more cynical terms Erick Heroux has observed that "The critique of alienation had to be buried so that an alienating mode of production could continue."[78] In the contemporary theoretical climate, the familiar critique of alienation (as a critical conceptual tool) is that it introduces an outdated form of humanism/essentialism (and, thus, of the subject). According to this critique, as Heroux puts it, "The reason 'alienation' remains untenable is that it always depends upon the ground of a 'true' self, of a primal unalienated nature beneath the artifices of power … Thus the whole theory of alienation becomes an embarrassing anachronism, a regression to the romantic juvenilia of a vaguely conceived 19th Century Humanism."[79] However, a critique of alienation in the terms outlined in the previous section can be rehabilitated as an immanent rather than a transcendent one – a concern with the way in which social relations thrive on thwarting the very freedoms and capacities they invoke. Separation is conserved in this updated approach as a defining characteristic of alienation. In both instances, alienation is understood not in terms of a betrayed, abstract, individual, ahistorical essence, but rather in terms of domination and the social relations that reproduce it. The consequence for a critical approach, as Heroux observes, is that "Disalienation would not somehow be more 'true to nature' but it would change the balance of power relations."[80] These are the stakes of critique – not simply the attempt to address sentiments of disaffection or discontent (although these are surely also important), but an invitation to examine the way in which existing social relations reproduce conditions that separate modes of existence from their power of acting.

On the one hand, there is a certain appeal to the Tofflerian claim of the "overthrow of matter" associated with digitization – at least insofar as it suggests that we turn our glance away from questions of physical infrastructure and ownership of the means of communication and interaction.[81] What does it matter who owns the Internet backbone or YouTube or Google, as long as these facilitate original, unique, and unfettered forms of individual and collaborative creativity? On the other hand – the one that has grown a bit too invisible – the critique of exploitation directs us back to these questions. It urges us to consider the ways in which the commercialization of the platform turns our own activity back upon ourselves in the service of priorities that are not our own, and it reminds us of the double duty done by the privately controlled interactive infrastructure. This infrastructure might serve as a platform for new forms of creativity, deliberation, communication, interaction, and consumption. At the same time, though, it works to assemble the most comprehensive system for mass monitoring in human history. The accusation associated with the critique of exploitation reminds us of the ways in which new forms of marketing-driven surveillance help turn our own productive activity back upon ourselves in the service of ends that are not our own. In so doing, to borrow Smith's formulation, the interactive infrastructure "separates a mode of existence from its power of acting."[82] Countering alienation, then, would not mean the same thing as restoring value by compensating users. It would entail rethinking and transforming relations of control over and access to the communicative infrastructure. Such transformations would, in turn, mean radically altering the economic strategies we have adopted for supporting the development of new media technologies and applications. The profound difficulty we have in even imaging possible alternatives to these strategies is perhaps one more symptom of the system they would replace. In an era of digitization and emergent data clouds, such a change would mean recognizing that matter still matters, and that the ostensibly outdated concerns about relations of private ownership and the imperatives these reinforce stubbornly persist.

It will not be enough, however, to gain control over the infrastructure of our communicative lives. We will also need to gain control over the forms of post-comprehension knowledge that promise to populate the databases and contest their displacement of comprehension, models, theories, and narratives.

This is the critical challenge posed by the Big Data era and the new forms of control it ushers in: not simply to reimagine infrastructural arrangements, but also the knowledge practices with which they are associated. Just turning the databases back on the data miners will not be enough: we need to develop resources for reviving the experience of diremption, alienation, and exploitation as such. In other words, we need to find a way of re-inscribing (suppressed) forms of knowledge back upon the new ways of knowing associated with the database/algorithm assemblage. If this sounds like a perversely negative assessment of new technological capabilities, products, and services, it is an assessment driven by a consideration of the political, economic, and environmental background against which the recent promise of digital media technologies unfolds: the ascendance of conservative forms of neoliberalism in many nations, the increasing income gap in many industrialized countries (and the systematic dismantling of their social safety nets and labor unions), new regimes of austerity associated with the global financial crisis, and the inability of governments to address the looming threat of global warming. Against this background the technological promise starts to look like little more than an alibi. To experience the failure of this promise as such is to simultaneously imagine the possibility of its redemption.

NOTES

Chapter 1

1 Dana Priest and William Arkin. "Top Secret America: A Hidden World Growing Beyond Control," *The Wall Street Journal*, 19 July 2010, http://projects. washingtonpost. com/top-secret-america/articles/a-hidden-world-growing-beyond-control/print/ (accessed 10 August 2012).
2 Ibid.
3 Ibid.
4 Ibid.
5 Jorge Luis Borges. *Ficciones* (New York: Grove Press, 1994), p114.
6 David Shenk. *Data Smog* (New York: Harper Collins, 1997), p38.
7 *PR Newswire*. "Americans Slam News Media on Believability," 9 January 2008.
8 Karl Marx and Friedrich Engels. *The German Ideology, Part 1* (New York International Publishers, 1970), p5.
9 James Glanz, William Broad, and David Danger. "Huge Cache of Explosives Vanished from Site in Iraq," *The New York Times*, 25 October 2004, http://www.nytimes.com/2004/10/25/international/middleeast/25bomb.html (accessed 10 August 2012).
10 Slavoj Zizek. *Iraq: The Borrowed Kettle* (London, Verso: 2004), p22.
11 James Glanz, William Broad, and David Danger. "Huge Cache of Explosives Vanished from Site in Iraq," *The New York Times*, 25 October 2004, http://www.nytimes.com/2004/10/25/international/middleeast/25bomb.html (accessed 10 August 2012).
12 *Agence France Presse*. "Discrepancy Found in Amount of Explosives at Iraqi Facility," *Newswire*, 28 October 2004.
13 David Sanger. "The 2004 Campaign: The Candidates," *The New York Times*, 26 October 2004, pA1.
14 David Halbfinger. "Kerry Attacks Bush Over Loss of Explosives," *The New York Times*, 27 October 2004, p17.
15 CNN. "Lou Dobbs Tonight," 26 October 2004.
16 Shenk. *Data Smog*, p101.

17 Brian Massumi. "The Future Birth of the Affective Fact," Conference proceedings, *Ethics and Politics of Virtuality and Indexicality*, University of Leeds, 30 June 2005, p5, http://browse.reticular.info/text/collected/massumi.pdf (accessed 10 August 2012).

18 As quoted in Shenk, *Data Smog*, p78.

19 Naomi Oreskes and Erik Conway. *Merchants of Doubt: How a Handful of Scientists Obscured the Truth on Issues from Tobacco Smoke to Global Warming* (New York: Bloomsbury Press, 2010).

20 Ibid, p34.

21 Ibid, p63.

22 James Fallows. "Bit by Bit It Takes Shape: Media Evolution for the 'Post-Truth' Age," *The Atlantic*, 9 August 2012, http://www.theatlantic.com/politics/archive/2012/08/bit-by-bit-it-takes-shape-media-evolution-for-the-post-truth-age/261741/ (accessed 10 August 2012).

23 See, for example, Clay Shirky. "Newspapers and Thinking the Unthinkable," Clay Shirky (blog), 13 March 2009, http://www.shirky.com/weblog/2009/03/newspapers-and-thinking-the-unthinkable/ (accessed 10 August 2012).

24 Stephen Coleman. "A Tale of Two Houses: The House of Commons, The Big Brother House", *The Hansard Society*, 2003, p35, www.clubpublic.org/eve/030708/Hansardb_b.pdf (accessed 24 July 2011).

25 Lev Grossman. "You – Yes, You – Are Person of the Year," *Time*, 25 December 2006, http://www.time.com/time/magazine/article/0,9171,1570810,00.html (accessed 10 September 2011).

26 Cathy Bryan, Rosa Tsagarousianou, and Damian Tambini. "Electronic Democracy and the Civic Networking Movement in Context," in *Cyberdemocracy: Technology, Cities, and Civic Networks*, ed. Cathy Bryan, Rosa Tsagarousianou, and Damian Tambini (London: Routledge, 1998), p5.

27 Celia Pearce. *The Interactive Book* (New York: Penguin, 1997), p183.

28 Bruno Latour. "Why has Critique Run out of Steam? From Matters of Fact to Matters of Concern," *Critical Inquiry*, vol 30, Winter 2004, pp225–245, 230.

29 Ibid, 225.

30 Coleman. "A Tale of Two Houses," p35.

31 Sherry Turkle. *Life on the Screen: Identity in the Age of the Internet* (New York: Simon & Schuster, 1997), p18.

32 Stephen Coleman. "Connecting Parliament to the Public via the Internet: Two Case Studies of Online Consultations," *Information, Communication & Society*, March 2004, p2, http://depts.washington.edu/ccce/assets/documents/coleman1.pdf (accessed 10 August 2012).

33 Slavoj Zizek. *The Ticklish Subject* (London: Verso, 1999).

34 Slavoj Zizek. *The Indivisible Remainder: An Essay on Schelling and Related Matters* (London: Verso, 1996), p196.

35 Zizek. *The Ticklish Subject*, p323.

36 Ibid. The Groucho Marx quote, according to Zizek, is: "Whom do you believe, your eyes or my words?"

37 Slavoj Zizek. *How to Read Lacan* (New York: W.W. Norton, 2007), p27.

38 Immanuel Kant. *"What is Enlightenment,"* *On History*, ed. and trans. Lewis White Beck (New York: Macmillan, 1963), p3.

39 Jonathan Chait. "Who's Smarter, Obama or Bush?," *The New Republic*, 14 April 2012, http://www.tnr.com/blog/jonathan-chait/whos-smarter-obama-or-bush# (accessed 10 August 2012).

40 Mark Danner. "Words in a Time of War: On Rhetoric, Truth and Power", in ed. Szántó, András, *What Orwell Didn't Know: Propaganda and the New Face of American Politics* (New York, PublicAffairs: 2007), p17.

41 Ron Suskind. "Faith, Certainty, and the presidency of George W. Bush," *The New York Times Magazine*, 17 October 2004, http://www.nytimes.com/2004/10/17/magazine/17BUSH.html (accessed 18 August 2012).

42 Jean Baudrillard. *Simulacra and Simulation* (Ann Arbor: University of Michigan Press, 2001), p1.

43 Ibid, p2.

44 William E. Connolly. *Neuropolitics: Thinking, Culture, Speed* (Minneapolis: University of Minnesota Press, 2002), p10.

45 Aaron Weller. "Quote of the Day: Here Today, Gone More Valuable Tomorrow," *Forbes*, 3 October 2012, http://www.forbes.com/sites/kashmirhill/2012/10/03/quote-of-the-day-here-today-gone-more-valuable-tomorrow/ (accessed 10 August 2012).

Chapter 2

1 Holman Jenkins. "Can Data Mining Stop the Killing?," *The Wall Street Journal*, 24 July 2012, http://online.wsj.com/article/SB10000872396390443570904577546671693245302.html (accessed 10 August 2012).

2 Ibid.

3 William Bogard. *The Simulation of Surveillance* (Cambridge: Cambridge University Press, 1996), p33.

4 Colleen McCue. *Data Mining and Predictive Analysis* (New York: Butterworth-Heinemann, 2006), pxiii.

5 Ibid, p30.

6 Jean Baudrillard. *Simulations and Simulacra* (New York: Semiotext(e), 1983), p27.

7 Jean Baudrillard. "The Virtual Illusion: Or the Automatic Writing of the World," *Theory, Culture & Society*, vol 12, 1995, p97.

8 As quoted in: Ian Hacking. *The Taming of Chance* (Cambridge: Cambridge University Press, 1990), p12.

9 Bogard, p134.

10 Philip K. Dick. *The Collected Stories of Philip K. Dick, Volume 4: The Minority Report* (New York, Citadel: 1994), p72.

11 Michel Foucault. *Security, Territory, Population: Lectures at the Collège de France 1977–1978* (New York: Picador, 2009), p20.

12 Colleen McCue. "Data Mining and Predictive Analytics: Battlespace Awareness for the War on Terrorism," *Defense Intelligence Journal*, vol 13, no 1&2, 2005, p47.

13 Ryan Singel. "FBI Mined Grocery Store Records to Find Iranian Terrorists, CQ Reports," Wired.com, 6 November 2007, http://www.wired.com/threatlevel/2007/11/fbi-mined-groce/ (accessed 10 August 2012).

14 Charles Duhigg. "How Companies Learn Your Secrets," *The New York Times*, 16 February 2012, http://www.nytimes.com/2012/02/19/magazine/shopping-habits.html?pagewanted=all (accessed 10 August 2012).

15 Ibid.

16 Ibid.

17 Ibid.

18 Ibid.

19 Bogard. *Simulation of Surveillance*, p90.

20 McCue. *Data Mining*, p29.

21 David Weinberger. *Too Big to Know* (New York: Basic Books, 2011), p130.

22 An excerpted version of Weinberger's argument appears in *The Atlantic* under the title: "To Know, but Not Understand: David Weinberger on Science and Big Data." David Weinberger, "To Know, but Not Understand," *The Atlantic*, 3 January

2012, http://www.theatlantic.com/technology/archive/2012/01/to-know-but-not-understand-david-weinberger-on-science-and-big-data/250820/ (accessed 10 August 2012).

23 McCue. *Data Mining and Predictive Analysis*, p24.
24 Two Crows Corporation. "Introduction to Data Mining and Knowledge Discovery," Online publication, http://www.twocrows.com/intro-dm.pdf, 10 August 2010, p1.
25 Robert O'Harrow, Jr. *No Place to Hide* (New York: Free Press, 2005), p78.
26 Darryl Taft. "IBM Takes Its Big Data Analytics to Academia," *TechWeek Europe*, 22 December 2011, http://www.techweekeurope.co.uk/news/ibm-takes-its-big-data-analytics-to-academia-51145 (accessed 10 August 2012).
27 Brad Hamilton. "Misfortune Telling: Can the NYPD Predict a Crime Before it Happens? A Tech Guru Thinks So," *The New York Post*, 17 April 2011, p25.
28 Quentin Hardy. "IBM: Big Data, Bigger Patterns," *Bits* (*The New York Times*'s tech blog), 15 February 2012, http://bits.blogs.nytimes.com/2012/02/15/i-b-m-big-data-bigger-patterns/ (accessed 10 August 2012).
29 IBM. "IBM SPSS Predictive Analytics in Fusion Centers," White Paper, 2010, http://home.comcast.net/~leslie.corkill/Portfolio/2010_IBM_TechE.pdf (accessed 10 August 2012).
30 ENP Newswire. "Scala Introduces Advanced Analytics," Press Release, 7 March 2012.
31 *The Edge* (Malaysia). "Net Value: Digital Predictions for 2011," 17 January 2011, p1.
32 Carly Weeks. "Advertising Closing in on *Minority Report*-Style Marketing," *The Globe and Mail*, 15 June 2011, p1.
33 Business Wire. "*Adobe Digital Marketing Suite Tackles Big Data with Predictive Marketing*," Press release, 21 March 2012.
34 Ibid.
35 Ibid.
36 Rachel Nolan. "Behind the Cover Story: How Much Does Target Know?" *The New York Times*, 21 February 2012, http://6thfloor.blogs.nytimes.com/2012/02/21/behind-the-cover-story-how-much-does-target-know/ (accessed 10 August 2012).
37 Ian Ayres. *Super Crunchers: How Anything Can be Predicted* (London: John Murray, 2007), p48.
38 Beth Pearsall. "Predictive Policing: The Future of Law Enforcement?" *NIJ Journal* 266, June 2012, http://www.nij.gov/journals/266/predictive.htm (accessed 10 August 2012).
39 Martine Powers. "Policing by the Numbers: Cambridge Officials Credit Data Analysis for a Drop in Serious Crime," *The Boston Globe*, 16 February 2012, pB1.
40 Erica Goode. "In the U.S.: A New Computer Program Aims to Fight Crime by Predicting It," *The International Herald Tribune*, 17 August 2011, p4.
41 Bartholomew Sullivan. "Godwin Touts Blue CRUSH in Washington," *The Commercial Appeal*, 1 April 2011, pB6.
42 Pearsall. *Predictive Policing*.
43 Goode. "In the U.S.," p4.
44 Martin Beckford. "Foreign Powers Will Be Allowed to Access Email and Phone Records," *The Telegraph*, 4 July 2012, http://www.telegraph.co.uk/news/uknews/law-and-order/9372965/Foreign-powers-will-be-allowed-to-access-email-and-phone-records.html (accessed 10 August 2012).
45 Chris Calabrese. "The Biggest New Spying Program You've Probably Never Heard Of," ACLU Website, 30 July 2012, http://www.aclu.org/blog/national-security-technology-and-liberty/biggest-new-spying-program-youve-probably-never-heard (accessed 10 August 2012).

46 Colleen McCue. "Data Mining: And Predictive Analytics," *Defense Intelligence Journal*, vol 13, no 1&2, 2005, pp47–63, 48.

47 As quoted in Ibid, pp49–50.

48 Ibid, p48.

49 Andrew Zammit-Mangionab, Michael Dewarc, Visakan Kadirkamanathand, and Guido Sanguinettia. "Point Process Modelling of the Afghan War Diary," *Proceedings of the National Academy of Sciences (PNAS)*, 16 July 2102, http://www.pnas.org/content/early/2012/07/11/1203177109.full.pdf+html (accessed 10 August 2012).

50 Irfan Kahn. "Strategic Weapon: Unstructured Data Yields Battlefield Edge," IT World Blog, 9 August 2012, http://www.itworld.com/big-datahadoop/289177/strategic-weapon-unstructured-data-delivers-battlefield-edge (accessed 10 August 2012).

51 Ibid.

52 Ibid.

53 Hari Pulakkat. "Elegant Scientific Theories, Techniques Being Used to Analyse Messy Social Conflicts," *The Economic Times*, 25 September 2011, http://articles.economictimes.indiatimes.com/2011-09-25/news/30198477_1_social-science-social-media-computer (accessed 10 August 2012).

54 Kade Crockford. "Private Spies and Our Growing Surveillance State," *The Nation*, 4 September 2012, http://www.thenation.com/article/169727/private-spies-and-our-growing-surveillance-state (accessed 10 August 2012).

55 Bill Gates. *The Road Ahead* (New York: Penguin, 1996), p33.

56 James Banford. "The NSA is Building the Country's Biggest Spy Center (Watch What You Say!)," *Wired Magazine*, 15 March 2012, http://www.wired.com/threatlevel/2012/03/ff_nsadatacenter/ (accessed 10 August 2012).

57 Gus Hunt. "Big Data: Operational Excellence Ahead in the Cloud," Presentation to the Amazon Web Services Government Summit 2011, 26 October, Washington, DC, http://www.youtube.com/watch?v=SkIhHnoPpjA (accessed 10 August 2012).

58 Ibid.

59 Ibid.

60 Ibid.

61 Ibid.

62 Timothy Lee. "House Approves Another Five Years of Warrantless Wiretapping Reauthorization of the FISA Amendments Act Must Still Be Passed by the Senate," ArsTechnica.com, 12 September 2012, http://arstechnica.com/tech-policy/2012/09/house-approves-another-five-years-of-warrantless-wiretapping/ (accessed 20 September 2012).

63 Ibid.

64 The caption of the original cartoon by Peter Steiner in the 5 July 1993 issue of *The New Yorker* is "On the Internet, nobody knows you're a dog."

65 Tomio Geron. "Kaggle's Predictive Data Contest Aims to Fix Health Care," *Forbes*, 4 April 2012, http://www.forbes.com/sites/tomiogeron/2011/04/04/kaggles-predictive-data-contest-aims-to-fix-health-care/ (accessed 10 August 2012).

66 Bogard. *The Simulation of Surveillance*, p132.

67 Michael Barbaro and Tom Zeller, Jr. "A Face Is Exposed for AOL Searcher No. 4417749," *The New York Times*, 9 August 2006, http://www.nytimes.com/2006/08/09/technology/09aol.html?pagewanted=all (accessed 10 August 2012).

68 Jacqui Cheng. "Netflix Settles Privacy Law Suit; Ditches $1 Million Contest," Ars Technica, 12 March 2010, http://arstechnica.com/tech-policy/2010/03/netflix-ditches-1-million-contest-in-wake-of-privacy-suit/ (accessed 10 August 2012).

69 Tania Karas. "10 Things Online Data Collectors Won't Say," SmartMoney.com, 6 April 2012, http://www.smartmoney.com/spend/technology/10-things-online-data-collectors-wont-say-1333598586287/ (accessed 10 August 2012).

70 Ibid.

71 Nolan. "Behind the Cover Story."

72 Chris Anderson. "The End of Theory: The Data Deluge Makes the Scientific Method Obsolete," *Wired Magazine*, 23 June 2008, http://www.wired.com/science/discoveries/magazine/16–07/pb_theory (accessed 30 August 2008; 12 March 2012).

73 See, for example, Malcolm Gladwell. "The Science of Shopping," *The New Yorker*, 4 November 1996, pp23–44.

74 Ibid, p28.

Chapter 3

1 For an in-depth discussion of the notion of "digital enclosure," see: Mark Andrejevic. *iSpy: Surveillance and Power in the Interactive Era* (Lawrence, KS: University of Kansas Press, 2007).

2 Biztech2.com. "IBM Helps Cities Measure Public Social Sentiment on Critical Issues," 13 September 2012, http://biztech2.in.com/news/social/ibm-helps-cities-measure-public-social-sentiment-on-critical-issues/143572/0 (accessed 10 August 2012).

3 Steve Lohr. "The Age of Big Data," *The New York Times*, 11 February 2012, http://www.nytimes.com/2012/02/12/sunday-review/big-datas-impact-in-the-world.html?pagewanted=all (accessed 10 August 2012).

4 Randy Saaf. "Case Study: *AlphaGenius*, Sentiment Investing – Above Market Returns Extracting & Analyzing Twitter & the Social Internet Plenary Session," Presentation to the Predictive Analytics World Conference, 25–26 June 2012, Chicago, http://www.predictiveanalytic world. com/chicago/2012/agenda.php (accessed 10 August 2012).

5 Ibid.

6 Thomas Davenport and D. J. Patil. "Data Scientist: The Sexiest Job of the 21st Century," *Harvard Business Review*, October 2012, http://hbr.org/2012/10/data-scientist-the-sexiest-job-of-the-21st-century/ar/pr (accessed 10 August 2012).

7 Maurizio Lazzarato. "Immaterial Labour," in *Radical Thought in Italy: A Potential Politics* eds. P. Virno and M. Hardt (Minneapolis: University of Minnesota Press, 1996), pp133–150, 137.

8 Michael Hardt. "Affective labor," *Boundary*, vol 2, no 2, 1999, pp89–100, 93.

9 Genevieve Bell. "Anthropology at Intel: A Thrice Told Tale," Keynote Talk, Australian Anthropological Society Conference, 2012, September, Brisbane, pp26–28.

10 Lohr. "The Age of Big Data."

11 Alex Wright. "Mining the Web for Feelings, Not Facts," *The New York Times*, 23 August 2009, viewed 28 November 2009, http://www.nytimes.com/2009/08/24/technology/internet/24emotion.html (accessed 10 August 2012).

12 Attensity. "Learn more about Attensity," Corporate home page, 20 January 2010, http://www.nytimes.com/2009/08/24/technology/internet/24emotion.html (accessed 10 August 2012).

13 Patricia Clough. "The New Empiricism: Affect and Sociological Method," *European Journal of Social Theory*, vol 12, no 1, 2009, pp43–61, 53.

14 Ibid.

15 Noah Shachtman. "Exclusive: U.S. Spies Buy Stake in Firm That Monitors Blogs, Tweets," *Wired.com*, 19 October 2009, http://www.wired.com/dangerroom/2009/10/exclusive-us-spies-buy-stake-in-twitter-blog-monitoring-firm/ (accessed 10 August 2012).

16 Brian Massumi. "The Future Birth of the Affective Fact," in Conference proceedings, *Ethics and Politics of Virtuality and Indexicality*, University of Leeds, 30 June 2005,

pp1–12, http://browse.reticular.info/text/collected/massumi.pdf (accessed 10 August 2012).

17 Ron Suskind. "Faith, Certainty, and the presidency of George W. Bush," *The New York Times Magazine*, 17 October 2004, http://www.nytimes.com/2004/10/17/magazine/17BUSH.html (accessed 18 August 2012).

18 Massumi, "The Future Birth of the Affective Fact," p7.

19 Clough. "The New Empiricism," p50.

20 Public Policy Polling. "Fox the Most Trusted Name in News?," Press release, 26 January 2010, http://www.publicpolicypolling.com/pdf/PPP_Release_National_126.pdf (accessed 10 August 2012).

21 Ibid.

22 Cass Sunstein. *Republic.com* (Princeton: Princeton University Press, 2001).

23 Cass Sunstein. "The Daily We: Is the Internet Really a Blessing for Democracy," *Boston Review*, Summer, 26, no. 3, 2001, http://www.bostonreview.net/BR26.3/sunstein.html (accessed 10 August 2012).

24 John Hockenberry. "Thinking Like a Scientist: Solution to Politics," *The Takeaway*, WNYC, 27 September 2012, http://www.thetakeaway.org/2012/sep/27/thinking-scientist-solution-politics/?utm_source=local&utm_media=treatment&utm_campaign=featuredcomment&utm_content=article.

25 Ibid.

26 Ibid.

27 Henry Jenkins. *Convergence Culture: Where Old and New Media Collide* (New York and London: New York University Press, 2006).

28 Ibid, p319.

29 Ibid, p62.

30 Ibid, p63.

31 Ibid, p69.

32 Ibid, p70.

33 Ibid, p93.

34 Daniel W. Smith. "Deleuze and the Question of Desire: Toward an Immanent Theory of Ethics," *Parrhesia*, no 2, 2007, pp66–78, 74.

35 Patricia Clough. "Affect and Control: Rethinking the Body 'Beyond Sex and Gender,' *Feminist Theory*, vol 4, no 3, 2003, pp359–364, 360.

36 Ibid.

37 Massumi. "The Future Birth of the Affective Fact," p45.

38 Ibid, p27.

39 Eric Shouse. "Feeling, Emotion, Affect," *M/C Journal*, vol 8, no 6, 2005, http://journal.media-culture.org.au/0512/03-shouse.php (accessed 10 August 2012).

40 Massumi. "The Future Birth of the Affective Fact," p28.

41 Clough. "The New Empiricism," p48.

42 Ibid, p50.

43 Ibid, p52.

44 Sysomos. "Products," Corporate Website, 2010, http://www.sysomos.com/products/features (accessed 10 August 2010).

45 Jodi Dean. *Blog Theory: Feedback and Capture in the Circuits of Drive* (Cambridge: Polity Press, 2010), p89.

46 Ibid.

47 Listening Station. "Home," Homepage, 2010, http://www.listening-station.com/index.html (accessed 10 August 2010).

48 Ibid.

49 Jodange. "Home," Homepage, 2010, http://www.jodange.com/index.html (accessed 10 August 2010); Scout Labs. "Product," Homepage, 2010, http://www.scoutlabs.com/product/ (accessed 10 August 2010).

50 24/7 Customer. "Tweetview," 2010, http://www.247tweetview.com/tweetview/ (accessed 10 August 2010).
51 Jenkins. *Convergence Culture*, p80.
52 Ibid.
53 Ibid, p218.
54 Ibid, p223.
55 Clough. "Affect and Control," p361.
56 ReadWriteWeb. "5 Ways Sentiment Analysis Is Ramping Up in 2009," Blog, http://www.readwriteweb.com/archives/sentiment_analysis_is_ramping_up_in_2009. php (accessed 25 May 2010, italics added).
57 Slavoj Zizek. "Unbehgan in der Natur," ["Ecology Against Nature"] *Bedeutung Magazine*, vol 1, 2008, http://www.bedeutung.co.uk/index.php?option=com_ content&view=article&id=10:zizek-unbehagen-in-der-natur&catid=6:contents& Itemid=16 (accessed 22 May 2010).
58 Michael Sisk. "Tools to Analyze Buzz Are Generating Some More of It," *American Banker*, 16 October, 2009, p6.
59 ScoutLabs. "Product."
60 *Business Wire*. "PowerReviews Announces BrandConnect™; Helps Brands Drive Sales by Listening to and Engaging Customers; New Data Shows Brands Are Hungry for Social Tools that Help Them Drive Engagement, Loyalty and Word-of-Mouth Among Customers," 22 September 2009, http://findarticles.com/p/articles/ mi_m0EIN/is_20090922/ai_n35683272/?tag=content;coll (accessed 10 August 2011).
61 Ibid.
62 Ibid.
63 Massumi. "Future Birth of the Affective Fact," p6.
64 Ian Ayres. *Super Crunchers: How Anything Can be Predicted* (London: John Murray, 2007).
65 Ibid, p50.
66 Ibid, p49.
67 Chris Anderson. "The End of Theory: The Data Deluge Makes the Scientific Method Obsolete", *Wired Magazine*, vol 16, no 7, 23 June 2008, http://www. wired.com/science/discoveries/magazine/16–07/pb_theory (accessed 30 August 2011).
68 Brian Massumi. *Parables of the Virtual: Movement, Affect, Sensation* (Durham & London: Duke University Press, 2002), p23.
69 Ayres. *Super Crunching*, p44.
70 Massumi. "The Future Birth of the Affective Fact"; Clough. "Affect and Control."
71 Clough. "Affect and Control," p361 (internal quotes are from Massumi 1998).
72 Clough, "The New Empiricism," p50.
73 Jenkins. *Convergence Culture*, p260.
74 Ibid, p226.
75 Clough. "Affect and Control," p360.
76 Thanks to Jack Bratich for proposing the notion of "divergence culture" in conversation.
77 Jenkins. *Convergence Culture*, p223.
78 Ibid, pp293–294.

Chapter 4

1 Andy Sullivan. "Clinton Dismisses 'Elite' Economists on Gas Tax Plan," *Reuters*, 4 May 2008, http://www.reuters.com/article/idUSNO4324440 (accessed 10 August 2012).

2 Alison Mitchell. "Bush Derides Gore for Rejecting Debate Plan," *The New York Times*, 5 September 2000, pA22. The proposed gas tax holiday fit with Bush policy in more ways than one. The general consensus of the experts was that any reduction in the tax would quickly be erased by increased demand, driving prices back up and leading to a transfer of money from the public to the private sector. Consumers would end up paying the same amount, the government would get less, and oil companies would realize additional profits. At least that's what the "elite" experts were saying.

3 Alison Mitchell. "Bush Says that Bottom Line on Gore's Proposals Would Consume the Surplus," *The New York Times*, 7 September 2000, pA27.

4 The Colbert quote from his famous appearance at the White House Correspondents' Dinner in 2006 is "Reality has a well-known liberal bias." For coverage of the talk, see: *Editor & Publisher* Staff. "Colbert Lampoons Bush at White House Correspondents Dinner – President Not Amused?," *Editor & Publisher*, 29 April 2006, http://www.editorandpublisher.com/Headlines/Article/Colbert-Lampoons-Bush-at-White-House-Correspondents-Dinner-President-Not-Amused (accessed 10 August 2012).

5 *The O'Reilly Factor*. Fox News Channel, First aired 5 February 2010.

6 David Shenk. *Data Smog* (San Francisco: Harper Collins, 1997), p81.

7 Josh Marshall. "The Post-Modern President. Deception, Denial, and Relativism: What the Bush Administration Learned from the French," *Washington Monthly*, September 2003, http://www.washingtonmonthly.com/features/2003/0309.marshall.html (accessed 10 August 2012).

8 David Leonhard. "When the Crowd Isn't Wise," *The New York Times*, 8 July 2012, pE1.

9 Liz Benston. "Markets Pick 'Em Better than Polls," *Las Vegas Sun*, 16 January 2008, p1.

10 David Leonhardt. "Making Bets on Elections, Traders Buy Online Contracts," *International Herald Tribune*, 14 February 2008, second ed., p16.

11 David Alexander. "Political Markets See Clinton vs. Giuliani Contest," *Reuters News*, 29 October 2007, http://www.reuters.com/article/idUSN2636611520071029 (accessed 10 August 2012).

12 I owe the formulation of "divergence culture" to Jack Bratich, in a personal conversation.

13 James Surowiecki. "Q&A with James Surowiecki," *The Wisdom of Crowds*, 2004, http://www.randomhouse.com/features/wisdomofcrowds/Q&A.html (accessed 10 August 2012).

14 Robin Hanson. "Shall We Vote on Values, But Bet on Beliefs?" Author homepage, October 2007, http://hanson.gmu.edu/futarchy.html (accessed 10 May 2010).

15 Paul Parsons. "Predicting the Future with the Power of Betting," *The Telegraph*, 18 August 2008, http://www.telegraph.co.uk/science/science-news/3349800/Predicting-the-future-with-the-power-of-betting.html (accessed 10 August 2012).

16 Michael Abramowicz. *Predictocracy: Market Mechanisms for Public and Private Decision Making* (New Haven, CT: Yale University Press, 2008).

17 Ibid.

18 James Surowiecki. *The Wisdom of Crowds* (New York: Anchor Books, 2004).

19 James Surowiecki. "Q&A with James Surowiecki," *The Wisdom of Crowds*, 2004, http://www.randomhouse.com/features/wisdomofcrowds/Q&A.html (accessed 10 August 2012).

20 Surowiecki. *The Wisdom of Crowds*, p23.

21 Michael Lewis. *The Big Short: Inside the Doomsday Machine* (London: Penguin Books, 2010), p244.

22 Ibid, p61.

23 Peter Rowe. "Decision Markets Tap 'Wisdom of the Crowd,'" *San Diego Union-Tribune*, 1 February 2012, pE1.

24 Danny O'Brien. "Gambling Dressed up in a Well Street Suit?" *Irish Times*, 7 March 2008, p8.

25 Ibid.

26 Michael Schrage and Sam Savage. "If This Is Harebrained, Bet on the Hare," *The Washington Post*, 3 August 2003, pB4.

27 Robert Hahn and Paul Tetlock. "When Gambling Is Good," *The Wall Street Journal*, 11 May 2007, pA10.

28 Surowiecki. *The Wisdom of Crowds*, p250.

29 David Saltonstall. "You'da Made Bundle Even on Small 'O7 Bet on Bam,'" *New York Daily News*, 3 November 2008, p28.

30 June Kronholz. "Campaign '08: Prediction Traders Put Their Money on Obama," *The Wall Street Journal*, 13 February 2008, pA8.

31 Gordon Crovitz. "Information Age: Trading on the Wisdom of Crowds," *The Wall Street Journal*, 28 April 2008, pA17.

32 *The Economist*. "Economic Focus: Guessing Games", 20 November 2004, http://bpp. wharton.upenn.edu/jwolfers/Press/Mentions/GuessingGames(The%20Economist). pdf (accessed 10 August 2012).

33 Mitchell Dean. *Governmentality: Power and Rule in Modern Society* (London: Sage, 1999), p162.

34 Paul Rhode and Koleman Strumpf. "Historical Presidential Betting Markets," *The Journal of Economic Perspectives*, vol 18, no 2, Spring, 2004, pp127–141, 129.

35 Paul Parsons. "Predicting the Future with the Power of Betting," *The Telegraph*, 18 August 2008, http://www.telegraph.co.uk/science/science-news/3349800/Predicting-the-future-with-the-power-of-betting.html (accessed 10 August 2012), p25.

36 Ibid.

37 Thanks to Anna Pertierra for her discussion of this shift during a Work in Progress session at the Centre for Critical and Cultural Studies, University of Queensland.

38 David Pennock. "The Good Side of the 'Terror Futures' Idea (Yes, There Is One)," *Yahoo! Research*, 5 August 2003, http://dpennock.com/pam.html (accessed 5 May 2010).

39 Slavoj Zizek. *The Sublime Object of Ideology* (London: Verso, 1989), p28.

40 Ibid, p28.

41 Ibid, p28.

42 Slavoj Zizek. *In Defense of Lost Causes* (London: Verso, 2008), p453.

43 Brit Hume. "Fox Special Report with Brit Hume," Fox News, 3 March 2003. The 90 percent statistic is from: ABC News. "Persian Gulf Ally Dragging Its Feet," 8 January 2003, http://abcnews.go.com/WNT/story?id=129901&page=1 (accessed 1 October 2011).

44 Christopher Walker. "Get Ready for the War in Europe," *The Independent, Independent on Sunday*, 23 February 2003, p2.

45 Slavoj Zizek. "Unbehgan in der Natur," ["Ecology Against Nature"] *Bedeutung Magazine*, vol 1, 2008, http://www.bedeutung.co.uk/index.php?option=com_content &view=article&id=10:zizek-unbehagen-in-der-natur&catid=6:contents&Itemid=16 (accessed 10 August 2010).

46 Ibid.

47 Slavoj Zizek. "Against the Populist Temptation," *Critical Inquiry*, vol 32, Spring, pp551–574, 555.

48 Ibid, p556.

Chapter 5

 1 John Durham Peters. "John Locke, the Individual, and the Origin of Communication," *The Quarterly Journal of Speech*, vol 75, 1989, pp387–399.

2 Kevin Warwick. "Cyborg 1.0," *Wired Magazine*, February 2000, http://www.wired.com/wired/archive/8.02/warwick_pr.html (accessed 10 August 2012).

3 Malcolm Gladwell. *Blink: The Power of Thinking Without Thinking* (Back Bay Books, Little Brown, 2005).

4 Ibid.

5 Malcolm Gladwell. "The Second Mind," Online excerpt from the book *Blink*, 2005, http://www.gladwell.com/blink/blink_excerpt1.html (accessed 10 August 2011).

6 Malcolm Gladwell. "What Is *Blink* About," Online Q&A about the book *Blink*, 2005, http://www.gladwell.com/blink/blink_excerpt1.html (accessed 20 January 2010).

7 Ibid.

8 *The Mentalist.* "Pilot," Primrose Hill Productions, Warner Brothers Television, first aired 28 September 2008.

9 *The Mentalist.* "Crimson Casanova," Primrose Hill Productions, Warner Brothers Television, first aired 8 February 2009.

10 *Lie to Me.* Television program, Fox Television, Network Ten, Brisbane, broadcast 10 March 2009.

11 Ibid.

12 Ibid.

13 CBS News: *The Saturday Early Show.* "Interview: Joe Navarro, 'What Every Body is Saying,' Discusses Body Language of Candidates at Presidential Debate," CBS Worldwide, aired 27 September 2008.

14 CBS News: *The Early Show.* "Profile: Body Language Expert Joe Navarro on Hillary Clinton's Body Language During her Speech at the DNC," CBS TV, aired 27 August 2008a.

15 See, for example, Carol Kinsey Goman. *The Nonverbal Advantage: Secrets and Science of Body Language at Work* (San Francisco: Berrett-Koehler Publishers, 2008); Kevin Hogan. *The Secret Language of Business: How to Read Anyone in 3 Seconds or Less* (New York: Wiley, 2008); Joe Navarro. *What Every BODY is Saying: An Ex-FBI Agent's Guide to Speed-Reading People* (New York: Harper Paperbacks, 2008); Tonya Reiman. *The Power of Body Language: How to Succeed in Every Business and Social Encounter* (New York: Pocket Books, 2008).

16 Anand Giridharadas. "India's Novel Use of Brain Scans in Courts Is Debated," *The New York Times*, 17 July 2008, http://www.nytimes.com/2008/09/15/world/asia/15brainscan.html?scp=1&sq=champadi&st=cse (accessed 9 March 2009).

17 Clive Thompson. "There's a Sucker Born in Every Medial Prefrontal Cortex," *The New York Times Magazine*, 26 October 2003, http://query.nytimes.com/gst/fullpage.html?res=9b07e1de113ef935a15753c1a9659c8b63&sec=&spon=&&scp=1&sq=brighthouse%20institute&st=cse (accessed 2 March 2009).

18 Ibid.

19 Bruno Latour. "Why Has Critique Run out of Steam: From Matters of Fact to Matters of Concern," *Critical Inquiry*, vol 30, no 2, winter, 2004 (pp25–248), p228.

20 Copies of these ads, both of which were delivered via e-mail to online subscribers to *Human Events*, are available at http://www.investorsdailyedge.com/ad/mediaads/bndeagle022509.html?fc_c=1368349x2852852x61007965 and http://www.isecureonline.com/Reports/HSI/LHSIJB07/?fc_c=1315494x2636898x61007965.

21 Slavoj Zizek. *The Ticklish Subject* (London: Verso, 1999); Ulrich Beck. *Risk Society: Towards a New Modernity* (London: Sage, 1992).

22 Slavoj Zizek. *Enjoy Your Symptom! Jacques Lacan in Hollywood and Out* (London: Routledge, 2001), p219.

23 Ibid, p220.

24 Sherry Turkle. *Life on the Screen: Identity in the Age of the Internet* (New York: Simon & Schuster, 1997), p19.

25 Ibid, p22. The story about the Facebook breakup was recounted to me by a student.

26 Stephen Coleman. "A Tale of Two Houses: The House of Commons, The Big Brother House," *The Hansard Society*, 2003, www.clubepublic.org/eve/030708/Hansardb_b.pdf, p35 (accessed 24 July 2005).

27 Fox News: *The O'Reilly Factor*. "Body Language: Joe Biden, Sarah Palin, Barney Frank," Fox News Network, aired 6 October 2008.

28 Ibid.

29 David Kamien. *The McGraw-Hill Homeland Security Handbook: The Definitive Guide for Law Enforcement, EMT, and all other Security Professionals* (New York: McGraw-Hill, 2005), p132.

30 IAT Home. "Project Implicit," Website, https://implicit.harvard.edu/implicit/demo/ (accessed 8 March 2009).

31 *World Series of Poker*. "Main Event," Episodes 3, ESPN, 2007, iTunes download.

32 Ibid.

33 Ibid.

34 Ibid.

35 *Celebrity Poker Showdown*. "Tournament 7, Game 2," Bravo, Picture This Television, first aired 20 October 2005.

36 Walter Benjamin. "Notes on a Theory of Gambling," in *The Sociology of Risk and Gambling Reader*, ed. James F. Cosgrove (New York, Routledge, 2006), p214.

37 Ibid, p214.

38 Ad Council. "Homeland Security Readiness Campaign", http://www.adcouncil.org/campaigns/homeland_security (accessed 24 October 2005).

39 Elayne Rapping. "Aliens, Nomads, Mad Dogs and Road Warriors: The Changing Face of Criminal Violence on TV," in *Reality TV: Remaking Television Culture*, eds. Susan Murray and Laurie Ouellette (New York: New York University Press, 2004), p222.

40 Deborah Lupton. "Risk and Governmentality," in *The Sociology of Risk and Gambling Reader*, ed. James F. Cosgrove (New York, Routledge, 2006), p98.

41 Robert O'Harrow Jr. *No Place to Hide* (New York: Free Press, 2005).

42 *The Engineer*. "In Brief: Scientists to Prove Many a True Word is Spoken in Gestures," 19 September 2005, p7.

43 Jeffrey Kluger. "How to Spot a Lie," *Time Magazine*, 20 August 2006, http://www.time.com/time/magazine/article/0,9171,1229109,00.html (accessed 3 March 2009).

44 Ibid.

45 Slavoj Zizek. *The Indivisible Remainder: An Essay on Schelling and Related Matters.* (London: Verso, 1996), p196.

46 CBS News: *The Early Show*. "Interview: Joe Navarro Analyzes Sarah Palin's Acceptance Speech," CBS TV, aired 4 September 2008.

47 Ibid.

48 G. W. F Hegel. *Phenomenology of Spirit* (trans. A.V. Miller) (Oxford, New York, Toronto, Melbourne: Oxford University Press, 1977), p193.

49 Coleman. "A Tale of Two Houses: The House of Commons, The Big Brother House".

50 Ron Suskind. "Without a Doubt," *The New York Times Magazine*, 17 October 2004, http://www.cs.umass.edu/~immerman/play/opinion05/WithoutADoubt.html (accessed 1 March 2009).

51 NBC News: *Today*. "Interview: Joe Navarro Discusses Meaning of Body Language," NBC News, first aired 12 March 2007.

52 Ibid.

53 Fox News: *The Morning Show with Mike and Juliet*. "Interview: Tonya Reiman," Fox News, first aired 12 September 2008. Videos of Reiman's appearance are available online at http://www.youtube.com/watch?v=T3L6Y2OAuFo.

54 Ibid.
55 Ibid.
56 Ibid.
57 Ibid.
58 Ibid.
59 *New Zealand Press Association.* "Poker Players can Learn to Decipher Body Language," 20 October 2008 (accessed via Factiva 1 March 2009).
60 Joe Navarro. "Joe Navarro's Read 'Em and Reap Poker Course: A Spy-Catcher's Video Guide to Reading Tells," 2007, Excerpt viewed on YouTube: http://www. youtube.com/watch?v=7jUUHNmbfxM (accessed 12 March 2009).
61 Ibid.
62 Hegel. *Phenomenology of Spirit*, pp190–191.
63 Ibid.
64 Ian Ayres. *Super Crunchers: How Anything Can Be Predicted* (London: John Murray, 2007).

Chapter 6

1 Innerscope. "Our Approach", Innerscope Research, http://www.innerscoperesearch. com/flat/our_approach.html (accessed 12 December 2011).
2 Ilan Brat. "The Emotional Quotient of Soup Shopping," *Wall Street Journal*, 17 February 2010, p1.
3 Ibid.
4 Jessica Tsai. "Are You Smarter than a Neuromarketer," *CRM Magazine*, vol 14, no 1, 2010, p19.
5 Ibid.
6 Caitlin Johnson. "Cutting through the Advertising Clutter," *CBSnews.com*, 11 February 2009, http://www.cbsnews.com/stories/2006/09/17/sunday/main2015684. shtml (accessed 10 August 2010).
7 Scott Vrecko. "Neuroscience, Power and Culture: An Introduction," *History of the Human Sciences*, vol 23, no 1, 2010, p1.
8 Francisco Ortega and Fernando Vidal. "Mapping the Cerebral Subject in Contemporary Culture," *Reciis: Electronic Journal of Communication Innovation*, vol 1, no 2, 2007, p256.
9 Nikolas Rose. "A Neurobiological Complex? Governing Human Beings in the Age of the Brain," Keynote talk, *Governing Human Beings in the Age of the Brain: A Symposium with Nikolas Rose*, Centre for the History of European Discourses at the University of Queensland, 16 November 2011.
10 Vrecko. "Neuroscience, Power and Culture: An Introduction", p3.
11 Ortega and Vidal. "Mapping the Cerebral Subject in Contemporary Culture", p257.
12 Ibid.
13 Ibid.
14 Jonna Brenninkmeijer. "Taking Care of One's Brain: How Manipulating the Brain Changes People's Selves," *History of the Human Sciences*, vol 23, no 1, 2010, p107.
15 Free Brain Age Games. "Results," Website, http://www.freebrainagegames.com/ index.php (accessed 12 December 2011).
16 Joseph Hardy. "The Science Behind Lumosity," 12 December 2009, www.lumosity. com/documents/the_science_behind_lumosity.pdf (accessed 10 August, 2012), p3; Foresight Mental Capital and Wellbeing Project. *Final Project Report – Executive Summary* (London: Government Office for Science, 2008), p1.
17 Ibid, p10.
18 Ibid, p10.

19 Nikolas Rose. *Powers of Freedom: Reframing Political Thought* (Cambridge: Cambridge University Press, 1999), p164.
20 Nikolas Rose. "The Politics of Life Itself," *Theory, Culture & Society*, vol 18, no 6, 2001, p6.
21 Email Wire. "Keros Client Bark Group Partners with Mindmetic in New Field of Neuromarketing," Press release, 15 December 2009, http://emailwire.com/release/31185-Keros-Client-Bark-Group-Partners-With-Mindmetic-in-New-Field-of-Neuromarketing-.html (accessed 10 August 2011).
22 *PR Newswire*. "Draftfcb Launches Institute of Decision Making; Agency Forms Part- nerships with Leading Academics at Stanford and Berkeley," Press release, 2 July 2010.
23 Carrie Dahlberg. "'Neuromarketing' Science Probes Subconscious Reasons for Buying," *Sacramento Bee*, 4 April 2004, p4.
24 NeuroFocus. "Advertising," NeuroFocus Webpage, http://www.neurofocus.com/Advertise.htm (accessed 12 December 2011),
25 Fernando Vidal. "Brainhood, Anthropological Figure of Modernity," *History of the Human Sciences*, vol 22, no 1, 2009, pp5–36, 6.
26 NeuroFocus. "Entertainment," NeuroFocus Webpage, http://neurofocus.com/entertainment.htm (accessed 10 August 2012).
27 *Asia Pulse*. "Korea's Economy Emerging as World Leader in Brainwave Measure- ment," Press release, 24 June 2009, p1.
28 Antonio Damasio. *Descartes' Error: Emotion, Reason, and the Human Brain* (New York: Harper Perennial, 1995), p171.
29 Ibid, p172.
30 Jonah Lerner. *How We Decide* (New York: Houghton-Mifflin, 2009).
31 Damasio. *Descartes' Error: Emotion, Reason, and the Human Brain*, p45.
32 Ibid, p174.
33 Ibid, p174.
34 Jonah Lerner. *How We Decide* (New York: Houghton-Mifflin, 2009), p23.
35 Ibid, p47.
36 Malcolm Gladwell. *Blink: The Power of Thinking without Thinking* (New York: Little, Brown, and Company, 2005), p22.
37 The Daily Show. "Weathering Fights", Comedy Central, first aired 26 October 2011.
38 Ibid.
39 Hendrik Hertzbert. "Comment: Alt-Newt," *The New Yorker*, 19 December 2011, http://www.newyorker.com/talk/comment/2011/12/19/111219taco_talk_hertzberg (accessed 10 August 2012).
40 Ibid.
41 Ibid.
42 Ruth Leys. "The Turn to Affect: A Critique," *Critical Inquiry*, vol 37, no 3, 2011, pp434–472.
43 Damasio. *Descartes' Error: Emotion, Reason, and the Human Brain*, p436
44 *PR Newswire*. "Draftfcb Launches Institute of Decision Making; Agency Forms Partnerships with Leading Academics at Stanford and Berkeley," Press release, 2 July 2010.
45 Andrew Stark. "Science Comes to Selling," *The Wall Street Journal*, 22 October 2008.
46 Ibid.
47 Slavoj Zizek. *In Defense of Lost Causes* (London: Verso, 2008).
48 *PR Newswire*. "Out of Sync, Out of Sales," Press release, 26 October 2009.
49 Ibid.
50 Samantha Ellis. "You've Seen the Movie, Now Take the Brain Scan," *The Guardian*, 3 June 2004, p8.

51 Robert Hotz. "Songs Stick in Teens' Head," *The Wall Street Journal*, June 2011, http://online.wsj.com/article/SB10001424052702303848104576381823644333598. html (accessed 10 August 2012).
52 Ibid.
53 Vance Packard. *The Hidden Persuaders* (New York: IG Publishing, 1980).
54 Patricia Clough. "The New Empiricism: Affect and Sociological Method," *European Journal of Social Theory*, vol 12, no 1, 2009, p50.

Chapter 7

1 Slavoj Zizek. *The Ticklish Subject* (London: Verso, 1999), p362.
2 Ibid.
3 Ibid.
4 Jodi Dean. "Theorizing Conspiracy Theory," *Theory & Event*, vol 4, no 3, 2000, p2. Dean is referring to: George Marcus, ed. *Paranoia within Reason: A Casebook on Conspiracy as Explanation*, vol 6 (Chicago: University of Chicago Press, 1999).
5 Ibid, p3.
6 Ibid, p1.
7 Paul Krugman. "Gilded Once More," *The New York Times*, 27 April 2007, http://select.nytimes.com/2007/04/27/opinion/27krugman.html (accessed 10 August 2012).
8 DeWayne Wickham. "Is Trump Hype over Obama's Birth Newsworthy?," *USA Today*, 12 April 2011, pA9.
9 Jerome Corsi. "Obama Blinked: Now Game Begins," *World Net Daily*, 27 April 2011, http://www.wnd.com/2011/04/292213 (accessed 10 August 2012).
10 Mark Fenster. *Conspiracy Theories: Secrecy and Power in American Culture* (Minneapolis: University of Minnesota Press, 2008), p123.
11 Mark Fenster and Jack Z. Bratich. "Dialogues in Communication Research: Bratch, J. Z. (2008). Conspiracy Panics: Political Rationality and Popular Culture," *Journal of Communication Inquiry*, vol 33, no 3, 2009, p282.
12 Cass Sunstein and Adrian Vermeule. "Conspiracy Theories," Harvard University Law School Public Law & Legal Theory Research Paper Series, University of Chicago Law School Public Law & Legal Theory Research Paper, 15 January 2008, http://ssrn.com/abstract=1084585 (accessed 10 August 2012), p4.
13 Dean. "Theorizing Conspiracy Theory", p2.
14 Ibid.
15 Ibid.
16 Slavoj Zizek. *The Parallax View* (Cambridge, MA: MIT Press, 2006), p304.
17 Slavoj Zizek. *The Sublime Object of Ideology* (London: Verso, 1989), p49.
18 Mark Fenster. *Conspiracy Theories: Secrecy and Power in American Culture* (Minneapolis: University of Minnesota Press, 2008), p103.
19 Dean. "Theorizing Conspiracy Theory", p2.
20 Fenster. *Conspiracy Theories*, p202.
21 Ibid.
22 Ibid, p225.
23 As quoted in Fenster, *Conspiracy Theories*, p70.
24 Glenn Beck. "The Puppet Master," *Fox News: Glenn Beck*, Fox News Network, 8–11 November 2010, 9 November.
25 Glenn Beck. "The Puppet Master," *Fox News: Glenn Beck*, Fox News Network, 8–11 November 2010, 10 November.
26 Glenn Beck. "The Puppet Master," *Fox News: Glenn Beck*, Fox News Network, 8–11 November 2010, 11 November.
27 Glenn Beck. *Fox News: Glenn Beck*, Fox News Network, 14 February 2011.

28 Glenn Beck. *Fox News: Glenn Beck*, Fox News Network, 22 April 2011.
29 Glenn Beck. *Fox News: Glenn Beck*, Fox News Network, 24 March 2011.
30 Fenster. *Conspiracy Theories*, p123.
31 Glenn Beck. *Fox News: Glenn Beck*, Fox News Network, 5 April 2011.
32 Ibid.
33 As quoted in Fenster, *Conspiracy Theories*, p94.
34 Glenn Beck. *Fox News: Glenn Beck*, Fox News Network, 22 April 2011.
35 Alexander Zaitchik. *Common Nonsense: Glenn Beck and the Triumph of Ignorance* (Hoboken, NJ: John Wiley & Sons, 2010), p200.
36 Ibid, p35.
37 Ron Suskind. "Faith, Certainty, and the Presidency of George W. Bush," *The New York Times Magazine*, 17 October 2004.
38 Glenn Beck. *Fox News: Glenn Beck*, Fox News Network, 22 April 2011.
39 Harold Pollack. "Do Liberals Disdain the Disabled," *The New York Times*, 27 February 2012, http://www.nytimes.com/2012/02/27/opinion/do-liberals-disdain-the-disabled.html?_r=0 (accessed 10 August 2012).
40 Hwa Yol Jung. *Transversal Rationality and Intercultural Texts: Essays in Phenomenology and Comparative Philosophy* (Toledo: University of Ohio Press, 2011), p17.
41 Glenn Beck. *Fox News: Glenn Beck*, Fox News Network, 30 June 2011.
42 Glenn Beck. *Fox News: Glenn Beck*, Fox News Network, 23 June 2011.
43 Slavoj Zizek. "Against the Populist Temptation," *Critical Inquiry*, vol 32, Spring, 2006, p555.
44 Glenn Beck. *Fox News: Glenn Beck*, Fox News Network, 23 June 2011.
45 Zizek. "Against the Populist Temptation", p555.
46 Ibid, p556.
47 Dean. "Theorizing Conspiracy Theory", p2.
48 Jodi Dean. *Blog Theory: Feedback and Capture in the Circuits of the Drive* (Cambridge: Polity Press, 2010), p12.
49 Zizek. "Against the Populist Temptation", p567.
50 Fenster. *Conspiracy Theories*, p220.
51 Glenn Beck. *Fox News: Glenn Beck*, Fox News Network, 29 March 2011.
52 The Daily Show. "The Socialist Network," Comedy Central, 3 March 2012.
53 Michel Foucault. "What Is Critique?" in *The Politics of Truth*, eds. Sylvère Lotringer and Lysa Hochroth (New York: Semiotext(e), 1997), transcript by Monique Emery, revised by Suzanne Delorme et al, translated into English by Lysa Hochroth. This essay was originally a lecture given at the French Society of Philosophy on 27 May 1978, subsequently published in *Bulletin de la Société française de la philosophie*, vol 84, no 2, 1990, p37.
54 Judith Butler. "What Is Critique? An Essay on Foucault's Virtue," EIPCP Website, 2001, http://eipcp.net/transversal/0806/butler/en (accessed 10 August 2012), p5.
55 Ibid, p7.

Chapter 8

1 James Bennett. "'We're Not Going to Let Our Campaign Be Dictated by Fact-Checkers,'" *The Atlantic*, 28 August 2012, http://www.theatlantic.com/politics/archive/2012/08/were-not-going-to-let-our-campaign-be-dictated-by-fact-checkers/261674/ (accessed 10 September 2012).
2 L. Gordon Crovitz. "Double-Checking the Journalist 'Fact Checkers': Their Claims of Campaign Falsehoods Are Often a Matter of Opinion," *The Wall Street Journal*, 9 September 2012, http://online.wsj.com/article/SB10000872396390443686004577639743922340620.html (accessed 12 September 2012).

3 Ibid.
4 Ibid.
5 Jodi Dean. *Blog Theory: Feedback and Capture in the Circuits of the Drive* (Cambridge: Polity Press, 2010), p60.
6 Alenka Zupancic. *The Shortest Shadow: Nietzsche's Philosophy of the Two* (Cambridge, MA: MIT Press, 2003), p25.
7 Ben Zimmer. "On Language: Truthiness," *The New York Times*, 13 October 2010, http://www.nytimes.com/2010/10/17/magazine/17FOB-onlanguage-t.html (accessed 10 August 2012).
8 *CNN: Starting Point with Soledad O'Brien*, 14 August 2012. Interestingly, the moment during which Sununu shouts about "Democratic analysis" is omitted from the official transcript, which describes it as "crosstalk." The full exchange can be found readily online: http://www.youtube.com/watch?v=m2EfmX6LoAA.
9 Jonah Lehrer. "Beware Our Blind Seers," *The Wall Street Journal*, 30 October 2010, http://online.wsj.com/article/SB10001424052702303341904575576650877154216.html (accessed 10 August 2012).
10 Dean. *Blog Theory: Feedback and Capture in the Circuits of Drive*, p90.
11 Bennett. "We're Not Going to Let Our Campaign Be Dictated by Fact-Checkers."
12 Ibid.
13 Brad Knickerbocker. "Polls Favor Obama: A Conspiracy by Democrats and the Media?," *Christian Science Monitor*, 29 September 2012, http://www.csmonitor.com/USA/DC-Decoder/2012/0929/Polls-favor-Obama.-A-conspiracy-by-Democrats-and-the-media-video (accessed 10 August 2012).
14 David Graham. "Meet the Incredible, Incoherent Jobs-Report Truthers," *The Atlantic*, 5 October 2012, http://www.theatlantic.com/politics/archive/2012/10/meet-the-incredible-incoherent-jobs-report-truthers/263285/ (accessed 10 August 2012).
15 Ibid.
16 Dean. *Blog Theory: Feedback and Capture in the Circuits of Drive*, p90.
17 Nicholas Brown and Imre Szeman. "Twenty-five Theses on Philosophy in the Age of Finance Capital," in *A Leftist Ontology: Beyond Relativism and Identity Politics*, Carsten Strathausen, ed. (Minneapolis, University of Minnesota Press, 2009), p37.
18 Ibid.
19 Simon Jarvis. *Adorno: A Critical Introduction* (New York: Routledge, 1998), p25.
20 Ibid, p20.
21 Max Horkheimer and Theodor Adorno. *The Dialectic of Enlightenment* (Stanford, CA: Stanford University Press, 2002), p7.
22 Jane Bennett. *Vibrant Matter: A Political Ecology of Things* (Durham, NC: Duke University Press, 2010), p23.
23 James Taylor. "Analytics and Ending the Tyranny of the Anecdotal," *James Taylor on Everything Decision Management* (Blog), 8 October 2012, http://jtonedm.com/2012/10/08/analytics-and-ending-the-tyranny-of-the-anecdotal/ (accessed 12 October 2012).
24 Horkheimer and Adorno. *The Dialectic of Enlightenment*, p3.
25 Bennett. *Vibrant Matter: A Political Economy of Things*, p122. Adorno would likely have agreed that some chastening of fantasies of human mastery was in order, though not at the expense of the objectification of subjects.
26 Ibid, p20. She notes that an "actant never really acts alone" (p21), but this is what might be described as an aggregational understanding of agency – not a collaborative, deliberative, or collective one.
27 Ibid, p32.
28 Ibid, p34.

29 Slavoj Zizek. *"Unbehagan in der Natur,"* ["Ecology Against Nature"] *Bedeutung Magazine*, vol 1, 2008, http://www.bedeutung.co.uk/magazine/issues/1-nature-culture/zizek-unbehagen-natur-ecology-nature/ (accessed 10 August 2012).

30 Bennett. *Vibrant Matter: A Political Economy of Things*, p19.

31 Jorge Luis Borges and John M. Fein (translator). "Lottery in Babylon," *Prairie Schooner*, 1959, pp203–207.

32 Zizek. "Unbehagen."

33 Bennett, p11.

34 Zizek. "Unbehagen."

35 Shoshan Magnet. *When Biometrics Fail: Gender, Race, and the Technology of Identity* (Durham, NC: Duke University Press, 2011), p46.

36 Alex Guazelli. "Predicting the Future, Part 1: What Is Predictive Analytics?" *IBM: Developer Works*, http://www.ibm.com/developerworks/industry/library/ba-predictive-analytics1/index.html (accessed 10 August 2012).

37 Slavoj Zizek. *Living in the End Times* (London: Verso, 2010), p338.

38 John McQuaid. "Prediction Markets Are Hot, But Here's Why They Can Be So Wrong," *Wired Magazine*, vol 16, no 6, 19 May 2008, http://www.wired.com/techbiz/it/magazine/16–06/st_essay (accessed 10 August 2012).

39 Guazelli. "Predicting the Future, Part 1: What Is Predictive Analytics?"

40 Adam Gordon. "The Uses and Limits of Prediction Markets in Forecasting," *FutureSavvy.net*, 20 August 2008, http://futuresavvy.net/2008/08/the-uses-and-limits-of-prediction-markets-in-forecasting/ (accessed 10 August 2012).

41 Cary Wolfe. *What Is Posthumanism* (Minneapolis, MN: University of Minnesota Press: 2008), pxx.

42 Jacques Derrida. *Limited, INC.* (Evanston, IL: Northwestern University Press, 1988), p146.

43 Michel Foucault. *Knowledge/Power: Selected Interviews and Writings, 1972–1977* (ed. Colin Gordon) (New York: Random House/Pantheon: 1980), p80.

44 Barbara Bradley Haggerty. "The Most Influential Evangelist You've Never Heard Of." Npr.org, 8 August 2012, http://www.npr.org/2012/08/08/157754542/the-most-influential-evangelist-youve-never-heard-of (accessed 10 August 2012).

45 Rick Green. "Attacks on David Barton as Tactics of Saul Alinsky," *Rick Green* (Blog), http://www.rickgreen.com/attacks-on-david-barton-same-as-tactics-of-alinsky-hitler/ (accessed 10 August 2012).

46 As quoted in Ruth Leys. "The Turn to Affect: A Critique," *Critical Inquiry*, vol 37, no 3, Spring, 2011, p435. The original quote is from Eric Shouse. "Feeling, Emotion, Affect," *M/C Journal*, vol 8, December, 2005, http://journal.media-culture.org.au/0512/03-shouse.php (accessed 10 August 2012).

47 Ruth Leys. "Affect and Intention: A Reply to William E. Connolly," *Critical Inquiry*, vol 37, no 4, Summer, 2011, p800.

48 Ibid, p800.

49 Ibid, p802.

50 Lee Spinks as quoted in Leys, "The Turn to Affect: A Critique." The original article is: Lee Spinks. "Thinking the Post-Human: Literature, Affect, and the Politics of Style," *Textual Practice*, vol 15, no 1, 2001, p24.

51 Leys. "Affect and Intention: A Reply to William E. Connolly," p805.

52 Leys. "The Turn to Affect: A Critique," p472.

53 Ruth Leys. "The Turn to Affect: A Critique," p471.

54 Ibid, p469.

55 Ibid, p436.

56 On mimesis see: Walter Benjamin. "On the Mimetic Faculty," in *Reflect-ions: Essays, Aphorisms, Autobiographical Writings* (New York: Schocken, 1986), pp120–125.

57 Martin Jay. "Mimesis and Mimetology," in *The Semblance of Subjectivity*, ed. Lambert Zuidervaart (Cambridge: MIT Press, 1997).

58 Shierry Weber Nicholsen. *Exact Imagination, Late Work: On Adorno's Aesthetics* (Cambridge: MIT Press, 1997), p140.

59 Bennett. *Vibrant Matter*, pix.

60 Ibid, p4. There is an unspoken affinity in this account to Benjamin's description of the "flashing" of contellational form. For more on this, see Nicholsen, pp167–180.

61 Ibid, p5.

62 Ibid, pp17, 3.

63 Ibid, p4.

64 J. M. Bernstein. "Why Rescue Semblance? Metaphysical Experience and the Possibility of Ethics," in *The Semblance of Subjectivity*, ed. Lambert Zuidervaart (Cambridge: MIT Press, 1997), p199.

65 Ian Bogost. "What Is Object-Oriented Ontology," *Ian Bogost: Video Game, Theory, Criticism, Design* (Blog), 8 December 2009, http://www.bogost.com/blog/what_is _objectoriented_ontolog.shtml (accessed 10 August 2012).

66 Slavoj Zizek and Glynn Daly. *Conversations with Zizek* (Cambridge: Polity Press, 2004), p97.

67 Ibid.

68 Theodor Adorno. *Negative Dialectics* (London: Continuum, 1981), p22.

69 Zizek and Daly. *Conversations with Zizek*, p97.

70 Zupancic. *The Shortest Shadow*, p35.

71 Ibid.

72 Zupancic. *The Shortest Shadow*, p58.

73 Ibid, p127.

74 Bernstein. "Why Rescue Semblance," p12.

75 Ibid, p12.

76 Ibid, p12.

77 Alistair Croll. "Big Data Is Our Generation's Civil Rights Issue, and We Don't Know It," *O'Reilly Radar*, 2 August 2012, http://radar.oreilly.com/2012/08/big-data-is-our-generations-civil-rights-issue-and-we-dont-know-it.html (accessed 10 August 2012).

78 Erick Heroux. "The Returns of Alienation," Cultural Logic, vol 2, no 1, 1998, http://clogic.eserver.org/2–1/2–1index.html (accessed 10 August 2012).

79 Ibid.

80 Ibid.

81 Alvin Toffler. *PowerShift: Knowledge, Wealth, and Violence at the Edge of the 21st Century* (New York: Bantam Books, 1991), p84.

82 Daniel W. Smith, "Deleuze and the Question of Desire: Toward an Immanent Theory of Ethics," *Parrhesia*, vol 2, 2007, p67.

BIBLIOGRAPHY

24/7 Customer. "Tweetview," Homepage, http://www.247tweetview.com/tweetview (accessed 28 January 2010).

Abramowicz, Michael. *Predictocracy: Market Mechanisms for Public and Private Decision Making*. New Haven, CT: Yale University Press, 2008.

Ad Council. "Homeland Security Readiness Campaign", http://www.adcouncil.org/campaigns/homeland_security (accessed 24 October 2005).

Adorno, Theodor W. *Negative Dialectics*. London: Continuum, 1981.

Adorno, Theodor and Max Horkheimer. *The Dialectic of Enlightenment*. Stanford, CA: Stanford University Press, 2002.

Agence France Presse. "Discrepancy Found in Amount of Explosives at Iraqi Facility," *Newswire*, 28 October 2004.

Alexander, David. "Political Markets See Clinton vs. Giuliani Contest," *Reuters News*, 29 October 2007, http://www.reuters.com/article/idUSN2636611520071029 (accessed 20 May 2010).

Anderson, Chris. "The End of Theory: The Data Deluge Makes the Scientific Method Obsolete," *Wired Magazine*, 23 June 2008, http://www.wired.com/science/discoveries/magazine/16–07/pb_theory (accessed 30 August 2008; 12 March 2012).

Asia Pulse. "Korea's Economy Emerging as World Leader in Brainwave Measurement," Press Release, 24 June 2009.

Attensity. "Learn More about Attensity," Corporate homepage, http://www.nytimes.com/2009/08/24/technology/internet/24emotion.html (accessed 20 January 2010).

Ayres, Ian. *Super Crunchers: How Anything Can Be Predicted*. London: John Murray, 2007.

Banford, James. "The NSA is Building the Country's Biggest Spy Center (Watch What You Say!)," *Wired Magazine*, 15 March 2012, http://www.wired.com/threatlevel/2012/03/ff_nsadatacenter/ (accessed 10 August 2012).

Barbaro, Michael and Tom Zeller, Jr. "A Face Is Exposed for AOL Searcher No. 4417749," *The New York Times*, 9 August 2006, http://www.nytimes.com/2006/08/09/technology/09aol.html?pagewanted=all (accessed 10 August 2012).

Baudrillard, Jean. *Simulations and Simulacra*. New York: Semiotext(e), 1983.

—— "The Virtual Illusion: Or the Automatic Writing of the World," *Theory, Culture & Society*, vol 12, no 4, 1995, pp97–107.

—— *Simulacra and Simulation*. Ann Arbor, MI: University of Michigan Press, 2001.

Beck, Glenn. "The Puppet Master," *Fox News: Glenn Beck*, Fox News Network, 8–11 November 2010.

—— *Fox News: Glenn Beck*, Fox News Network, 14 February 2011a.

—— *Fox News: Glenn Beck*, Fox News Network, 24 March 2011b.

—— *Fox News: Glenn Beck*, Fox News Network, 29 March 2011c.

—— *Fox News: Glenn Beck*, Fox News Network, 5 April 2011d.

—— *Fox News: Glenn Beck*, Fox News Network, 22 April 2011e.

—— *Fox News: Glenn Beck*, Fox News Network, 23 June 2011f.

—— *Fox News: Glenn Beck*, Fox News Network, 30 June 2011g.

Beck, Ulrich. *Risk Society: Towards a New Modernity*. London: Sage, 1992.

Beckford, Martin. "Foreign Powers Will Be Allowed to Access Email and Phone Records," *The Telegraph*, 4 July 2012, http://www.telegraph.co.uk/news/uknews/law-and-order/9372965/Foreign-powers-will-be-allowed-to-access-email-and-phone- records.html (accessed 10 August 2012).

Bell, Genevieve. "Anthropology at Intel: A Thrice Told Tale," Keynote Talk, Australian Anthropological Society Conference, Brisbane, 26–28 September 2012.

Benjamin, Walter. "Notes on a Theory of Gambling," in *The Sociology of Risk and Gambling Reader*, edited by James F. Cosgrove. New York: Routledge, 2006, pp211–214.

Bennett, James. "'We're Not Going to Let Our Campaign Be Dictated by Fact-Checkers,'" *The Atlantic*, 28 August 2012, http://www.theatlantic.com/politics/archive/2012/08/were-not-going-to-let-our-campaign-be-dictated-by-fact-checkers/261674/ (accessed 10 September 2012).

Bennett, Jane. *Vibrant Matter: A Political Ecology of Things*. Durham, NC: Duke University Press, 2010.

Benston, Liz. "Markets Pick 'Em Better than Polls," *Las Vegas Sun*, 16 January 2008, p1.

Bernstein, J. M. "Why Rescue Semblance? Metaphysical Experience and the Possibility of Ethics," in *The Semblance of Subjectivity: Essays in Adorno's Aesthetic Theory*, edited by Tom Huhn and Lambert Zuidervaart. Cambridge, MA: MIT Press, 1997, pp177–212.

Biztech2.com. "IBM Helps Cities Measure Public Social Sentiment on Critical Issues," http://biztech2.in.com/news/social/ibm-helps-cities-measure-public-social-sentiment-on-critical-issues/143572/0 (accessed 10 August 2012).

Bogard, William. *The Simulation of Surveillance*. Cambridge: Cambridge University Press, 1996.

Borges, Jorge Luis. *Ficciones*. New York: Grove Press, 1994.

Borges, Jorge Luis, and John M. Fein. "Lottery in Babylon." *Prairie Schooner*, Fall, 1959, pp203–207.

Brat, Ilan. "The Emotional Quotient of Soup Shopping," *Wall Street Journal*, 17 February 2010.

Brenninkmeijer, Jonna. "Taking Care of One's Brain: How Manipulating the Brain Changes People's Selves," *History of the Human Sciences*, vol 23, no 1, 2010, pp107–126.

Brown, Nicholas and Imre Szeman. "Twenty-Five Theses on Philosophy in the Age of Finance Capital," in *A Leftist Ontology: Beyond Relativism and Identity Politics*, edited by Carsten Strathausen. Minneapolis, MN: University of Minnesota Press, 2009, pp33–53.

Bryan, Cathy, Rosa Tsagarousianou, and Damian Tambini. "Electronic Democracy and the Civic Networking Movement in Context," in *Cyberdemocracy: Technology, Cities, and Civic Networks*, edited by Cathy Bryan, Rosa Tsagarousianou, and Damian Tambini. London: Routledge, 1998, pp1–17.

Business Times. "Don't Just Get Connected, Get Smarter Too," 18 January 2010, p8.

Business Wire. "Adobe Digital Marketing Suite Tackles Big Data with Predictive Marketing," Press release, 21 March 2012.

—— "PowerReviews Announces BrandConnect™; Helps Brands Drive Sales by Listening to and Engaging Customers; New Data Shows Brands Are Hungry for Social Tools that Help Them Drive Engagement, Loyalty and Word-of-Mouth Among Customers," http://findarticles.com/p/articles/mi_m0EIN/is_20090922/ai_n35683272/?tag=content;col1 (accessed 22 January 2010).

Butler, Judith. "What Is Critique? An Essay on Foucault's Virtue," EIPCP Website, 2001, http://eipcp.net/transversal/0806/butler/en (accessed 10 August 2012).

Calabrese, Chris. "The Biggest New Spying Program You've Probably Never Heard Of," ACLU Website, 30 July 2012, http://www.aclu.org/blog/national-security-technology-and-liberty/biggest-new-spying-program-youve-probably-never-heard (accessed 10 August 2012).

CBS News. "Interview: Joe Navarro Analyzes Sarah Palin's Acceptance Speech," *The Early Show*, CBS TV, aired 4 September 2008.

—— "Interview: Joe Navarro, 'What Every Body is Saying,' Discusses Body Language of Candidates at Presidential Debate," *The Saturday Early Show*, CBS Worldwide, aired 27 September 2008.

—— "Profile: Body Language Expert Joe Navarro on Hillary Clinton's Body Language During her Speech at the DNC," *The Early Show*, CBS TV, aired 27 August 2008.

Celebrity Poker Showdown. "Tournament 7, Game 2," Bravo, Picture This Television, first aired 20 October 2005.

Chait, Jonathan. "Who's Smarter, Obama or Bush?," *The New Republic*, 14 April 2012, http://www.tnr.com/blog/jonathan-chait/whos-smarter-obama-or-bush# (accessed 10 August 2012).

Cheng, Jacqui. "Netflix Settles Privacy Law Suit; Ditches $1 Million Contest," Ars Technica, 12 March 2010, http://arstechnica.com/tech-policy/2010/03/netflix-ditches-1-million-contest-in-wake-of-privacy-suit/ (accessed 10 August 2012).

Clough, Patricia. "Affect and Control: Rethinking the Body 'Beyond Sex and Gender'," *Feminist Theory*, vol 4, no 3, 2003, pp359–364.

—— "The New Empiricism: Affect and Sociological Method," *European Journal of Social Theory*, vol 12, no 1, 2009, pp43–61.

CNN. "Lou Dobbs Tonight," 26 October 2004.

—— "Starting Point with Soledad O'Brien," 14 August 2012, http://www.youtube.com/watch?v=m2EfmX6LoAA.

Coleman, Stephen. "A Tale of Two Houses: The House of Commons, The Big Brother House," *The Hansard Society*, 2003, www.clubepublic.org/eve/030708/Hansardb_b.pdf (accessed 24 July 2011).

—— "Connecting Parliament to the Public via the Internet: Two Case Studies of Online Consultations," *Information, Communication & Society*, March 2004, http://depts.washington.edu/ccce/assets/documents/coleman1.pdf (accessed 10 August 2012).

Corsi, Jerome. "Obama Blinked: Now Game Begins," *World Net Daily*, 27 April 2011, http://www.wnd.com/2011/04/292213 (accessed 10 August 2012).

Crockford, Kade. "Private Spies and Our Growing Surveillance State," *The Nation*, 4 September 2012, http://www.thenation.com/article/169727/private-spies-and-our-growing-surveillance-state (accessed 10 August 2012).

Croll, Alistair. "Big Data Is Our Generation's Civil Rights Issue, and We Don't Know It," O'Reilly Radar, 2 August 2012, http://radar.oreilly.com/2012/08/big-data-is-our-generations-civil-rights-issue-and-we-dont-know-it.html (accessed 10 August 2012).

Crovitz, Gordon. "Information Age: Trading on the Wisdom of Crowds," *The Wall Street Journal*, 28 April 2008, pA17.

—— "Double-Checking the Journalist 'Fact Checkers': Their Claims of Campaign Falsehoods Are Often a Matter of Opinion," *The Wall Street Journal*, 9 September 2012,

http://online.wsj.com/article/SB10000872396390443686004577639743922340620.
html (accessed 12 September 2012).

Dahlberg, Carrie. "'Neuromarketing' Science Probes Subconscious Reasons for Buying," *Sacramento Bee*, 4 April 2004, p4.

Damasio, Antonio. *Descartes' Error: Emotion, Reason, and the Human Brain*. New York: Harper Perennial, 1995.

Danner, Mark. "Words in a Time of War: On Rhetoric, Truth and Power," in *What Orwell Didn't Know: Propaganda and the New Face of American Politics*, edited by András Szántó, 17. New York: PublicAffairs, 2007.

Davenport, Thomas and D. J. Patil. "Data Scientist: The Sexiest Job of the 21st Century," *Harvard Business Review*, October 2012, http://hbr.org/2012/10/data-scientist-the-sexiest-job-of-the-21st-century/ar/pr (accessed 10 October 2012).

Dean, Jodi. "Theorizing Conspiracy Theory," *Theory & Event*, vol 4, no 3, 2000, pp1–16.

——— *Blog Theory: Feedback and Capture in the Circuits of the Drive*. Cambridge: Polity Press, 2010.

Dean, Mitchell. *Governmentality: Power and Rule in Modern Society*. London: Sage, 1999.

Derrida, Jacques. *Limited, INC*. Evanston, IL: Northwestern University Press, 1988.

Dick, Philip K. "The Minority Report," in *The Collected Stories of Philip K. Dick, Volume 4: The Minority Report*. New York: Citadel, 1994.

Duhigg, Charles. "How Companies Learn Your Secrets," *The New York Times*, 16 February 2012, http://www.nytimes.com/2012/02/19/magazine/shopping-habits.html?pagewanted=all (accessed 10 August 2012).

Ekman, Paul. *Telling Lies: Clues to Deceit in the Marketplace, Politics, and Marriage*. New York and London: W.W. Norton & Co., 2001.

Ellis, Samantha. "You've Seen the Movie, Now Take the Brain Scan," *The Guardian*, 3 June 2004, p8.

Email Wire. "Keros Client Bark Group Partners with Mindmetic in New Field of Neuromarketing," Press release, 15 December 2009, http://emailwire.com/release/31185-Keros-Client-Bark-Group-Partners-With-Mindmetic-in-New-Field-of-Neuromarketing-.html (accessed 10 August 2011).

ENP Newswire. "Scala Introduces Advanced Analytics," Press Release, 7 March 2012.

Fallows, James. "Bit by Bit It Takes Shape: Media Evolution for the 'Post-Truth' Age," *The Atlantic*, 9 August 2012, http://www.theatlantic.com/politics/archive/2012/08/bit-by-bit-it-takes-shape-media-evolution-for-the-post-truth-age/261741/ (accessed 10 August 2012).

Fenster, Mark. *Conspiracy Theories: Secrecy and Power in American Culture*. Minneapolis, MN: University of Minnesota Press, 2008.

Fenster, Mark and Jack Z. Bratich. "Dialogues in Communication Research: Bratch, J. Z. (2008). Conspiracy Panics: Political Rationality and Popular Culture," *Journal of Communication Inquiry*, vol 33, no 3, 2009, pp278–286.

Foresight Mental Capital and Wellbeing Project. *Final Project Report – Executive Summary*. London: Government Office for Science, 2008.

Foucault, Michel. "What is Critique?" in *The Politics of Truth*, edited by Sylvère Lotringer and Lysa Hochroth. New York: Semiotext(e), 1997. Transcript by Monique Emery, revised by Suzanne Delorme et al., translated into English by Lysa Hochroth (originally a lecture to the French Society of Philosophy, 27 May 1978, subsequently published in *Bulletin de la Société française de la philosophie*, vol 84, no 2, 1990, pp35–63).

——— *Security, Territory, Population: Lectures at the Collège de France 1977–1978*. New York: Picador, 2009.

Fox News: *The O'Reilly Factor*. "Body Language: Joe Biden, Sarah Palin, Barney Frank," Fox News Network, aired 6 October 2008.

Free Brain Age Games. "Results," Website, http://www.freebrainagegames.com/index. php (accessed 12 December 2011).

Gates, Bill. *The Road Ahead*. New York: Penguin, 1996.

Geron, Tomio. "Kaggle's Predictive Data Contest Aims to Fix Health Care," *Forbes*, 4 April 2012, http://www.forbes.com/sites/tomiogeron/2011/04/04/kaggles-predictive-data-contest-aims-to-fix-health-care/ (accessed 10 August 2012).

Giridharadas, Anand. "India's Novel Use of Brain Scans in Courts Is Debated," *The New York Times*, 17 July 2008, http://www.nytimes.com/2008/09/15/world/asia/15brainscan.html?scp=1&sq=champadi&st=cse (accessed 9 March 2009).

Gladwell, Malcolm. "The Science of Shopping," *The New Yorker*, 4 November 1996.

—— *Blink: The Power of Thinking Without Thinking*. Little Brown: Back Bay Books, 2005a.

—— "The Second Mind," Online excerpt from *Blink*, 2005b, http://www.gladwell. com/blink/blink_excerpt1.html (accessed 10 August 2011).

—— "What Is *Blink* About," Online Q&A about *Blink*, 2005c, http://www.gladwell. com/blink/blink_excerpt1.html (accessed 20 January 2010).

Glanz, James, William Broad and David Danger. "Huge Cache of Explosives Vanished from Site in Iraq," *The New York Times*, 25 October 2004, http://www.nytimes.com/2004/10/25/international/middleeast/25bomb.html (accessed10 August 2012).

Goode, Erica. "In the U.S.: A New Computer Program Aims to Fight Crime by Predicting It," *The International Herald Tribune*, 17 August 2011.

Gordon, Adam. "The Uses and Limits of Prediction Markets in Forecasting," *Future-Savvy.net*, 20 August 2008, http://futuresavvy.net/2008/08/the-uses-and-limits-of-prediction-markets-in-forecasting/ (accessed 10 August 2012).

Graham, David. "Meet the Incredible, Incoherent Jobs-Report Truthers," *The Atlantic*, 5 October 2012, http://www.theatlantic.com/politics/archive/2012/10/meet-the-incredible-incoherent-jobs-report-truthers/263285/ (accessed10 August 2012).

Green, Rick. "Attacks on David Barton as Tactics of Saul Alinsky," *Rick Green* (Blog), http://www.rickgreen.com/attacks-on-david-barton-same-as-tactics-of-alinsky-hitler/ (accessed 10 August 2012).

Grossman, Lev. "You – Yes, You – Are Person of the Year," *Time*, 25 December 2006, http://www.time.com/time/magazine/article/0,9171,1570810,00.html (accessed 10 September 2011).

Guazelli, Alex. "Predicting the Future, Part 1: What Is Predictive Analytics?," *IBM: Developer Works*, http://www.ibm.com/developerworks/industry/library/ba-predictive-analytics1/index.html (accessed 10 August 2012).

Hacking, Ian. *The Taming of Chance*. Cambridge: Cambridge University Press, 1990.

Haggerty, Barbara Bradley. "The Most Influential Evangelist You've Never Heard Of," Npr.org, 8 August 2012, http://www.npr.org/2012/08/08/157754542/the-most-influential-evangelist-youve-never-heard-of (accessed 10 August 2012).

Hahn, Robert and Paul Tetlock. "When Gambling Is Good," *The Wall Street Journal*, 11 May 2007, pA10.

Halbfinger, David. "Kerry Attacks Bush Over Loss of Explosives," *The New York Times*, 27 October 2004, p17.

Hamilton, Brad. "Misfortune Telling: Can the NYPD Predict a Crime Before It Happens? A Tech Guru Thinks So," *The New York Post*, 17 April 2011.

Hanson, Robin. "Shall We Vote on Values, But Bet on Beliefs?" Author homepage, October 2007, http://hanson.gmu.edu/futarchy.html (accessed 10 May 2010).

Hardt, Michael. "Affective Labor," *Boundary*, vol 2, no 2, 1999, pp89–100.

Hardy, Joseph. "The Science behind Lumosity", Website, www.lumosity.com/documents/the_science_behind_lumosity.pdf (accessed 12 December 2011).

Hardy, Quentin. "IBM: Big Data, Bigger Patterns," *Bits* (*The New York Times*'s tech blog), 15 February 2012, http://bits.blogs.nytimes.com/2012/02/15/i-b-m-big-data-bigger-patterns/ (accessed 10 August 2012).

Hegel, G. W. F. *Phenomenology of Spirit* (trans. A.V. Miller). Oxford, New York, Toronto, Melbourne: Oxford University Press, 1977.

Heroux, Erick. "The Returns of Alienation," *Cultural Logic*, vol 2, no1, 1998, http://clogic.eserver.org/2–1/2–1index.html (accessed August 10 2012).

Hockenberry, John. "Thinking Like a Scientist: Solution to Politics," *The Takeaway*, WNYC, 27 September 2012, http://www.thetakeaway.org/2012/sep/27/thinking-scientist-solution-politics/?utm_source=local&utm_media=treatment&utm_campaign=featuredcomment&utm_content=article.

Hotz, Robert. "Songs Stick in Teens' Head," *The Wall Street Journal*, 13 June 2011, http://online.wsj.com/article/SB10001424052702303848104576381823644333598.html (accessed 10 August 2012).

Hunt, Gus. "Big Data: Operational Excellence Ahead in the Cloud," Presentation to the Amazon Web Services Government Summit Washington, DC, 26 October 2011, http://www.youtube.com/watch?v=SkIhHnoPpjA (accessed 10 August 2012).

IAT Home. "Project Implicit," Website, https://implicit.harvard.edu/implicit/demo/ (accessed 8 March 2009).

IBM. "IBM SPSS Predictive Analytics in Fusion Centers," White Paper, 2010, http://home.comcast.net/~leslie.corkill/Portfolio/2010_IBM_TechE.pdf (accessed 10 August 2012).

Innerscope. "Our Approach", Innerscope Research, http://www.innerscoperesearch.com/flat/our_approach.html (accessed 12 December 2011).

Jarvis, Simon. *Adorno: A Critical Introduction*. New York: Routledge, 1998.

Jay, Martin. "Mimesis and Mimetology," in *The Semblance of Subjectivity*, edited by Lambert Zuidervaart, Amherst, MA: University of Massachusetts Press, 1998, pp374–422.

Jenkins, Henry. *Convergence Culture: Where Old and New Media Collide*. New York and London: New York University Press, 2006.

Jenkins, Holman. "Can Data Mining Stop the Killing?," *The Wall Street Journal*, 24 July 2012, http://online.wsj.com/article/SB100008723963904435709045775466716932 45302.html (accessed 10 August 2012).

Jodange. "Home," Homepage, http://www.jodange.com/index.html (accessed 18 January 2010).

Johnson, Caitlin. "Cutting through the Advertising Clutter," *CBSnews.com*, 11 February 2009, http://www.cbsnews.com/stories/2006/09/17/sunday/main2015684.shtml (accessed 10 August 2012).

Jung, Hwa Yol. *Transversal Rationality and Intercultural Texts: Essays in Phenomenology and Comparative Philosophy*. Toledo, OH: University of Ohio Press, 2011.

Kahn, Irfan. "Strategic Weapon: Unstructured Data Yields Battlefield Edge," IT World Blog, 9 August 2012, http://www.itworld.com/big-datahadoop/289177/strategic-weapon-unstructured-data-delivers-battlefield-edge (accessed 10 August 2012).

Kamien, David. *The McGraw-Hill Homeland Security Handbook: The Definitive Guide for Law Enforcement, EMT, and all other Security Professionals*. New York: McGraw-Hill, 2005.

Kant, Immanuel. *On History*, edited and translated by Lewis White Beck. New York: Macmillan, 1963.

Karas, Tania. "10 Things Online Data Collectors Won't Say," SmartMoney.com, 6 April 2012, http://www.smartmoney.com/spend/technology/10-things-online-data-collectors-wont-say-1333598586287/ (accessed 10 August 2012).

Kluger, Jeffrey. "How to Spot a Lie," *Time Magazine*, 20 August 2006, http://www.time.com/time/magazine/article/0,9171,1229109,00.html (accessed 3 March 2009).

Knickerbocker, Brad. "Polls Favor Obama. A Conspiracy by Democrats and the Media?" *Christian Science Monitor*, 29 September 2012, http://www.csmonitor.com/

USA/DC-Decoder/2012/0929/Polls-favor-Obama.-A-conspiracy-by-Democrats-and-the-media- video (accessed 10 August 2012).

Kronholz, June. "Campaign '08: Prediction Traders Put Their Money on Obama," *The Wall Street Journal*, 13 February 2008, pA8.

Krugman, Paul. "Gilded Once More," *The New York Times*, 27 April 2007, http://select. nytimes.com/2007/04/27/opinion/27krugman.html (accessed 10 August 2012).

Kuchler, Hannah. "Marketing Industry Turns to Mind Reading," *Financial Times*, 11 April 2010, http://www.ft.com/intl/cms/s/0/0bd88596-4426-11df-b327-00144feab49a.html#axzz1gVyqI7Mq (accessed 12 December, 2011).

Latour, Bruno. "Why Has Critique Run Out of Steam? From Matters of Fact to Matters of Concern," *Critical Inquiry*, vol 30, Winter, 2004, pp225–245.

Lazzarato, Maurizio. "Immaterial Labour," in *Radical Thought in Italy: A Potential Politics*, edited by Paolo Virno and Michael Hardt. Minneapolis, MN: University of Minnesota Press, 1996.

Lee, Timothy. "House Approves another Five Years of Warrantless Wiretapping; Reauthorization of the FISA Amendments Act Must Still Be Passed by the Senate," ArsTechnica.com, 12 September 2012**,** http://arstechnica.com/tech-policy/2012/09/house-approves-another-five-years-of-warrantless-wiretapping/ (accessed 20 September 2012).

Lehrer Jonah. *How We Decide*. New York: Houghton-Mifflin, 2009.

—— "Beware Our Blind Seers," *The Wall Street Journal*, 30 October 2010, http://online. wsj.com/article/SB10001424052702303341904575576550877154216.html (accessed 10 August 2012).

Leonhardt, David. "Making Bets on Elections, Traders Buy Online Contracts," *International Herald Tribune*, 14 February 2008, second ed., p16.

—— "When the Crowd Isn't Wise," *The New York Times*, 8 July 2012, pE1.

Lewis, Michael. *The Big Short: Inside the Doomsday Machine*. London: Penguin Books, 2010.

Leys, Ruth. "Affect and Intention: A Reply to William E. Connolly," *Critical Inquiry*, vol 37, no 4, 2011a, pp799–805.

—— "The Turn to Affect: A Critique," *Critical Inquiry*, vol 37, no 3, 2011b, pp434–472.

Lie to Me. Television program, Fox Television, Network Ten, Brisbane, broadcast 10 March 2009,

Lohr, Steve. "The Age of Big Data," *The New York Times*, 11 February 2012, http://www.nytimes.com/2012/02/12/sunday-review/big-datas-impact-in-the-world.html?pagewanted=all (accessed 10 August 2012).

Lupton, Deborah. "Risk and Governmentality," in *The Sociology of Risk and Gambling Reader*, edited by James F. Cosgrove. New York: Routledge, 2006, pp85–100.

Magnet, Shoshana. *When Biometrics Fail: Gender, Race, and the Technology of Identity*. Durham, NC: Duke University Press, 2011.

Marshall, Josh. "The Post-Modern President**.** Deception, Denial, and Relativism: What the Bush Administration Learned from the French," *Washington Monthly*, September 2003, http://www.washingtonmonthly.com/features/2003/0309.marshall.html (accessed 20 May 2010).

Marx, Karl and Friedrich Engels. *The German Ideology, Part 1*. New York: International Publishers, 1970.

Massumi, Brian. "Requiem for Our Prospective Dead," in *Deleuze and Guattari: New Mappings in Politics, Philosophy and Culture*, edited by Eleanor Kaufman and Kevin Jon Heller. Minneapolis, MN: University of Minnesota Press, 1998, pp40–64.

—— *Parables of the Virtual: Movement, Affect, Sensation*. Durham & London: Duke University Press, 2002.

—— "The Future Birth of the Affective Fact," Conference proceedings, *Ethics and Politics of Virtuality and Indexicality*, University of Leeds, 30 June 2005, p5, http://browse.reticular.info/text/collected/massumi.pdf (accessed 10 August 2012).

McCue, Colleen. "Data Mining and Predictive Analytics: Battlespace Awareness for the War on Terrorism," *Defense Intelligence Journal*, vol 13, no 1&2, 2005, pp47–63.

—— *Data Mining and Predictive Analysis*. New York: Butterworth-Heinemann, 2006.

McQuaid, John. "Prediction Markets Are Hot, But Here's Why They Can Be So Wrong," *Wired Magazine*, 19 May 2008, http://www.wired.com/techbiz/it/magazine/16–06/st_essay (accessed 10 August 2012).

Mitchell, Alison. "Bush Derides Gore for Rejecting Debate Plan," *The New York Times*, 5 September 2000a, pA22.

—— "Bush Says that Bottom Line on Gore's Proposals Would Consume the Surplus," *The New York Times*, 7 September 2000b, pA27.

Navarro, Joe. "Joe Navarro's Read 'Em and Reap Poker Course: A Spy-Catcher's Video Guide to Reading Tells," 2007, excerpt viewed on YouTube: http://www.youtube.com/watch?v=7jUUHNmbfxM (accessed 12 March 2009).

NBC News. "Interview: Joe Navarro Discusses Meaning of Body Language," *Today*, NBC News, first aired 12 March 2007.

NeuroFocus. "Advertising," NeuroFocus Webpage, http://www.neurofocus.com/Advertise.htm (accessed 12 December 2011).

—— "Entertainment," NeuroFocus Webpage, http://neurofocus.com/entertainment.htm (accessed 12 December 2011).

New Zealand Press Association. "Poker Players Can Learn to Decipher Body Language," 20 October 2008 (accessed via Factiva 1 March 2009).

Nichols, John and Robert McChesney. *It's the Media, Stupid*. New York: Seven Stories Press, 2000.

Nicholsen, Shierry Weber. *Exact Imagination, Late Work: On Adorno's Aesthetics*. Cambridge, MA: MIT Press, 1997.

Nolan, Rachel. "Behind the Cover Story: How Much Does Target Know?," *The New York Times*, 21 February 2012, http://6thfloor.blogs.nytimes.com/2012/02/21/behind-the-cover-story-how-much-does-target-know/ (accessed 10 August 2012).

O'Brien, Danny. "Gambling Dressed Up in a Well Street Suit?" *Irish Times*, 7 March 2008, p8.

O'Harrow, Robert Jr. *No Place to Hide*. New York: Free Press, 2005.

Oreskes, Naomi and Erik Conway. *Merchants of Doubt: How a Handful of Scientists Obscured the Truth on Issues from Tobacco Smoke to Global Warming*. New York: Bloomsbury Press, 2010.

Ortega, Francisco and Fernando Vidal. "Mapping the Cerebral Subject in Contemporary Culture," *RECIIS: Electronic Journal of Communication Innovation*, vol 1, no 2, 2007, pp255–259.

Packard, Vance. *The Hidden Persuaders*. New York: IG Publishing, 1980.

Parsons, Paul. "How Gambling Could Rule the World," *The Daily Telegraph*, 19 August 2008, p25.

Parsons, Paul. "Predicting the Future with the Power of Betting," *The Telegraph*, 18 August 2008, http://www.telegraph.co.uk/science/science-news/3349800/Predicting-the-future-with-the-power-of-betting.html (accessed 10 August 2012).

Pearce, Celia. *The Interactive Book*. New York: Penguin, 1997.

Pearsall, Beth. "Predictive Policing: The Future of Law Enforcement?," *NIJ Journal*, vol 266, June 2012, http://www.nij.gov/journals/266/predictive.htm (accessed 10 August 2012).

Pennock, David. "The Good Side of the 'Terror Futures' Idea (Yes, There Is One)," *Yahoo! Research*, http://dpennock.com/pam.html (accessed 5 May 2010).

Pollack, Harold. "Do Liberals Disdain the Disabled," *The New York Times*, 27 February 2012, http://www.nytimes.com/2012/02/27/opinion/do-liberals-disdain-the-disabled.html?_r=0 (accessed 10 August 2012).

Powers, Martine. "Policing by the Numbers: Cambridge Officials Credit Data Analysis for a Drop in Serious Crime," *The Boston Globe*, 16 February 2012.

PR Newswire. "Americans Slam News Media on Believability," 9 January 2008.

—— "Out of Sync, Out of Sales," Press release, 26 October, 2009.

—— "Draftfcb launches Institute of Decision Making; Agency Forms Partnerships with Leading Academics at Stanford and Berkeley," Press release, 2 July 2010.

Priest, Dana and William Arkin. "Top Secret America: A Hidden World Growing beyond Control," *The Wall Street Journal*, 19 July 2010, http://projects.washingtonpost.com/top-secret-america/articles/a-hidden-world-growing-beyond-control/print/ (accessed 10 August 2012).

Public Policy Polling. "Fox the Most Trusted Name in News?" Press release, http://www.publicpolicypolling.com/pdf/PPP_Release_National_126.pdf (accessed 26 January 2010).

Pulakkat, Hari. "Elegant Scientific Theories, Techniques Being Used to Analyse Messy Social Conflicts," *The Economic Times*, 25 September 2011, http://articles.economictimes.indiatimes.com/2011-09-25/news/30198477_1_social-science-social-media-computer (accessed 10 August 2012).

Rapping, Elayne. "Aliens, Nomads, Mad Dogs and Road Warriors: The Changing Face of Criminal Violence on TV," in *Reality TV: Remaking Television Culture*, edited by Susan Murray and Laurie Ouellette. New York: New York University Press, 2004, pp214–230.

ReadWriteWeb. "5 Ways Sentiment Analysis Is Ramping Up in 2009," Blog, http://www.readwriteweb.com/archives/sentiment_analysis_is_ramping_up_in_2009.php (accessed 25 May 2010).

Rhode, Paul and Koleman Strumpf. "Historical Presidential Betting Markets," *The Journal of Economic Perspectives*, vol 18, no 2, 2004, pp127–141.

Rose, Nikolas. *Powers of Freedom: Reframing Political Thought*. Cambridge: Cambridge University Press, 1999.

—— "The Politics of Life Itself," *Theory, Culture 30*.

—— "A Neurobiological Complex? Governing Human Beings in the Age of the Brain," Keynote talk, *Governing Human Beings in the Age of the Brain: A Symposium with Nikolas Rose*, Centre for the History of European Discourses at the University of Queensland, 16 November 2011.

Rowe, Peter. "Decision Markets Tap 'Wisdom of the Crowd'," *San Diego Union-Tribune*, 1 February 2010, pE1.

Saaf, Randy. "Case Study: *AlphaGenius*, Sentiment Investing – Above Market Returns Extracting & Analyzing Twitter & the Social Internet Plenary Session," Presentation to the Predictive Analytics World conference, 25–26 June 2012, Chicago, http://www.predictiveanalyticsworld.com/chicago/2012/agenda.php (accessed 10 August 2012).

Saltonstall, David. "You'da Made Bundle Even on Small 'O7 Bet on Bam,'" *New York Daily News,* 3 November 2008, p28.

Sanger, David. "The 2004 Campaign: The Candidates," *The New York Times*, 26 October 2004, pA1.

Schrage, Michael and Sam Savage. "If This Is Harebrained, Bet on the Hare," *The Washington Post*, 3 August 2003, pB4.

Scout Labs. "Product," Homepage, http://www.scoutlabs.com/product (accessed 25 January 2010).

Seigworth, Gregory. "From Affection to Soul," in *Gilles Deleuze: Key Concepts,* edited by Charles J. Stivale, Montreal: McGill-Queen's University Press, 2005, pp159–169.

Shenk, David. *Data Smog*. New York: Harper Collins, 1997.

Shirky, Clay. "Newspapers and Thinking the Unthinkable," Clay Shirky (Blog), 13 March 2009, http://www.shirky.com/weblog/2009/03/newspapers-and-thinking-the-unthinkable/ (accessed 10 August 2012).

Shouse, Eric. "Feeling, Emotion, Affect," *M/C Journal*, vol 8, no 6, 2005, http://journal.media-culture.org.au/0512/03-shouse.php (accessed 24 November 2009).

Singel, Ryan. "FBI Mined Grocery Store Records to Find Iranian Terrorists, CQ Reports," *Wired.com*, 6 November 2007, http://www.wired.com/threatlevel/2007/11/fbi-mined-groce/ (accessed 10 August 2012).

Sisk, Michael. "Tools to Analyze Buzz Are Generating Some More of It," *American Banker*, 16 October 2009, p6.

Smith, Daniel W. "Deleuze and the Question of Desire: Toward an Immanent Theory of Ethics," *Parrhesia*, vol 2, 2007, pp66–78.

Spinks, Lee. "Thinking the Post-Human: Literature, Affect, and the Politics of Style," *Textual Practice*, vol 15, no 1, 2001, pp23–46.

Stark, Andrew. "Science Comes to Selling," *The Wall Street Journal*, 22 October 2008, http://online.wsj.com/article/SB122463327520456683.html (accessed 12 December 2011).

Sullivan, Andy. "Clinton Dismisses 'Elite' Economists on Gas Tax Plan," *Reuters*, 4 May 2008, http://www.reuters.com/article/idUSNO4324440 (accessed 5 May 2010).

Sullivan, Bartholomew. "Godwin Touts Blue CRUSH in Washington," *The Commercial Appeal*, 1 April 2011.

Sunstein, Cass. "The Daily We: Is the Internet Really a Blessing for Democracy," *Boston Review*, vol 26, no 3, 2001a, http://www.bostonreview.net/BR26.3/sunstein.html (accessed 20 November 2009).

—— *Republic.com*. Princeton, NJ: Princeton University Press, 2001b.

Sunstein, Cass and Adrian Vermeule. "Conspiracy Theories," Harvard University Law School Public Law & Legal Theory Research Paper Series, University of Chicago Law School Public Law & Legal Theory Research Paper, 15 January 2008, http://ssrn.com/abstract=1084585 (accessed 10 August 2012).

Surowiecki, James. "Q&A with James Surowiecki," *The Wisdom of Crowds* (Website), http://www.randomhouse.com/features/wisdomofcrowds/Q&A.html (accessed 10 May 2010).

—— *The Wisdom of Crowds*. New York: Anchor Books, 2004.

Suskind, Ron. "Faith, Certainty, and the Presidency of George W. Bush," *The New York Times Magazine*, 17 October 2004a, http://www.nytimes.com/2004/10/17/magazine/17BUSH.html (accessed 18 August 2012).

—— "Without a Doubt," *The New York Times Magazine*, 17 October 2004b, http://www.cs.umass.edu/~immerman/play/opinion05/WithoutADoubt.html (accessed 1 March 2009).

Sysomos. "Products," Corporate website, http://www.sysomos.com/products/features (accessed 20 May 2010).

Taft, Darryl. "IBM Takes Its Big Data Analytics to Academia," *TechWeek Europe*, 22 December 2011, http://www.techweekeurope.co.uk/news/ibm-takes-its-big-data-analytics-to-academia-51145 (accessed 10 August 2012).

Taylor, James. "Analytics and Ending the Tyranny of the Anecdotal," *James Taylor on Everything Decision Management* (Blog), 8 October 2012, http://jtonedm.com/2012/10/08/analytics-and-ending-the-tyranny-of-the-anecdotal/ (accessed 12 October 2012).

The Daily Show. "Weathering Fights," Comedy Central, first aired 26 October 2011.

—— "The Socialist Network," Comedy Central, 3 March 2012.

The Economist. "Economic Focus: Guessing Games," 20 November 2004, http://bpp.wharton.upenn.edu/jwolfers/Press/Mentions/GuessingGames(The%20Economist).pdf (accessed 19 May 2010).

The Edge (Malaysia). "Net Value: Digital Predictions for 2011," 17 January 2011.

The Engineer. "In Brief: Scientists to Prove Many a True Word is Spoken in Gestures," 19 September 2005.

The Listening Station. "Home," Homepage, http://www.listening-station.com/index. html (accessed 22 January 2010).

The Mentalist. "Pilot," Primrose Hill Productions, Warner Brothers Television, first aired 28 September 2008.

—— "Crimson Casanova," Primrose Hill Productions, Warner Brothers Television, first aired 8 February 2009.

Fox News Channel. *The O'Reilly Factor*, first aired 5 February 2010.

Thompson, Clive. "There's a Sucker Born in Every Medial Prefrontal Cortex," *The New York Times Magazine*, 26 October 2003, http://query.nytimes.com/gst/fullpage.html? res=9b07e1de113ef935a15753c1a9659c8b63&sec=&spon=&&scp=1&sq=brighthouse %20institute&st=cse (accessed 2 March 2009).

Toffler, Alvin, *PowerShift: Knowledge, Wealth, and Violence at the Edge of the 21st Century*. New York: Bantam Books, 1991.

Tsai, Jessica. "Are You Smarter than a Neuromarketer," *CRM Magazine*, vol 14, no 1, 2010, p19.

Turkle, Sherry. *Life on the Screen: Identity in the Age of the Internet*. New York: Simon & Schuster, 1997.

Two Crows Corporation. "Introduction to Data Mining and Knowledge Discovery," Online publication, http://www.twocrows.com/intro-dm.pdf (accessed 10 August 2010).

Vidal, Fernando. "Brainhood, Anthropological Figure of Modernity," *History of the Human Sciences*, vol 22, no 1, 2009, pp5–36.

Vrecko, Scott. "Neuroscience, Power and Culture: An Introduction," *History of the Human Sciences*, vol 23, no 1, 2010, pp1–10.

Warwick, Kevin. "Cyborg 1.0," *Wired Magazine*, February 2000, http://www.wired. com/wired/archive/8.02/warwick_pr.html (accessed 10 August 2012).

Weeks, Carly. "Advertising Closing in on Minority Report-Style Marketing," *The Globe and Mail*, 15 June 2011.

Weinberger, David. *Too Big to Know*. New York: Basic Books, 2011.

—— "To Know, but Not Understand," *The Atlantic*, 3 January 2012, http://www. theatlantic.com/technology/archive/2012/01/to-know-but-not-understand-david-weinberger-on-science-and-big-data/250820/ (accessed 10 August 2012).

Weller, Aaron. "Quote of the Day: Here Today, Gone More Valuable Tomorrow," *Forbes*, 3 October 2012, http://www.forbes.com/sites/kashmirhill/2012/10/03/quote-of-the-day-here-today-gone-more-valuable-tomorrow/ (accessed 10 August 2012).

Wolfe, Cary. *What is Posthumanism*. Minneapolis, MN: University of Minnesota Press: 2008.

Wolfers, Justin and Eric Zitzewitz. "Prediction Markets," *Journal of Economic Perspectives*, vol 18, no 2, 2004, pp107–126.

World Series of Poker. "Main Event," Episodes 1–16, ESPN, 2007, iTunes download.

Wright, Alex. "Mining the Web for Feelings, not Facts," *The New York Times*, 23 August 2009, http://www.nytimes.com/2009/08/24/technology/internet/24emotion.html (accessed 28 November 2009).

Zaitchik, Alexander. *Common Nonsense: Glenn Beck and the Triumph of Ignorance*. Hoboken, NJ: John Wiley & Sons, 2010.

Zimmer, Ben. "On Language: Truthiness," *The New York Times*, 13 October 2010, http://www.nytimes.com/2010/10/17/magazine/17FOB-onlanguage-t.html (accessed 10 August 2012).

Zizek, Slavoj. *The Sublime Object of Ideology*. London: Verso, 1989.

—— *The Indivisible Remainder: An Essay on Schelling and Related Matters*. London: Verso, 1996.

—— *The Ticklish Subject*. London: Verso, 1999.

—— *Enjoy Your Symptom! Jacques Lacan in Hollywood and Out*. London: Routledge, 2001.

—— *Iraq: The Borrowed Kettle*. London, Verso: 2004.

—— "Against the Populist Temptation," *Critical Inquiry*, vol 32, Spring, 2006, pp551–574.

—— *How to Read Lacan*. New York: W.W. Norton, 2007.

—— "Unbehagen in Der Natur," ["Ecology against Nature"] *Bedeutung Magazine*, May 2008, http://www.bedeutung.co.uk/magazine/issues/1-nature-culture/zizek-unbehagen-natur-ecology-nature/ (accessed 10 August 2012).

—— *In Defense of Lost Causes*. London: Verso, 2009.

—— *Living in the End Times*. London: Verso, 2010.

Zizek, Slavoj and Glynn Daly. *Conversations with Zizek*. Cambridge: Polity Press, 2004.

Zupancic, Alenka. *The Shortest Shadow: Nietzsche's Philosophy of the Two*. Cambridge, MA: MIT Press, 2003.

INDEX